TEACHERS

TEACHERS

Frank E. Huggett

Weidenfeld & Nicolson   London

First published in Great Britain in 1986
by George Weidenfeld & Nicolson Limited
91 Clapham High Street
London SW4 7TA

ISBN 0 297 787918

Photoset by Deltatype, Ellesmere Port
Printed in Great Britain by
Butler & Tanner Ltd.,
Frome and London

Acknowledgements

I should like to thank all fifty teachers who were so very generous in giving me their time, their views and their hospitality. Not one of them let me down, which is a tribute in itself. I cannot thank them openly as I should like to do, as the names are all fictitious to conceal their identity. Some other details have also been changed and the locations of their schools have been moved to equivalent areas of the country. My thanks and apologies to all the other teachers who contacted me but whom I did not see, mainly because the substance of their views had already been expressed by someone else.

I would also like to thank the courteous and helpful staff at the DES, where I did some of my preliminary research. And finally, I am deeply grateful to the editors of *Contact, Education, Report, The Teacher, Time Out* and the *Times Educational Supplement* for their kindness in publishing my appeal for help.

As education has its own jargon, a glossary of the more uncommon terms and acronyms that teachers use is provided for the general reader at the back of the book; and for the more serious student, there is a brief index of types of schools, as some teachers who are included in one section of the book have also had experience in other kinds of schools.

Contents

Introduction

In the last few years, teachers have rarely been out of the headlines. Politicians have condemned them for a lack of professionalism; parents have accused them of being incompetent, lazy and scruffy; business-men have protested that far too many school leavers can't add up or spell. There have been many other allegations about political in-doctrination of children, a decline in classroom discipline and falling standards. Although teachers constantly discuss all these criticisms among themselves, a traditional sense of defensive secrecy has pre-vented them from making their own views more widely known outside the privacy of the staffroom. As a result, very few outsiders have any real idea what goes on in schools today, what teachers are trying to achieve, and what kind of difficulties and problems they have to face. Yet, if we do not understand teachers and their points of view, it is impossible to come to any balanced judgments about education, which is still one of the most vital agencies for the present and future well-being of the whole community. As one idealistic teacher told me: 'You could change the whole world with one generation of children, if you could only get it right.'

My aim was to discover what teachers thought and felt about their lives and work, their colleagues, their pupils and their parents, to learn about their hopes and fears, their ambitions and their frustrations. There was an enormous variety of schools to be covered, including nursery, infant, junior, first, middle, comprehensive and grammar schools, plus schools for children with special needs, sixth-form colleges and independent schools. It was a daunting task which took me up and down, and across, the country several times.

From the start, it was obvious that it was going to be impossible to find representative teachers (if, indeed, they do exist), but I did make strenuous efforts to find the widest possible cross-section. One or two were contacted through personal recommendation; a few through letters which had appeared in the educational press; but the majority through appeals for help in newspapers and magazines, which produced an astonishingly good response. From the hundreds of letters and telephone calls I received, some of which I followed up with a brief questionnaire, I selected fifty teachers who not only seemed to have the most important and revealing things to say, but who also provided in aggregate the widest range of attitudes, age, experience and geographical location. Their political attitudes ranged from ultra-conservative to libertarian anarchist; their experience, from probationers in their first job to others who had recently retired after years of service; their level of skills, from those who still found teaching difficult to others who had a natural vocation; and their favoured teaching methods from formal to free schooling.

In accordance with my brief, I dutifully travelled from one part of the country to another, but it soon became abundantly clear that the catchment area of a school was far more important than its geographical location. Apart from other variables, such as the size of the school and the quality of the head, both of which have enormous impact, I found one suburban comprehensive to be very much like any other, and both entirely different from an inner-city comprehensive, regardless of whether they were located in the same city or three hundred miles apart. A number of the teachers I saw had also come to similar conclusions.

I thought it would be instructive, too, to interview some teachers who had been so greatly disillusioned that they had been forced to retreat from secondary schools into more child-centred primary schools, into supply or even voluntary, one-to-one teaching, into independent schools, or into the wider world by leaving the profession altogether, which many other teachers would also like to do. (*See Individual Retreats, pages 157–180.*)

In addition, I believed it would be interesting to talk to some exchange teachers working temporarily over here, whose contrasting experiences might enable them to see British schools in a new light. It was striking how many of their opinions confirmed what British teachers said, and have been saying, privately for many years.

Initially, I used a structured scheme of questions, based on much preliminary research, in which my own voice was quite apparent. I quickly realised that one of their main complaints was that everyone else's views of education were always being heard, and never *theirs*, so I immediately abandoned that method and let them speak freely about whatever seemed most important to them. The results of my self-imposed reticence were rewarding. Teachers opened many more private doors into their classrooms, their staffrooms and their private lives. Their opinions, which reveal both their limits and their horizons, were so very different from anything that I had read about education elsewhere, that I decided to let them come through, abbreviated and collated, but as pristine as when they were expressed to me.

At first, about the only thing the teachers all seemed to have in common was the courage to speak frankly to me and a desire to make their views more widely known, though one or two were troubled that this might be mere self-indulgence. There didn't appear to be much of a consensus. Opinions were divided on many issues, even on their shamefully low pay; I found one or two teachers, admittedly with higher Scale posts, who were not unduly bothered about it and another teacher who has such a high sense of vocation that she has devoted much of her life to voluntary, unpaid teaching. There were even bigger disagreements over whether it was unprofessional for teachers to strike, which is reflected in the opposing views of teachers' unions. The question of discipline also produced a wide variety of opinions, ranging from one public school master who looked on corporal punishment as a first resort, to others who had thought more reflectively about the subject and believed that reason and group therapy provided a better exemplar for the future conduct of the child and the well-being of society. Classroom control was another issue which provoked widely divergent views. Some teachers, mainly – but not exclusively – young, wanted to be personally and emotionally involved with their pupils, while others thought it essential to preserve remoteness, which tended to increase with age. Support for particular teaching methods also appeared to be greatly influenced by a teacher's age, personality and training. There were some who favour talk and chalk, while others find the free discovery, child-centred methods practised in many primary schools most stimulating and rewarding.

From all that I had read, seen and heard, I had a very strong impression that, however many teachers I had interviewed, I would have found a similar mixture of attitudes on these and other topics. But as I assiduously restudied the transcripts of the tapes, which amounted to well over a million words, a common pattern began to emerge, connected not so much with attitudes as with the problems that afflict all sectors of State education to a greater or lesser extent. A few of them, such as the effects of education cuts and of appalling administrative blunders, have already been fairly well publicised, though teachers were able to give some particularly telling examples: a cookery class of twenty-five with only two vegetable knives; a fully equipped gymnasium in a special school with many of the pupils in wheelchairs; a school only fifteen years old which has leaking walls and roof and a heating system that has never worked properly. But the teachers were also conscious of three main categories of problems, largely ignored in public comment and debate, which have an equal or even more devastating impact on their daily work and lives. These three problems – governmental interference, the attitude of parents and the powers of headmasters and headmistresses – are so fundamental that they bring into question the whole structure and nature of the present educational system and the changes that are currently being made.

Practically none of the changes made by the present government find much favour among teachers. In all my travels, I found no one who had a kind word to say for Sir Keith Joseph. I felt that if they had to mark his work, they might have given him $\frac{1}{2}$ out of 10 – for trying. They believe that, even with more adequate preparation and funding, most of his schemes simply will not work in classroom terms, of which, they, obviously, can be the only arbiters. The CPVE, the latest vocational-based scheme on which the government has pinned so many of its hopes, is a fair example. Too much has to be covered in too short a time; some of the work was already being done in a different form anyway; and many of the concepts are beyond the children's understanding. Even teachers find all the attendant jargon of core competencies, modules and vocational families difficult to understand and feel sure that children, parents and employers will find it even more incomprehensible. The associated pupil profiles might have more merit if adequate classroom time were available to negotiate seriously about the comments that go into them; but teachers believe that few employers are going to take the trouble to study such bulky documents, particularly as they exclude all negative statements about the child. Neither do they believe that the children will be greatly impressed by the value of the certificate if it fails to provide them with a job. One head of science with seventeen years' experience, who has just left teaching to open a general store, told me that some kids, even on the pilot scheme, had realised that it was just another useless exercise dreamed up by the system. Teachers also have equally serious reservations about the new GCSE, teacher assessment, the integration of pupils with special needs into ordinary schools and many other changes and proposals.

As one impractical scheme after another is imposed on schools in rapid succession, both the teachers and the pupils become more bewildered and demoralised. Teachers question whether there should be such great emphasis on work-related courses, when jobs seem to be getting more and more scarce. They suspect they are being introduced for the new non-academic sixth form mainly to prevent the formation of an educated dole queue, as they neglect whole areas of creativity and imagination which the majority of teachers see as vital ingredients in a full and rounded education. Their suspicions are increased by the fact that most of these innovations are confined to low-ability children, while the academicism of the bright child remains a self-sufficient justification. As youth unemployment grows, the 16+ scene has become a battlefield with schools competing against colleges and MSC-funded courses to retain their pupils and to remain viable. Should education be based on this kind of competition on a battleground whose boundaries are dictated by the government? For most teachers, real education has no intellectual, moral or aesthetic limits. The current tendency to force reluctant children to take courses which do not lead to paid employment only alienates them and has made a number of teachers question the fundamentally conscripted nature of education itself, with several advocating that formal education might stop at twelve or thirteen, when children can write and read, but with the right of re-entry at any age guaranteed. They realise that such proposals might be impractical or economically unviable, but as one comprehensive teacher said: 'How does progress come about except through idealists dreaming openly?'

Parents of all social classes are another weak link in the educational chain in both State and independent schools. Their assessments of schools are too frequently based on recollections of the sterner discipline and more formal methods of their own school-days, for which, unfortunately, they are too often not much of a personal recommendation. Some of the least educationally useful work in schools is done to satisfy their demands for pretty displays of perfect work on classroom walls at open evenings, when most modern teachers feel that real education should be concerned with the taking of intellectual risks with all its attendant errors. Unfortunately, falling rolls have made it necessary to waste even more time on such work to keep schools viable. Some ignorant parents are opposed to any innovations, such as team teaching or creative writing, without trying to understand the rationale that lies behind them. Professional, middle-class parents, who think they know far more about education than teachers, pose an equivalent threat, particularly at the primary level. In all schools, teachers suffer from the unrealistic demands of some parents for their children, which once brought a tart response from the headmistress of an independent school, 'If you want your daughter to do that, I suggest a brain transplant.' Only totally unsupportive parents cause more problems.

One school has had to put up Health Education Council posters asking parents to talk to their children when they come home. Teachers are now increasingly having to cope with disruptive children of inadequate parents who were themselves disaffected by the educational system. But the problem of inadequate parental support is not confined to one social class. A junior school teacher finds that some middle-class parents are such great believers in self-reliance that they neglect the affectionate side of their relationship with their children.

Even when parents are more involved, much of their efforts go not into genuinely educational development, but into fund-raising (a result of education cuts), social activities and the defence of the school uniform, that badge of class distinction which State schools have copied from the grammar schools and the independent sector. Many teachers find that valuable classroom time is wasted on policing the wearing of the correct uniform and similar non-educational matters, which has made a few call into question the whole vague and outdated concept of *in loco parentis*, which remains the basic legal contract between the teacher and the parent. Too often it is based on the concept of some stern paterfamilias from the Victorian past instead of the open-minded parent of today.

Teachers do not want to ignore parents and, indeed, they could scarcely do so in some nursery and infant schools where they regularly cry on their shoulder or threaten them with physical violence. They see parents as an essential element in a three-way partnership between the child, teacher and parents, and have fairly clear ideas of what the partnership should be; but the ignorance, prejudice or indifference of some parents makes them less than useful allies.

Some heads also cause many needless problems for teachers. Many are authoritarian figures from the past, unskilled and usually untrained in administration and personnel management, who impose their own views and values far too frequently on reluctant teachers and fail to provide the necessary support in areas which should be their chief concern. Even though lip-service has increasingly been paid in recent years to the democratic management of schools, many staff meetings remain parodies of democracy with vital decisions being made before the meeting or in closed rooms afterwards. Some Commonwealth teachers were astonished by the lack of democracy in our schools and the proprietorial attitudes of some heads. One teacher with extensive experience in five countries complained that he had been to information meetings, but never staff meetings, over here. He did not think it would be tolerated in many North American schools.

On the whole, the main plea of the British teachers was for much greater understanding and co-operation both inside and outside schools and for their professional expertise and judgments to be accorded much more attention and respect. Since the end of the war, they have made a sustained attempt to provide an education for each child which accords with his needs and abilities. They have had to make great changes in their own methods, attitudes and conduct to cope with the increasingly intrusive problems of society and the changed children of today, who are far more sceptical, demanding and assertive. As one teacher in a suburban comprehensive told me: 'In the past, a teacher could go in and bellow at his class, but you wouldn't get far with that now.' Teachers can no longer expect immediate respect because of their position, but have to earn it. Their ability to survive in the classroom depends on a negotiated contract, either implicit or explicit, in which the pupil is treated as an individual in his own right whose potentialities will be developed to the fullest possible extent. To accomplish this, they have developed many new professional skills, including a much greater stress on individualised learning to cope with mixed ability classes, collaborative learning to encourage the development of the less literate child, action-research to check on their classroom performance and many more. At the same time, they have had to cope with many reflected problems from society, including an increasing number of disruptive children from deprived and broken homes, a growing lack of motivation among children as jobs become scarcer, racism, sexism, political apathy. No one but teachers can fully appreciate the constant stresses and demands that are made on them hour after hour, day after day, term after term, as they try to provide a full education for each child by dashing from a class of children with special needs to a bright form of A-level students who are going to university, and then on to a class of horrendously naughty third-years. As one mathematics teacher in a comprehensive school told me: 'You don't decide when you're going to change your activity or your *persona*. When the bell goes, you jump!'

This is the first time that a sustained attempt has been made to provide education for all, and it has produced some spectacular failures, as teachers acknowledge, but a much greater number of individual successes, acknowledged by many grateful pupils and parents, though rarely gaining much public praise. Most teachers would not like to return to the more formal methods and the divisive educational system of the past, especially those who lived through it, like one junior teacher I met who can still vividly recall the solemn children – 'real puddens' – from her teaching practice in Norfolk during the Second World War, and the silent rows of children in an inner-city elementary, visited regularly by Nitty Nora, the school nurse who inspected children's heads for lice. But they are deeply concerned that the present trends could put education into reverse, with a greater stress on more formal methods and separate subjects in primary schools and a re-emergence of division in secondary education, with academic high-fliers taking the top grades in GCSE, the less bright taking lower grades possibly in separate classes, and the rest, the majority, taking vocational-orientated courses like CPVE, and going on to unemployment or community work. This is not what the children need or the teachers want, so one consequence might be that we will end up with a majority of teachers and their pupils equally disaffected. Teachers' morale is lower than it has ever been.

I

NURSERY AND INFANT

1

A Drop-Out Before He Starts

People always say there's a very homely atmosphere here. The health visitors especially love coming in for coffee. One of them said to me the other day, 'Oh, I do like it here; I always feel so welcome.' But that's something I can never understand. Why wouldn't they be welcome? We've got what I call an open house here. That's very important in an area like this. Why do we exist if it's not to help the parents of the children, too? They want security; they want someone to talk to, who's even-tempered and friendly. When they go to the social security, the first question is, 'Why are you here?' It's always 'Why?' We never ask them that, but just say, 'Oh, do come in and sit down.' The mums are always surprised when they hear that for the first time. And then we say, 'Would you like a cup of coffee?'

Linda McClune runs a nursery school on an arterial road flanked by rather shabby council houses and flats in a northern industrial city. The school, a squat, single-storey building, is protected from the perils of the road by a chain mesh fence and tall iron gates with child-proof latches. Although there is a well-tended flowerbed in the small side garden and several plant containers beside the path, it looks almost as dispiriting from the outside as its bleak surroundings.

But inside, there is an almost magical transformation. Fresh white paint glistens on the rough brick walls; there are colourful pictures and posters everywhere; and groups of very smartly-dressed little boys and girls are sitting in small contented groups around low tables with their teachers. For such small children, the level of concentration seems high. There are two quiet areas in the open-plan unit and a smaller room at the end of the passage for the youngest children. There are sixty pupils in all, including a number from different ethnic groups and four teachers, plus nursery assistants and students, including some from the Manpower Services Commission scheme. The majority of the parents are on social security and many are one-parent families.

Linda, who has been head for two terms, is a slim, neatly-dressed unmarried woman in her early thirties, who has the quiet, friendly serenity and the inner toughness of a nun. Although she is modest about her achievements, it is obvious that she is very capable and dedicated to her school. She is firmly convinced that nursery education has a vital part to play in children's emotional and social development, especially in the sort of deprived area where she works.

It's very necessary to be warm to our mums, as they have every kind of social problem. They're always coming in to see me. Only this morning, just before you arrived, one came in and said that her son was having nightmares. You have to stop everything and say, 'Do sit down and talk'. She wanted to know the best person to consult. Was it the child guidance? So I told her to go to her own doctor first. That sort of thing goes on every day.

Some of the dads bring the children to school. You may have noticed that. Many of them are not working, you see, and mum may have a job on the sly, some little thing, that no one ever mentions and we're not supposed to know about. But we don't mind.

The mums are very supportive to the school. If we ask for clothes for a jumble sale, they'll bring them in, even though they're often not up to the standard wanted. They all take a great pride in their children. You must have noticed how well they're dressed. They never go to jumble sales themselves for their children's clothes: they only want the newest and the best. I think they can get money from the social services. When we had all that snow a few weeks back, a mother said she'd have to see the social services about getting a pair of boots for her little girl. The next day she was wearing green wellingtons.

Although they take a great pride in their children's appearance, they're not nearly so concerned with their development. My first week here was very difficult. I suppose you'll find it hard to believe, but many of them can't use a knife and fork when they come to school. My stomach was really turned up by the mess they made at the table, pulling meat apart with their little fingers. You see, at home, they don't sit at a table, but in front of the telly, eating fish fingers and beefburgers and all that sort of thing.

The mums would never think of taking their little Johnnie to the park and sitting there with him. It would be too much trouble. So a few weeks ago, when it was such lovely weather, we took all the children to the park. They went berserk with excitement, like animals let out of a zoo. You could hardly get them back here again.

You see, the mothers' priorities are all wrong; but they can't be blamed for that, because so many of them are inadequate. There's often no one here to pick the children up at half past three. Occasionally one of us has to wait with a child till six o'clock. I took one child home the other day and the door was opened by big brother. When I asked him why he hadn't answered the phone, he said he'd only just come in. They've always got some reason why the child hasn't been collected. Dad was supposed to do it, or the boy-friend, more likely. They'd just forgotten. And that happens at least once a week, if not twice.

The children don't mind the first time. It's a novelty to come home and wait with me. They love it. But the next day, they'll be apprehensive that they're not going to be picked up again and you can see the tears coming into their eyes. Some of the mothers do come in the next day and apologise. I tell the others off and say it's not fair on the children, but I don't pursue it with them. It just wouldn't do any good. Oh, yes, I get annoyed sometimes, but what can I do? Nothing! If I get angry, I'm the one who's upset afterwards, not the parents.

Many of the mums simply haven't got a clue. We had notices all over the school about rate-capping. And one mum came in – she was one of many – and said, 'I just can't understand why there are all these notices everywhere. I go down to the library and, you won't believe it, they had one up there. And then I went to the swimming-baths and they had one, too.' So I asked her if she knew what rate-capping meant and she replied, 'No, but they must have plenty of money to put up all those notices.' She wouldn't even wait for me to explain it to her.

I think, perhaps now, after many months, the penny's dropped; but they believe they're going to be okay. They've got a feeling of security, because they're on social security. It's a strange mentality, but lovely in a way, because it's innocent. They're like young children. Many of them can't read or write. Yes, that's true! Some of them can just about sign their own name. That's an awful thing to have to say in this day and age, but it's our fault, way back. They can't be blamed for that.

They always think that the same thing won't happen to their children; but it will, without their support. It's so important that mum and dad – if he's there – should be behind the children all the time. But I think they look on this place as more of a club, not realising that it's an educational establishment.

Although we don't have a curriculum, we do have a structured programme, otherwise it would be absolute chaos. The staff come in between half past eight and a quarter to nine and lay out the room for all the different activities: constructional, perceptual, manipulative, creative. We use all sorts of things, jigsaws, matching cards, old radios, big bricks. Of course, we always have pencils, crayons and paper around and we have the painting out all the time, so that they're free to do their little pictures whenever they like.

We have sand and water all the time. We vary the containers in the sand. One day it will be cylindrical objects, like spools from toilet rolls and kitchen towels, and the next day it might be just spades and buckets. In playing with the water, they use anything from cups to washing-up-liquid bottles. But it's never the same containers every day. Everything is geared to language development. For example, we'll say, 'Fill the bottle; fill the container.' Some children won't know what fill means. Then you'll say, 'Can you empty it?' We don't just sit down and say we're going to do a shape or a colour today. We have a general plan that we're going to cover the numbers from one to ten, say, in the course of so many weeks. So we might have a lot of stories related to five in one week.

It's a fascinating job – there's no doubt about it – but it can be very frustrating at times. You might have organised a lovely activity and spent an hour at home in the evening getting all sorts of gadgets together. And then, just before you're going to start, a child is sick or wets itself. You have to be adaptable all the time. And that's where it becomes so demanding. It's a total dedication, a way of life. There's no getting away from that.

This local authority has given us every support. We have a nursery adviser, who's very helpful and keen that we should do a good job. But some authorities have very few nursery places, even though they're very, very important for all aspects of social and emotional development, particularly in areas like this. First, and most importantly, they get the children away from a very tense situation at home, which often has very cramped accommodation. The children are able to get their tantrums out without their mums telling them to stop it all the time. They learn to play with other children, which they find very difficult sometimes, because they're so aggressive. They have to learn to share, which is not easy for them. Sometimes it takes a whole year. And obviously it helps with their language development, which is important in this particular area. Many of them can't speak English when they come to school, but after a couple of terms there's not a single child who can't relate to us in English.

Speech defects can also be detected much earlier. I take a little boy to speech therapy myself every week. When he speaks, you can't understand a single word. They've been trying to get his mum to take him, but she won't do it, because she's got a young baby and all sorts of problems; probably not being able to get up in the morning is more like it. But I feel it's very important for him to have speech therapy, because when he gets to school next year, he's going to be jeered at and he's never going to learn. He would be a drop-out before he starts. I think that would be so unfair.

2

An Epidemic Can Be Bliss

When I got up, it was raining, so I dashed off to school to let the children in early because there's nowhere for them to shelter in the playground. Usually, there are only two or three children there, but it always creates a problem, as they don't understand – and you can't expect them to – that you're not really on duty yet, and they want to chat to you and get a bit of special attention, which stops you doing your preparation.

But, by the time I arrived, about half past eight, it had stopped raining. The children came in at five to nine and I took the register and so on. Then I started talking to them about stories. Previously, most of them had only written news about what had happened to them, which infants tend to do a lot. So we discussed the difference between a made-up story and a true story and different kinds of stories – animal stories, fairy stories, legends, funny stories, that sort of thing. They settled down to work at half past nine. Most of them worked on their stories for about an hour, but a part-time teacher took some of the very poor readers out to give them extra attention.

Just before half past ten, they had their milk and then they went into the playground. It was wet, but it wasn't actually raining. They came in at ten to eleven. At the beginning of every session, I sit them down on the carpet and teach them as a class. We did a bit of spelling, I think. They went back to their work for about ten minutes and then we all read silently for another ten minutes. I also sit and read at this time because I want the children to see that I regard reading as a worthwhile activity. Of course, the children who are good readers love it; but I insist that they all do it, even if they can't read yet and are just looking at the words. We only do it once a week. Then we went to the hall and did PE before lunchtime. I occupied myself with putting up pictures, sorting through work, getting out new reading books and the million jobs that always need to be done all the time.

In the afternoon, they were doing artwork: rubbing over leaves to make patterns, cutting them out, forming them into pictures and sticking them on pieces of paper. I gave them this work not so much because I thought it was a very worthwhile activity in itself, but because I badly wanted to hear children read individually. It's an eternal problem to get enough time for that, because when you're writing stories or doing maths, they need your help and attention all the time. This went on until afternoon playtime.

When they came back, I read them stories as I do every day. After the children had departed at half past three, I labelled their pictures, cut them out more neatly, drew borders round them, and put them all up on the wall. Plus, more sorting through reading books and the work they'd done and making some decisions about the next day. I left school just after half past four.

Jane Brookbank teaches in an infant school in a prosperous city not far from the south coast. In her late forties, she is slim and bespectacled, with a rather tense, authoritarian appearance but her features softened and her eyes glowed whenever she talked about the children in her care. Her main problems are lack of time, large classes and professional parents who think they know more about education than she does.

When I was young, I never thought of becoming a teacher. I distinctly remember when I passed the 11+ and went to the grammar school for an interview, my parents primed me: 'Don't say you want to be a teacher or a civil servant.' I'd no idea why they said that. So I came up with this rather fanciful idea that I'd like to be a secretary to an author who travelled. I'm not exactly a feminist, but nowadays it makes me quite angry that I was only going to be the secretary, not the author. I didn't really come up with the idea of teaching until I was about sixteen.

I quite enjoyed the teacher training course, but in retrospect I feel that it was very inadequate. That was a long time ago; I don't know what they're like today. Apart from the fact that they called us by our surnames, it was just like being at school. In fact some of the girls who had come straight there from school, which I had not, wore ankle socks. The principal, who was a very imposing lady, terrified the life out of me. The maths lecturer annoyed me most. She only ever came to about four lectures in the two years. The rest of the time she either didn't turn up at all, or else she'd come in and say, 'Oh, I'm so exhausted, darlings, just run off and amuse yourselves.' I think she drank heavily. That was the impression I got. I liked the lecturer in my special subject. She knew her subject well, but she was one of the most nervous persons I have ever met. She had a terrible nervous tic and was endlessly blinking and screwing up her face. At first, it was terribly disconcerting, but after a while you didn't notice it. The education lecturer was about the best, but there wasn't nearly enough teaching practice. I don't say she was outstanding, though she inspired enough interest for me to do a lot of reading.

They were absolutely screaming out for teachers in those days. I remember the chairman of the education committee in my home town trying to convince me that I had a duty to work there, because they had paid for my education. It seems very strange now when some teachers can't get jobs.

My first job was an utterly disastrous experience. I only stayed for a week,

8

because the headmaster hated me and I hated him. He came into my room about every ten minutes or so and kept saying, 'Why aren't they writing in ink? Why aren't they doing joined-up writing? Why aren't they doing harder sums?' And there was I with forty tough little kids trying to get on top of them. I'm not saying that there weren't faults on my side, but it was a very unnerving experience. On the Thursday I rang the education office and said that I couldn't stay there. The head had apparently rung the office, too.

So, on Friday, the inspector arrived. It was a very amusing experience. He came into the room and had a few fatherly words with me and said, 'I'll show you how to control the class.' He clapped his hands and started to talk, but the children just called out ribald remarks. They really were tough little kids. So he quickly realised that he wasn't going to be able to do anything with them, certainly not show off to a younger teacher. As he fled, he turned in the doorway and said, 'I'll ring you from the office.' And sure enough I got a phone call later telling me to report to the office on Monday. I was sent to another school where I settled down happily.

After I'd been teaching for a few years, I left to have a family, and when they were all at secondary school, I got my present job. The school was only built about fifteen years ago, but it's falling apart. It's really dreadful. They're doing the roof at this moment. The rain comes in under the walls and soaks the carpets. It's freezing cold. The heating system has never worked properly from the start. If I do complain about the cold, the caretaker, who is bone idle, brings a portable heater into the classroom, which keeps the temperature just above sixty degrees. The doors open directly on to the playground, which faces north, so there's a most fearful draught in the winter. The whole building was very badly designed.

There are hardly any working class or ethnic minority children in the school, which is a great pity as it does create a rather sterile atmosphere. Most of the children come from comfortably-off, professional homes. The main social problem is these professional parents who think they know at least as much and usually a great deal more than teachers. For the first year or two I felt very threatened, but I've learnt to cope now. I resent excessive interference. Not so long ago, I confiscated a little boy's toy for a day because he'd been doing something with it that I'd specifically forbidden. Apparently on the way home, he must have had a tantrum, because the mother came rushing back and demanded the toy. When I explained what had happened, she was incredibly rude and shouted, 'You've got no right to take it.' I won't stand that sort of behaviour.

Nevertheless, I do feel that education is absolutely a three-way partnership, if you can have such a thing, between the child, the parent and the teacher. There's no valid argument for denying parents the chance to be involved. We send reading books home regularly. I have parents in to hear children read, though not to teach them. And on odd occasions I might have parents in to help with cookery. Considering their expressed concern about their children's education, not nearly as many parents volunteer as you might think.

There are thirty pupils in my class which is far too many. Nine of them are below par in reading, but they're lucky if they get extra help twice a week. In the winter, when an epidemic cuts the numbers to twenty-two or twenty-three, it's bliss! Even twenty-five is nice. It makes a big difference to the noise level.

The atmosphere in my classroom is all-important to me. I work very hard to create a good relationship between the children and myself, which doesn't mean that I give in to them. I'm regarded as very strict, but I feel children need that firmness to feel safe. Sometimes I shout at them. I always feel ashamed afterwards. I encourage the class to discuss discipline. If there's been an epidemic of aggression in the playground, for example, instead of talking to the offender in the corner, I discuss it in front of the class. I think it's good for the offender to hear what other children think about his behaviour.

We don't get many really disruptive children, but there are a few you just can't reach. One little boy made me feel totally impotent. He was extremely bright and had taught himself to read, but he did practically no other work. He spent most of his time being quietly disruptive, breaking a rubber into pieces, or taking things out of one child's drawer and putting them into another's. All his behaviour was very attention-seeking. I was quite convinced that he was in urgent need of psychiatric help, but the headmistress did not agree. He's moved on to a church school now and I'm told that all they do for him there is to pray for him at their weekly staff prayer-meeting.

In spite of these problems, I find teaching very stimulating. You never know what each day is going to bring and you build up a tremendous store of memories – some sad, others amusing. There was quite an amusing incident in the classroom today. As I told you, I was talking about stories and I asked if anyone could tell me the name for real stories that happened a long time ago. Somebody knew the word history. I asked them if they knew anyone who was famous in history. That was difficult for them, which surprised me. Nobody answered at first and then somebody said 'Nelson'. And I think somebody else said 'Queen Victoria'. Then one able little boy said, 'I know a lot of people but I can't remember their names. There was one . . . It was something like Boots.' Well, I didn't cotton on, so I said, 'Perhaps you'll remember it later.' We went on talking and then all of a sudden he said, 'I know who it was. It was Wellington.'

I try to make the children responsible for their own learning instead of just standing there and saying, 'I've got this body of knowledge and I'm going to impart some of it to you.' That doesn't work, in my opinion, with any children, though some secondary schools are still light-years away from seeing that. Another important thing is to treat each child as an individual. I

10

give each one appropriate work and don't expect them all to do the same thing just because it's convenient. In many primary schools, the days are completely unstructured with each child doing assignments at their own speed and spending part of every day playing with toys. I haven't got the courage or organising ability to do that, and my classes are too large anyway. I only let them play with toys one afternoon a week normally. Curiously, it needs much more planning to have an unstructured day.

My greatest stress is having too little time to achieve what I want. I also find it stressful if colleagues are inadequate because that puts a great strain on everybody else. Some teachers, mainly in secondary schools, but also in primary, do the absolute minimum. I don't think this new contract of employment would be much help. It might make some of them do a bit more work, but there are many ways of evading contractual obligations. The only way is to weed out bad teachers.

I'm afraid teachers' esteem has fallen greatly in the last five years. Some of the more militant teachers have not inspired confidence in the public through their strikes, their very casual dress and so on. I'm coming over as someone who knocks secondary teachers and I don't want to do that. All of my own children went to State secondary schools and some of their teachers were very dedicated, caring people, but there were others who had no real interest in the children at all. I despise people for whom teaching is merely a nine to three thirty job.

I don't want to sound terribly pious about myself, but I really do hope every week that I shall reach the children and see some of them grow a bit. Sometimes, however, I just think, 'Oh, God! Monday! It's raining.'

3

Little Demi-Gods

Ruby Pearman, a pleasant, motherly-looking woman with an infectious chuckle and a bright smile, has been teaching in infant and junior schools since the early 1960s, including a five-year spell in Canada. She now works in an infant school in East Anglia. As a result of her experiences in Canada, she believes that infant teaching should be far more structured in Britain than it is. Before the interview began, she warned me that her eleven-year-old son was determined to have a word with 'that gentleman who is coming to see you', which he did.

I work in an infant school which takes rising fives. I take the children after they've been in the school for one or two terms. Before I went to Canada, I worked in an infant school serving a large council estate, teaching mainly six-year-olds, though I did take one reception class. I've also done a lot of supply work with juniors and infants.

What attracted me to primary teaching? I think it was because I'd done a lot of voluntary work with young children, such as helping out with a Brownie pack and teaching a Sunday school class. I was the eldest of a large family so I was used to looking after my little brothers and sisters. The youngest was sixteen years younger than me.

I like teaching infants, though juniors are not such a strain on your nervous energy. Infants are always crowding round you asking, 'How do I do this?' or 'How do I do that?' I don't think most men would be psychologically geared to doing my job. I'm sure you wouldn't stand it for five minutes. The children would be all round you, saying how much they loved you and wanting to sit on your knee. In top infant classes, however, I don't see any reason why a man shouldn't be just as successful as a woman.

I've got twenty-six children in my class, but I've had as many as forty, and for one notorious term it went up to forty-four. It's a pretty tough school serving a London slum clearance estate, which was built in the 1950s. It's a difficult area in general with a lot of social problems. The parents come into the classroom a lot. Many of the mothers are in quite dire straits and are worried and insecure and don't know which way to turn. Very often a teacher is the one secure person they can talk to. I've had many mothers burst into tears for one reason or another, mainly inability to cope with their child or marital problems. So, you're not only doing your own work as a teacher, but also a social worker's job.

I'm not saying that kind of thing is the norm, but it tends to come up very frequently in our school. Whatever has happened to the child, I don't make exceptions: they're all expected to do the things I say. Perhaps I do make allowances privately for a child's inability to cope because their dad has gone off the previous day. I obviously treat them with a certain amount of understanding; but I feel it's no good cushioning them, because they've got to learn to accept hardship, difficult though that may be.

As I have such a wide range of ability in my class, ranging virtually from the non-reader to the child who's reading quite fluently, I stay on at school for two hours every day – and one day until a quarter to seven – getting work ready for the following day. I make a lot of individual work cards or write work in their books and try to create a stimulating atmosphere in the classroom by putting their work and paintings up on the walls. As many of them are language-deprived, I make word cards for the classroom walls to cover practically every experience they're likely to write about: places they're likely to visit, the family and so on. So if they ask how to spell a word, I can say, 'Well, it's in the classroom. Go and look for it.' I can't do very much formal teaching . . .

The telephone rings and Ruby goes to answer it. No sooner has she gone than her eleven-year-old son appears, looking very determined. He is a thin open-faced boy with brown curly hair, wearing jeans and a white shirt. He says he would like to have a word with me.

It isn't very nice to have a mum who's a teacher. She doesn't like it at all. She hates it. She would have liked it, maybe, if she did the same work as in any other job. My mum works from 9 to 3.30. Well, she's supposed to work from 9 to 3.30, but she spends at least two hours afterwards, preparing and making cards and everything else, because she's in a primary school.

My mum's always tired. She has to get all this school work done. On Wednesdays she goes to an evening class, so she has to work until seven or seven thirty on Tuesday evening. She was going to do some of that work on Wednesday evening, but she can't do it, because she has the evening class. My mum has to spend at least three and a half hours working so that she can have one night free. I think it's awful. People who say teachers have an easy life haven't got teachers as mums.

Teachers should get more pay. Bankers get £16,000 a year, new cars, cheap loans, everything like that. It's inflation. Teachers were richer a few years ago. And now, because of all those nuclear missiles Mrs Thatcher wants, inflation is rising. Teachers' pay is not declining, but it's not rising. It's just the same, at a standard below inflation.

Teachers work hard at my school. One teacher I know worked till five in the morning, marking, writing reports. He should have got paid for that.

No, I'm not going to be a teacher. Never! I'm going to be a banker. Maths is one of my best subjects.

My mum really wears herself out. When she's tired she gets in a bad mood. It makes everyone's life a misery. I think teachers should finish work at 3.30 and do all their marking and everything else until five and get paid till 5 o'clock. Plus they should have a twelve per cent pay rise. Then they'd be with inflation, and we'd be richer and have a better life. Has that been recorded? What are you going to do with it? Use it? Really!

It was a little difficult to decide whether his views were based on personal conviction or on the received opinions he had heard at home. Probably as with most children of that age, they were a confused mixture of both.

As I was saying, I can't do very much formal teaching with the whole class, as about half of them wouldn't know what I was talking about. I can only do it when the work is on a physical, rather than an intellectual, level. I do a lot of work on letter formation. I draw a letter on the board and while they're copying it in their books, I parade around with a rubber to erase the odd poor attempt. This is about the only way I can teach the whole class.

In Canada, it was very different. There was a very structured syllabus, which meant that even if a child came from another school, he'd been doing the same work, which was a big advantage. Each unit of work took several weeks. If you found they hadn't learnt it, you'd go back over it again. If some of them didn't make the grade, you got a group offshoot that you had to teach separately. At the end of the year, those who didn't make the final grade, didn't go up. That was one of the biggest differences: they didn't teach children by age. They were six when they came to school, so they were far more mature. It was a professional area and the children were fairly bright and ready to learn. They all had their own workbooks, which could be bought in the local drugstore, and many of the parents had prepared them already before they came to school. Whereas over here my colleague in the reception class has to go through the nitty-gritty from the beginning.

We definitely need more nursery education as the children would be far more mature, socially and emotionally, when they came to school. One of their biggest problems is their inability to express themselves. If you ask them a question about something they've done in class, a lot cannot find the words to describe it. Nursery schools do a lot to train the child to talk and to sort out their emotional hang-ups as they have a chance to play out situations. There's a great deal of value in constructive play, especially in domestic play in Wendy houses. A child learns to come to terms with himself and the world around by coming into contact with other children and adults. As for painting, drawing, modelling and all that sort of thing, it's very therapeutic. A child can often unburden himself in creative work. All of this obviously has a place in infant schools, but it's very difficult to find the time when you're trying to get them to master the basic skills.

On afternoons when I can face the paint, I mix it up and put it out. I tend to link painting with project work. We're doing a bit about Holland now that the bulbs are coming into bloom. I've got a lot of Dutch things to show them, like clogs and tiles, which I brought back from a holiday. We'll probably do a big picture with windmills and tulips, as I like to have an objective in view, and not just slap paint on paper for the sake of it, not being all that creative myself.

When I started teaching in the sixties, there was a very free approach. The school I was in had a kind of integrated day. When the children came in, one of them would go off and paint a picture or model something in clay. The theory was that they would just learn automatically, but I found that it didn't work that way. With the large numbers in classes in those days, some children could get away with doing virtually nothing. By the time I came back from Canada, things had changed quite a lot. The pendulum had swung back to a more formal approach in the early seventies, because junior and secondary schools had been asking, 'What on earth have you taught them?' There were also a lot of public complaints about low standards. I must admit that you can still go into many infant schools which are fairly free and easy. It usually depends on the head teacher. Some heads are far too dominant, little demi-gods, who can intimidate teachers who don't think their way. It's usually better in a JMI with a headmaster, who often knows very little about infant teaching, and will accept virtually anything the infant staff does. I get on very well with my present head who leans towards the formal. And in that atmosphere, I thrive.

II
JUNIOR

4

A Very Ordinary Person

What is a typical day? Is there such a thing, as the unexpected is the norm whenever you're dealing with children? But let's try Friday.

After registration and assembly, three first-year classes split up into setted groups for English before play and setted groups (not necessarily the same children) for maths after play. During the English lesson there will be a variety of work: reading, writing, phonic work, discussion. Each child will need individual help. I will grumble at the lazy one, comfort the tearful one, praise the one who has made a superhuman effort by getting everything right and remembered to write on the lines. After play, I welcome my thirty-two children for maths, while a colleague looks after the 'bottom group' of seventeen. This is a large group for my small classroom as we are doing base work in which the children are split into separate groups doing addition, multiplication, subtraction and division, using cards, worked examples and apparatus. It does ensure that each child can work at his or her own speed.

Once the class has been arranged, I see the children who have problems with maths – they have 'Ask' written on their books – deal with small groups who are all at the same stage in their work, mark books, deal with other problems as they arise, complain about the noise, show children the next step, quell arguments and at 11.30, dinner time, collect the books and collapse into a crumpled heap.

The afternoon starts with a home base lesson when children remain together as a class. At present I have twenty-three in my home base, but I have had as many as thirty-nine. We finish the creative writing we started on Wednesday or the RE we left on Thursday. Today it's my turn to use a computer so some of the children will be taking turns, using one of a variety of programmes. We have three computers with disc drives and a printer and they are in use all the time. After play we have environmental studies. Last term it was the child and his home; this term it's the child and his school and village. This involves a lot of talking, looking and discussion. It's the nearest I come to chalk and talk in the whole week.

Bella Flaxman, a fifty-eight-year-old widow, who lives alone apart from her cats, is a traditional junior teacher who has kept up with modern

developments. She has wide interests, which include reading, genealogy, music and archaeology, which she intends to expand after her
retirement. Her life has contained much adversity, including a serious
operation many years ago, which left her slightly disabled, and the loss
of her husband when she was forty-six, but she has come to terms with
herself and her life and is contented with her lot. She is in the relatively
rare position of having seen teachers from two angles, as a colleague and
also as a laboratory technician. She teaches in a junior school in Wales,
where she has been particularly concerned with teaching slow learners
to read.

I got the job in my present school in 1970 and I have never regretted it.
Previously, I worked in a JMI school in the Midlands. The staff there were
not particularly helpful; the head spent the entire day in his office emerging
only for meals and assembly; and there was no school library. I discovered
later that the books which should have been in my room had been taken over
by other members of staff before I arrived.

The head of my present school is a complete contrast: a perfect gentleman,
caring, courteous and considerate. He will listen to any pupil, parent, or
teacher who has a problem. The school has a good reputation which has been
created by example from the top, by maintaining standards including the
three Rs, and by a lot of hard work by the dedicated staff. There is an
enormous amount of new housing in the village which serves as a dormitory
for the city. Some new firms have moved out here from the city, but the old
core of mining has gone. There is a lot of coming and going and as a
consequence our roll of about two hundred and fifty can vary almost week by
week.

The school itself is on a pleasant site and is built around a central
courtyard with lawns, trees and flower-beds. A few years ago we raised
enough money to glaze the verandahs, which made it much warmer and
more comfortable. Through sponsored events, parents' support and careful
spending, we have everything we need. There is a good library with
thousands of books, three computers, TV and video, several tape recorders,
slide and movie projectors, duplicating and photocopying machines.

For a number of years, we have operated a mixed system of team and class
teaching, which has enormous benefits for both children and staff, as they
meet all of us and we meet all of them. Mostly, I get on well with parents and
nearly every week some parent pops in to see me. I'm not sure how much say
parents should have in the running of a school, as it's difficult for them to be
objective or to see the overall picture. I've had some parents who wanted to
change the whole system of team teaching because their child did not fit into
it. As a parent myself, I can sympathise with them; but as a teacher I have to
consider the greatest good of the greatest number.

I've had one or two battles with parents who think their child is a little angel when we teachers know he's a real devil. As many of the pupils in my remedial classes have emotional or psychological problems, I've had my share of disruptive children. One of the worst was Ken, who was academically bright, but totally self-willed and lacking in control. He would kick, bite, thump, scratch and head-butt. He would scribble or spit on another child's work and tear it up; roll on the floor; crawl under the tables to nip legs; or stand on a table and shout. Every lesson with him was a succession of incidents. If all else failed to rouse me, he would sit in a corner and moan. Every teacher suffered. Punishment or praise were equally ineffectual with him.

Ever since I was at school myself I had wanted to be a teacher, but family circumstances forced me to leave at sixteen and take a job doing chemical analysis for the wartime Ministry of Supply. After the war, I worked in a steel plant. I became a lab assistant almost by chance. After a protracted spell of illness, my doctor advised me to get a job working with people. My previous scientific work was the only training I needed for a lab technician's job. The rest was common sense. I worked in a high school and a comprehensive and was treated with courtesy and respect by the teachers. From watching teachers at work, I learnt much. I saw that when I became a teacher – for that was still my ambition – I would need vast reserves of stamina, a sense of humour, an ability to wield an iron hand in the softest of velvet gloves, the capacity to admit that I might be wrong or that I did not know the answer to a child's question. I resolved that I would treat children with courtesy, not make fun of them, encourage rather then hector, always keep a promise, and treat them as people which they are.

Eventually, I went to a training college when I was thirty-nine. My fellow-students were drawn from all walks of life and some of them had given up well-paid responsible jobs. Just talking to them was an education in itself. I was fortunate to have two of the best tutors in the college for my main and subsidiary subjects. Their lectures, and even more, their tutorials were excellent. I was less impressed by my education tutor, who had only taught for a year herself. But basically, it was a good course. I felt well prepared to tackle the job when I left.

What is the purpose of education? I could write a book about that. Briefly, it is to help a child develop his potential however great or small; to open a door, or indicate a pathway, to something new; to teach a child to question, to consider, to form an opinion; to develop logical thought and the ability to express it; to become a person in his own right and a person to be proud of; to develop socially so that you fit into today's world without losing too many standards of the past. Kipling has said it much better than I ever could in his poem, *If*.

I see myself as a very ordinary person, a bit square, with a few old-fashioned ideas about discipline and good manners, but hard-working, honest, trustworthy and resilient. I have bounced back after a great deal of adversity and ill health. Above all, I am contented with my lot.

5

The Door That's Never Closed

Since I started teaching, which is not all that long ago really, the job has got more and more difficult because of changes in parents' attitudes. They've become much more critical, simply for the sake of being critical in some cases. They often complain that we haven't covered a particular subject and when we tell them that we've done it already, they blame us for not letting them know. They just seem to have picked up a general mood of dissatisfaction from uninformed Press comment, which they then apply to their own children's school.

Steve Dashwood, who is in his late thirties, teaches nine- and ten-year-olds in a southern junior school, which has a very mixed catchment area, including some very large private houses, several local authority homes for children in care and a large council estate. Before he started teaching seven years ago, he had had a successful career as a trust manager in a City solicitor's office. A fluent speaker, with very decided and occasionally extreme views, he sat upright in his armchair, a little tense throughout the interview, which was punctuated by quick chuckles at the most controversial points. He believes that parents have no right to interfere in his professional judgments and also that secondary schools would benefit from a more child-centred approach.

The parents are constantly complaining that the staff don't get involved enough in activities with children in the lunchtime and after school. Some of us do and others don't. Half of us spend most of our free time with the children and the other half spend no time at all. But it's quite a small staff – only seven plus the head for two hundred children – so we said that if any suitably qualified parents wanted to come in and help we would provide a teacher to supervise. Two of the fathers came in to do football, but they concentrated so much on competitiveness, to the neglect of skill training, that it had to be stopped, because it was having such a bad effect on the children. Altogether, we had only three offers of help and all of the helpers were very unreliable. You couldn't guarantee that they'd show up from one week to the next.

Over-protective parents are another big problem. They inhibit the child and put worries into his head which he wouldn't otherwise have. For instance, a child will go home and say, 'I had to do this work today and I found it very hard.' The parents will instantly write a letter or rush up to the school and complain, 'Why are you giving my child such terribly difficult work?' I've even had parents who told their children, 'Well, if it's too hard for you, don't do it.'

On the other hand, it's becoming far more difficult to get some parents to talk to their children at all when they come home. Too many children are left to their own devices. I was interested to see that the Health Education Council has felt the need to produce a poster saying, 'Talk to your children about what they've done at school'. We're going to put them up, because we find that so many children with learning difficulties are starved of a proper emotional relationship with their parents. Oh, no, it's not only a working class thing. Some middle-class parents are such great believers in self-reliance that they neglect the affectionate side of their relationship with their children. The remedial teacher has told me that the biggest improvement she ever sees is when she can persuade parents to sit down regularly and talk to their children and read to them.

In my classroom work at the third-year level, I don't really need any help from parents, as the children are already learning to use their reading and expand their skills. The only outside helper I have is a sixth-form girl from a local school who comes in one morning a week to work with a child who has English as a second language. She gives him a lot of individual attention which he wouldn't otherwise get in a class of thirty-five. He is also getting some help from a remedial teacher four times a week. Unfortunately, he's stuck in the nursery unit of a local authority home, so he's getting no real language experience where he lives.

Parents could help me most if they'd just come in and talk to me. I've never used a closed door since I started teaching. But I'm always rather disgusted when parents won't put themselves out to come, even when I've asked them. I get particularly annoyed with parents who come in to complain at the end of the year, when we haven't been able to get them near the school. In fact, I give them very short shrift.

We're very lucky in our head teacher because she allows each member of staff to develop his own style and methods of teaching. She hardly ever comes into your classroom, but is sufficiently experienced to know that she'll find out soon enough if anything is going wrong. She judges results by what she sees of the children, because she is far more concerned with their character and personality development than examination results, though we do take a couple of NFER papers once a year, just to check on the general level throughout the school.

I'm very independent in a lot of the things I do in the classroom, as, over the years, I've evolved my own methods. Too many teachers try to squeeze children into a fixed system, as if they were things, numbers, calculations, instead of spending some time first looking at the children, finding out about them, and then deciding how you do your job. That's why I'm opposed to having a centrally-determined curriculum. It gets you back to having a system and squeezing the child into it.

You're probably familiar with Postman and Weingartner. Their book, *Teaching as a Subversive Activity*, has influenced me most with its message that before you can teach a child, you have to love the child. I adopted that approach right from the start and I found it infallible. I can't conceive of any other way of teaching.

To me, the most important job in a junior school is to produce literate children who can enjoy their reading and benefit from it. That's why I stopped using graded reading books. A lot of children, who are at the take-off stage, are put off reading by the idea that they have to read this before they can read that. So I evolved my own method, after I'd experimented with it for a term. I get loads of fiction from the local library regularly, fifty to a hundred books at a time, graded roughly according to their age. They have to read a book a week, and I don't usually interfere with their choice, though I'll occasionally discuss it with them. Then we talk about the book when they bring it back. They get away from simply needing a story or a plot and begin to appreciate style and atmosphere and start to enjoy the sheer pleasure of being lost in books.

Even by the age of nine or ten, so many children have closed minds. They're terrified of attempting things and getting them wrong. So with their written work, I encourage them to realise that school is a place for making mistakes, for risking things, as long as they're using their minds in doing so. Therefore, I'm not in favour of wallpapering classrooms with written work. If the children want to put something up, they can do so. When we have open evenings, I give each of them a wallspace and say, 'You know what you like people to see, so you prepare it and then put it up. If you don't want to, I don't mind.'

It's got to the point where I put a note on letters going out to parents saying 'books by request only', because I don't believe they really have the knowledge to interpret exercise books. They can look at them if they like, but they must leave the interpretation to me. It's what I'm trained for and experienced in. In fact, I'd much rather throw books away as soon as they're finished, certainly at primary level, when children don't look back at their work.

Even though I've developed these methods over many years, I still sometimes look at their books with an outsider's eye and wonder if I'm doing the right thing, because their written work doesn't look beautiful and there are a lot of mistakes in it. But there's nothing I hate more than seeing a book with page after page of ticks, though I'm afraid I'm still in a minority in this.

In the same way, I dislike the idea of children not being allowed to think for themselves in maths. Being fond of the subject myself, I encourage them to use whatever methods they find most suitable. Maths is a science, so they're perfectly entitled to experiment. Too many third-year children learn an enormous system of rules without the slightest idea of why they're applying them.

This is one way in which the primary syllabus has been expanded to a ludicrous extent. Until fairly recently, the work was very basic, consisting of a firm grounding in literacy and numeracy and whatever you cared to put around it. But secondary schools are now making increasing demands about what children should be able to do when they get there. To measure angles, you have to teach children a whole new number base, which can perfectly well be delayed until they're thirteen.

I feel sure that secondary schools should be more child-centred. Although they do have year tutors, there's no one they can feel really close to. They haven't got a personal relationship with the teachers. The change is so traumatic that it's responsible for much of the disillusion and loss of interest in the early years of secondary education. That's why children suddenly come alive again when they're in the sixth form. They're in smaller groups, they're far more closely involved with their teachers again, and get to know each other as people.

6

No Innocence in the Playground

The other kids definitely look down on the Bangladeshi children. I just don't believe in the innocence of the playground. Research has proved that children notice racial differences at the age of three. There have been racial fights in my schools. They're easy to stop. You have rules that you don't have fights and that you don't call them 'Bengalis' or 'Pakis', but that doesn't change attitudes. It's difficult. I haven't got the answers, though getting children to work together in mixed groups is a start, as the other children might see that the Bangladeshi children have something to offer, instead of being an alien group huddled together in a corner.

Mary Draffin, who is in her early thirties, has worked as a peripatetic teacher with Bangladeshi children in inner-city schools in the north for eight years. Previously she worked in one of the schools as an ordinary junior teacher for four years. She is very concerned with social attitudes and thinks that one of the answers to racism might be to have more bilingual education in schools.

When I first started my present job, you were seen as someone who was meant to teach English to Bangladeshi kids, but now I work alongside the class teacher in the mainstream classroom, almost as a support teacher really. Usually I take a group of children who have English as a first or second language and work on a specific topic that the teacher, or the teacher and myself, has chosen. I focus on the children learning English as a second language and give them a bit of extra support.

Ideally, you have a planning meeting with the teachers. In one school I work with five teachers, and I know from week to week what I'm going to do. One of the topics we covered last week was time. One of the advantages of having a mixed group is that the Bangladeshi children learn English as a by-product. I wouldn't want the other children to think, 'Those Bangladeshi kids don't know anything because they can't speak English.' When I started this job, some of the Bangladeshi children who hadn't come over here until they were nine, did need a lot of support; but those who have been through the system from the age of five are pretty fluent and equal to their peers who have English as a first language.

26

Their parents are much more confident than they were. Initially very few of them came to the school. When they started to come and collect their kids, you could feel the antagonism from the other mothers – a kind of electric hatred almost. No one actually said anything, but you knew that it was there. On open days, they're usually here in force now. They want their children to do well and to become doctors, things like that. Considering that some of them have not even completed the whole of primary education themselves, they have very high aspirations. The parents often want their daughters to go to an all-girls' school. They have mixed PE, but the girls usually keep their legs covered and if they swim, they go to all-girls' sessions.

Some of the mothers don't know a lot of English, but the fathers do because they've normally been here longer. I've visited some of them in their homes and even if the mother doesn't speak English, she'll sit and grin at you. The kids love me to come: they feel so pleased, so very proud. Yes, they usually feed you, but the meals are so big that you can't really eat them, so I try to go when I'm starving. It's good food, nicely spiced. I like it, anyway.

The parents would rather see more formalised work in primary schools, which comes from their own expectations and experience. I can't generalise, but I think a lot of the other parents too would like more formal teaching, stronger discipline, that sort of thing. There's a lot of misunderstanding but it's up to us as professional teachers to explain why we do things in a particular way, and, in doing that, it might help to clarify our own minds.

The parents are very keen for their children to learn English, but they also want them to keep their own language and culture. After school, they have two hours' extra schooling, learning Bengali and reading the Koran. I think it would be better if these classes were held in the school itself. It would give them more self-esteem. They tend to feel that Bengali isn't a good enough language, so that affects the way they view themselves. A lot of your own identity is wrapped up in your language.

No, I haven't read the Swann Report. It costs £24 for a start, so I shouldn't think it will be widely bought, but I've read about it in the *Times Ed*. Some of it is very good, like the recommendation that schools should be about changing attitudes and working together for what they call education for all. That kind of thing needs to be said.

I think it probably ducked the issue on racism in schools by calling it prejudice and discrimination instead. I also don't like the fact that it ducked out of bilingual education by saying that the children should go to community schools for education in their mother tongue. Research in Canada, where French and English exist alongside each other as equi-status languages, has shown that it's academically beneficial to work in two languages. I think it should have come down strongly in favour of bilingual education. I know that means more money, which is not available at the moment, but it should have been stated in principle.

We monolingual English people might benefit, too. This is probably beyond the pale for most people, but there's nothing academically wrong – or the children wouldn't suffer academically – if the English-speaking children also learnt in another language, Bengali or whatever. Given where they live, it would be useful to them. But there's a whole load of issues there.

By and large, the school system is still a purveyor of white, middle class values. I come from a traditional working class home myself, but the problem is that, whatever my background may have been, I'm seen now as middle class. There's no denying that. I am – now. My connections with working class homes are very limited. Their life experiences are quite different from mine. If the children go to their nan every weekend, we might think it boring; but streetwise, these kids are really on the ball. I don't know how we could change schools to make whatever children bring in more acceptable. Maybe we should make them feel their kind of knowledge is just as important as what's in the textbooks.

I remember having a very bright kid – a white kid – in my class, who really used to worry me, because I could see that he had brains, though he wasn't particularly interested in school work. When his parents came in, I used to say, 'He's really bright, really intelligent', but whether they thought that was important I don't know. They might not have wanted him to make it, because what the hell? Teachers! So what? The parents probably earn twice as much as me, if they are working, of course. There is *that* problem. I might have made it in one respect but not in others. There's a different value system within the working class.

7

Nitty Nora Came Regularly

Alice Fawson taught in inner-city schools for thirty-six years before she retired early on health grounds. She is a brisk, alert, well-preserved woman of sixty, whose thoughts were as well-arranged as her spotless sitting-room. During her long career she saw many changes, most of which were beneficial in her opinion, though she is still unsure where some lines should be drawn. But she is convinced that any attempt to drag education back into the past would not only be detrimental but also impossible with the changed children of today.

I went to college from 1942 to 1944. The entrance age had been lowered during the war, so I went when I was seventeen when I'd passed my Higher Schools Certificate. It was a church college for young ladies. When you went out you had to wear gloves and go in pairs. And you had to be back very early. There was a long list of other rules. It was very strict, lady-like in fact. I thought it was going to be like being in a nunnery for two years.

Then we got a new principal, a very understanding, enlightened woman, who was a friend of the Red Dean of Canterbury. The local people called her 'that red woman up at the college'. We were allowed a lot more freedom after she came, and most of the pre-war rules were changed, though we still had to be in at half past ten. They used to ring a bell on the steps and all the girls came rushing out of the shrubbery. There was an American airbase nearby, you see. Then, I suppose the Yanks went off and found their second girl-friend of the night, but there were no scandals while I was there.

I was trained for secondary, but a lot of chaps were coming back from the forces and, of course, men always thought that secondary schools were their preserve, so when it came to getting a job, it was primary for me. I'm glad now as primary work is far more varied. You teach children, not subjects, and you have your own class, your own classroom, your own little world. I always enjoyed that.

My first job was in an old elementary school, which took children right up to fourteen, which was the school-leaving age then, though it split into junior and secondary soon after I arrived. I was in the junior school. The headmistress was a dear old granny figure who never married. She was very helpful to me. When I arrived she met me off the train and found me lodgings with some friends of hers. She was a dear, even though she told me off later on for not wearing stockings to school and for painting my toenails.

It was a mixed staff which I've always liked. A totally female environment can be rather bitchy and you get bogged down in talk about the job and nothing else. The staff were very cynical and would say things like, 'It's an unprofessional activity to mark books in the staffroom', and things like that. But then if you're not cynical about education sometimes, you don't survive. I was the youngest member of staff by a long way. Consequently, I ended up with all the PE and games, which wasn't really my bag.

The classrooms were sandbagged and a lot of the children were still evacuated. There were sometimes so few children that we could just sit and read a book, but gradually the school got back to normal. When it did, there were forty or more in a class. Sometimes you had a double class. I remember having ninety-seven children for scripture. Some of them had to bring in chairs to sit in the aisles. Then you had to talk to them solidly for half an hour, or sing unaccompanied hymns, or give them moral diatribes.

The children lived in the little two-storeyed terrace houses round the school. They were very poor. In winter, the girls wore little cotton frocks and no socks. The school was heated by open fires and when they stood in front of them, they stank. A lot of them had lice. While I was playing a game with them, called 'pat the dog', in the playground, they all leant over and patted me and I became lousy as a result. The Nitty Nora [a nurse who inspected the children's heads for lice] came round regularly. To get a letter excluding you from school was shameful. I also got impetigo and had to have my face painted with gentian violet. But they were nice, perky kids, not solemn and quiet like the children in Norfolk where I'd done a teaching practice – *they* were real 'puddens', though they're not like that any more.

The children were expected to sit in their desks and listen to teacher, then. Of course, there were some who didn't. I remember one occasion when a child just ran out of her desk and jumped into my lap. I was quite taken aback. I think she must have regarded me as her big sister, because I was only nineteen. About a year later, when I hit a boy for something or other, he went home and cried to his mother. The next day, she came rampaging up, and flung back the door. When I'd told her what he'd done, she pulled him out by the scruff of his neck and clumped him round the ear again in front of the class. Parents wouldn't do that anymore. They don't want you to touch their children, and the younger the teacher, the worse it is. They're not going to have any chit of a girl telling their child what to do.

We had canes then and used them for boys and girls. I remember being on dinner duty once when some of the boys started mucking about. They were all close together on a form, jostling each other, and, like an idiot, I threatened to cane the next one who moved. Of course, they all did. So I had to cane six of those big boys. They just laughed and ran off, but I went in and had to be sick. I couldn't eat my school dinner.

In those days, I didn't have a bean. My first month's salary – it wasn't quite a whole month – was £8. It was very, very little. There were no Scale posts then. You had to serve about fifteen years on an incremental pay scale before you could apply for a deputy headship or a headship. Some counties, like Yorkshire, gave grants to student teachers, but mine didn't, so I had to have a loan to go to college. I couldn't afford to go anywhere much. I read all the books in the public library and went to bed at nine. When I was living with a girl-friend, we used to share a pair of gloves. We went around together with one glove each and the other hand in our pocket. But you must remember that clothes and many other things were rationed then.

I can't really remember how long I stayed at my first school. Quite a long time, I think. I was never one to move about. If I was comfortable where I was, I tended to stay. Altogether, I've only been in four schools in thirty-six years. Education changed tremendously in those years, particularly when new methods of teaching were introduced. At one time, people were getting headships on the strength of having no textbooks in the school and making teachers prepare all their own work. Ridiculous! It was just making the job more and more difficult for no good reason. Not all teachers have an imposing personality, and if you don't have a formal framework, you go under.

The modern methods were quite upsetting for a lot of teachers. We had one pretty little blonde, who was a very old-fashioned type of teacher. Nobody dared move in her class. She taught exactly the same things year after year, but they knew their tables and their grammar so well that to have a class after her was a piece of cake. She became so upset by the new methods that she became ill, left teaching and died not long afterwards.

Another big change was getting rid of streaming, which made the job totally different because you simply hadn't got time to give each child individual attention, so the loudest-mouthed and the most pushy children got most. It was a bit of social engineering which had the reverse effect to what was intended. They didn't want children to feel that they'd been relegated to the C or D stream, but the children who were thick – let's not mince words – were made continuously aware of it in a mixed ability class.

Then there was the great increase in the number of coloured children. When I started teaching, the Jewish children were the odd ones out. They were the brightest and the best at scripture, as they didn't choose to sit out. The Asian children are more like the Jewish children in that they work hard. The West Indians are noisy (I'm generalising now and could pick out lots of exceptions), but some of the brightest children I ever had were black. I remember two black girls in particular who were marvellous at English, drama and art. It's often forgotten that received English is as much a foreign language to blacks as it is to Asians. But, in general, I couldn't have told you whether certain children were black, white or khaki.

Teachers also changed. I think some of them now look a load of scruffs, but the younger teachers work very hard and are full of bright ideas. I picked up all sorts of ideas from them particularly in drama, music and art. Although I never liked the idea of team teaching, not wanting to share my little kingdom with anyone else, I had lots of student-teachers during my last years and I found them very good. If that is what team teaching is like, I would have enjoyed it.

With the introduction of the new methods, it became a far more interesting job. A lot of mistakes were made. There was too much project-based work and too many gaps in what was taught. But I don't think we could ever go back to formal teaching. That time has gone and we shouldn't mourn it, because the children are far more open and much better informed. They may not be as good at spelling or grammar, but they've got a wider knowledge of the world. They are freer; they can discuss things; and they can question the established wisdom. That's been the greatest improvement in my time in schools.

Although there's been a deterioration in the behaviour of juniors, expectations are different now. When I started to teach, nobody expected them to answer back, to query anything, or to tell you that you'd done something wrong. Now you encourage them to do so. You have to make it a bit of a game. Give them a team mark if they can catch you out. Give them ten out of ten if they can make you laugh. I think it's better that way, but there's a line to be drawn. I wouldn't be excessive. But you talk to them as human beings now instead of treating them as little wooden heads to drive nails of information into.

The biggest problem since I started teaching has been the decline in concentration caused by the noise and general movement in schools. One of the things that tired me out more than anything at the end of my time was the noise – not noise from bad behaviour, but controlled talking, not chatting. In those thin buildings with low roofs it was quite oppressive at times. I felt it most when I moved to my last school. It was a new school, with windows and doors open all the time, like Butlins. A terrible building, but so informal that you couldn't be anything else. It wasn't quite open-plan, thank God, which is distraction to the nth degree, but it was so noisy that it was like being inside a drum. You could hear everything going on everywhere. The libraries were only alcoves, so you could never find a quiet corner.

I've been out of teaching for four years and an awful lot has happened in that time. Morale has steadily gone downhill. Falling rolls in junior schools have meant redeployment and cutting staff, and there's nothing more unsettling in a small school than that, because unity is so important. And there's nowhere for people to go for promotion, so they're treading on each other's toes. The heads are driven into the ground with so many surveys and records to keep. And they haven't got enough supply teachers, so they end up teaching a lot as well.

Yes, morale is definitely very low. The answer isn't just more teachers or more money. It's the feeling that you're happily doing what you want to do without restraint. I've got no regrets about becoming a teacher. It was a job I always wanted to do and I loved it. It wore me out, but you don't spend your labour-power without some consequences, do you?

III

FIRST & MIDDLE

8

Honestly, They're Little Darlings

Would you like a beer, a whisky?

Looking younger than his thirty-two years, Ronald Marritt has a frank, open face; dark curly hair and bright blue eyes. He was very honest and self-deprecatory, with an irrepressible sense of humour which caused him to roll around the sofa with mirth from time to time. He teaches in a first school in East Anglia and believes that there will be no increase in teachers' morale until parents, public and politicians start to give teachers some praise for the increasing amount of work they have undertaken in the last few years.

I've only been teaching for eleven years, but it seems ages whenever I bump into my first pupils in the pubs around here. I recognise some of the lads I took for football; but most of the girls have changed out of recognition, all tarted up and that. Blimey! Where have you been all my life? One or two buy me a drink, like a chap who was working behind the bar before he went up to university. Quite amazing, really!

I'm thirty-two and I've reached the dizzy heights of Scale 2 – an extra £400 a year for doing three duties throughout the school. That annoys me, because one of my mates got a Scale 2 after only two years for looking after the school rabbit. But then Scale 2s were around in big junior schools in those days. Not any more. At one time, I wanted to become a head, but I've reached about as high as I want to go. Thanks very much! I've been promoted to my level of incompetence.

I'm on £8,886. A friend of mine, who's only twenty-two, has joined the MOD police and he's on £7,500 plus overtime, so he's picking up around what I earn now. Lord knows what would happen if we started a family and Dawn packed in her job. She earns more than me. I couldn't afford to keep this place.

For the last year, I haven't met a contented teacher, and I've met quite a few on courses. We're all saying, 'When is someone going to say, please, we're doing a good job?' We might not be, but if only someone would say it. I can name five teachers in this area who are looking for other jobs and another three who are just hanging on for early retirement. I don't want to stay in teaching for ever. My parents are getting on and if anything happened to them I'd have a bit of money and Dawn and I would probably set up a bed and breakfast place.

I have to take some stick from my mates, you know. 'Ah, bloody schoolteachers, away on holiday, off again, home again.' Ha! Ha! Ha! But when you think what we're expected to do now, it's ridiculous. In one six-week period, I have to provide the kids with painting, cookery, sewing, play, a project and practical maths, as well as keeping a record of all of it. At one time you could go into a classroom and say, 'Right, get out your comprehension books, page so-and-so, right, off you go.' Not that I ever liked doing that, but there are times when it would be nice to have that option.

The trouble is that we're getting it now from all quarters. No one's got a good word to say for us, especially the *Daily Mail*. Occasionally, someone brings in a cutting and we sit and fume over it in the staffroom. Our public esteem is pretty low, very low in fact. That came out when you read some of the letters in the papers about our pay claim. Okay, with my friends a lot of it's a joke, but some people really mean it.

We had some HMIs in the other day, which is always guaranteed to cheer you up. I think, honestly, that's the closest I came to packing in teaching. Nothing I'd done was good. They didn't say, 'That's a nice piece of work' or 'I'm impressed by that.' Instead it was 'What about this?', 'What about that?' One was very nice and I had a long chat with him about computers, because I'm a sort of whizz-kid on the staff, as I know what a floppy disc is. I do know a bit. More than they do anyway. But the other inspector got very shirty because I called my pupils first- and second-year juniors. He immediately picked me up. 'Not first and second juniors. They're third- and fourth-years in the first school.' We're supposed to be running an integrated day with topic work integrated, but he said, 'If I asked one of your pupils what they'd done in RE or science, what would they say?' I don't know if the pendulum is swinging back to separate subjects again. I honestly don't know. It's just a merry-go-round.

I chose junior teaching because when I started college I was only five feet two and weighed seven stone. That's what put me off secondary. And as for infants, anyone who teaches them deserves about £1,000 a day. How they do it, I just don't know. Little things around your feet, with smells coming up at both ends.

I don't know when I first wanted to teach. I've been dreading you asking that question. I really don't know. It was that – or being a train driver. My father was a minister, so I had a lot to do with the church social club. My cousin was a teacher. I just drifted into it.

My training course was pretty good, really. They slung us out into the schools in the third week. We weren't expected to do much, just observe and take one lesson, but a lot of people left after that. Basically, I think we didn't do enough in schools – three weeks in the first year, four in the second and six in the third. It was a bit of an ordeal when your tutor came into your classroom. You just prayed that the Dean or Sharon in your class would behave. Usually, they were very good. Kids are very perceptive about that sort of thing. They'd had so many student-teachers that they could probably have taught us how to teach.

The first time you stand in front of a class and focus, not on a mass of people, but individuals just staring at you, is a harrowing experience. I'd done a bit of public speaking, reading the lesson and that sort of thing, but after the first teaching practice, I was absolutely shattered. The voice was going. In the evening, I went round to the bar, but by about ten o'clock I was ready for bed. The biggest fear was keeping discipline. Even now, before I go back in September, I still have a nightmare, well, not exactly, a dream that I'm standing in front of this class and they're not doing what I say. I know a couple of other people like that.

I could have stayed for a fourth year to do a B Ed if I'd pulled my finger out, but I was getting into cricket then, beer drinking, girl-friends, things like that. So I left it very late to apply for a job and didn't get one by September. So I went back and shared a flat with two friends who were doing a B Ed. I was on social security. Then I got a job in a junior school, in spite of turning up early for the interview. My dad kept on to my mother, 'He's got to go! Make sure he goes!' So I did – a week early.

It was a very formal school with most of the kids sitting in rows and the fourth year streamed. Basically, I was dumped into a classroom and left to get on with it. I think they're far more aware now of the problems of being a probationary teacher in knowing what other people are getting from the kids.

I didn't agree with what was going on. I found the school very repressive on the children. It was just: You sit there – you be quiet – I stand up – and you copy it down. I didn't really have the expertise then to do class-based projects with them. I suppose I was a bit immature, so I tended to side with the kids. I had almighty up-and-downers with the deputy head, the head, and I nearly got the sack. It was a stupid thing. I stayed behind to play football with some of the kids in the hall and two or three dinner plates got smashed. Instead of reporting it, I tried to cover up for myself and the kid. I knew I was under pressure. I thought, 'Blimey! That's it! Curtains! . . .'

Have another beer? . . . It's difficult to pour from these plastic bottles . . .

Yes, as I was saying, I was under a fair bit of pressure. I had an advisory teacher coming in to help me to organise myself. I must admit I wasn't doing my job properly. I was behind with the marking. But it was all basically because I didn't believe in what the school was doing. I couldn't find the right way to fight against it. You know what I mean? So I decided to get right away and work in a different county for a bit.

The new school, a junior and infants, was a real culture shock. It was the first time a kid of ten had told me to eff off. I'd never had kids run out of lesson and threaten to go home. There were fights all over the place, especially when it was windy. No, I don't know why it happens. It's an age-old problem. Some American psychologist has counted the incidence of fights on windy days. Most teachers will tell you that kids are more aggressive on a windy day, particularly in a confined space like a playground.

There was one lad there, John, who I think would be a real good football hooligan. He wasn't too bright, quite vicious in a nasty sort of way and a bit sly. He was fairly tall with very angular features, and hair down like this, around his cheeks. He was quite a good footballer – I've still got a photo of him in the team – when he wasn't kicking someone instead of the ball. The main thing wrong with him, and lots of other kids, was that they just couldn't take it when things went wrong. Yet there was something likeable about him. After he'd left, he'd shout out 'Ullo, Mr Marritt' whenever he saw me, and wave.

Mind you, I'm painting a bit of a black picture. There were some super kids there, really great ones. Going away with them was great. I love that. You see a totally different side of them. We took them away to the seaside on an adventure week, and some of them had never seen the sea. One of them just stood on the edge of the beach with the tide coming in over her boots, amazed that she was getting wet. I don't know if you've been to that coast, but the tide goes out for miles. When she saw this, she couldn't believe it and asked 'Where's the water gone?' But those kids came up trumps. They behaved beautifully, much better than they did in school. The school was very heavily weighted down to the lower ability. Some of the parents expected us to work miracles, but when you get kids coming in at the age of five and their language is 'Me poohs', you're not going to turn them into geniuses by the age of eleven. It was an open-plan school, which I'd never taught in before, and it was from then on that I really felt that I was starting to do the job properly.

While I was there, I got married for the first time. I hadn't been there long, about eight months, when the wife left me. The pressures of the job were partly responsible. The first hour when I come home, I'm very ratty and just want to sit down in front of the TV and lose myself in cartoons. My wife wasn't working and wanted to know what sort of day I'd had, which was the last thing I wanted to talk about. Also she wanted a family, but I didn't want kids of mine brought up in a two-bedroomed flat and I couldn't afford anything better. She left in December so I rang the head and said, 'Look, can you ask everybody not to ask me what kind of holiday I've had, as I'm likely to burst into tears.' The whole staff was tremendously supportive. I just threw myself totally into the job. I've never worked so hard before or since.

Then this job in a first school came up and I moved back here. We've got about two hundred pupils, mainly Council, from about the second roughest estate. As I'm sure you're aware, councils have different grades of estates. I suppose about 70 per cent of our kids come from the Council. That sounds really terrible, doesn't it, but it's true. So there's a lot of broken homes, but no coloured kids unfortunately. That's one thing about East Anglia. We did have one coloured boy once and there are a couple of Chinese. We've got one lad, who's Welsh, with a very sallow skin, and some of the other kids call him 'wop', 'Indian' or 'darkie', so Lord knows what would happen if they came across a real coloured kid. Generally I take the kid who's been calling names on one side and try to reason it out, but on other occasions I just shout 'Watch it, paleface!' It's always difficult to know how much to bring it into focus, because if you mention it, perhaps you're emphasising the problem. It's very dodgy – and a shame.

This school isn't as tough as my previous school. We only take kids up to the age of nine. They've got a lot of problems on the estate because there's nowhere for them to play. There's nothing up there for them – just a few swings. There's all the grass area, but no ball games are allowed. Most of them are outside the club at night waiting for mum and dad to come out. There isn't much home back-up, which is very, very sad . . . very sad. How many of the parents actually talk to their children? It's 'Right! Sit down! Shut up!' And then on goes the TV. That's a lot to do with it.

By the time the kids leave us, they do get 'leavingitis', the feeling that they're beyond all this. So when I go up to the middle school and see some of them at ten or eleven, I look at them and think, 'Yes, I could see that happening . . . Oh, no, that doesn't surprise me.' They're adolescing, of course, really kicking out against things, trying to establish themselves. Kids are far more confident than I ever was. I mean, coo, at their age I wouldn't have said boo to a goose. That sounds awful, doesn't it, looking back at my age and saying 'Well, blimey, when I was a kid . . . ' but I am.

The school is again very low weighted. Most of the kids have an IQ between eighty and ninety-five, so when a kid comes along who's about a hundred and ten or a hundred and fifteen, you think 'Great', and in a way you mislead the parents, because their child stands out. It's very difficult to find time to push the bright kids and extend them, particularly since we've had to spend so much more time on these statement things about children with special needs. By law, we've got to provide specialised teaching for kids with emotional, physical or academic problems – and there's one more I've forgotten. Anyway, the acronym spells APES. If a child is deaf in one ear, you've got to be aware of it and show you are. Or if a kid's got an emotional problem and wets himself every time you say 'rabbit' or something, you've got to put it down in his statement and show that you're providing for him. It's created a lot more work but it's only what we've been doing from time immemorial. It's just something else for us to do in addition to the other records we have to keep. We're being overloaded with paper and policies . . .

Let's have another beer . . .

The kids I teach range from seven years of age to just nine. There are thirty-one in the class. At the beginning of the year I tend to do a lot of classwork, so that I can judge what they're capable of. No matter how many records come up from below, you've got to form your own opinions. One kid who might not work with one teacher will click with you, and vice versa, of course. Then later on in the year, my teaching becomes far more group-based. Usually, I call the groups after planes. 'Right! Concorde, first of all I want this piece of art work, then your maths, then a piece of writing and then, if you get that done, free choice, maybe.' It would be nice to give them more time for painting, but most parents want to see writing and arithmetic when they come in.

I often set them a piece of writing, talk about it, give them a stimulus and say, 'Right, you've got twenty minutes.' While they're working, I walk round and talk about it with them. I never mark at home. I mean, I take books home to let them know that I'm keeping an eye on them and I might tick something to show that I've read it. But if I mark, I sit down with the kid. That sounds great, I know, but someone has a bleeding nose, someone's having a fight because they've lost a pencil-sharpener, or whatever. Some days I just give over to writing, maybe about once a month. Or I might say, 'This is a practical day.' It's difficult to strike a balance. I envy any teacher who can. There are some who are a hundred times more organised than me. I wish I could be more organised but I'm not that sort of creature. In the last few years it's just been one thing after another. You just get your science going and someone will come in and say, 'What about your art?' So you start on that and then somebody else will say, 'How about your RE?'

My favourite project? I think it's usually the last one. I took five of my kids to a field study centre, where I did a project on village life. We talked about it in general, then we all made clay cottages. I invented a village community and made out a census showing who lived in each house and how long they'd lived there. Yes, that went well. But some projects, you can spend perhaps two weeks in the summer preparing them, and they'll go off like a damp squib. Another time, a project might fizzle out after a week, and you've got nothing prepared, but something crops up, and for some unknown reason the kids love it and they're away. Then you're going down to the resource library, taking books and slides home and it will go on for two or three weeks. No problem! It's strange, really. You can never tell.

We've got one computer between six classes at the moment, so if you take a twelve-week term, you don't really get a long enough run at it. The ideal would be to have one between two classes to begin with and then possibly one in each classroom. Then it would be just like a library. If a kid was doing something in maths, you could say 'Oh, look, there's a programme that might help you.'

At the moment, it's still being used very much as an introduction to project work. It's still a bit false, you know. 'There's the COMPUTER. We'll have to use it.' No one asks what you're doing with it, but unless it's on from nine to three thirty, you feel you're not making much use of it. At the moment we're doing co-ordinates. There's a programme called 'Pirates', where the computer hides a treasure on a grid. It can be any size you like; you can work in three dimensions and all that. The kids love it. They like the game element, I'd be lying if I said they didn't, but computers do have terrific potential, though I'd hate to see them take over completely.

The kids don't find reading desirable anymore: it's slowly becoming a social skill. I'm a great believer that if they've got a model at home of mum or dad reading, then they'll read. If mum and dad don't, what are they going to copy? I knew a teacher who made the kids get out their reading books for half an hour every week. The teacher sat there reading too, just to give them a model. I don't know whether HMIs would approve but it seems perfectly justifiable to me.

As you can see, I'm surrounded by books. I've got loads more upstairs. I often take one of them in and say, 'Hey, look, here's a book.' One kid is into model railways, so I brought some books along for him. Because Chris was interested, some of the other kids became interested too. I've got about five or six lads and a girl into it now.

I prefer teaching boys as they get older, but most teachers now are aware that you mustn't be sexist and gender-cast the kids. The boys do cookery and needlework. Some of the boys enjoy needlework, but a lot can't get the co-ordination right. Sewing is good for improving fine control. The girls can do football if they like. It's nice to see them out there. If you see a boy in tears, it's still very tempting to say, 'Come on, lad, big boys don't cry', but now I say, 'Let it go. It does you good.' Crying *is* nice, I must admit. When my first wife left I did an awful lot of it and it made me feel a hell of a lot better.

Sex now is far more blurred. You glance at someone and think 'Is that a boy or a girl?' We have discos for the kids and when you see a five- or six-year-old with the old make-up on, and the sparkle, and the real disco gear, you think, 'Oh, they've lost something!' A lot of the boys have girl-friends, going steady and things, which I didn't achieve until I was eighteen. I must have been a late developer. Some of them don't like sitting next to girls, but by the time they leave us, the majority are taking an interest in girls.

In spite of all the problems, I still like my job, especially the kids. It's terrific, there's no two ways about it. At the end of the year, I like to think that we've got a tremendous camaraderie. I'm lucky. I've got a fairly good rapport with the kids. I slip into it easily. I like having a laugh and a joke with them. When we took those kids to a field studies centre, we had a sing-song, I taught them a rugby song, cleaned up, you know, but lots of action. We did daft things. We made them give an after-dinner speech. It's a chance for them to see you're human.

If you're feeling down, the kids are terrific. I tend to tell them, to say, 'Look, I didn't sleep very well last night, so tread carefully.' So one of them will come up and say something daft or make an awful joke, or offer to do a job for me.

'Any jobs, sir?'

'Yes, tidy my desk.'

'Oh, no. Not *that*.'

My advice to any probationary teacher would be to tell the kids you have a sore throat and you can't shout. Honestly, they're little darlings! Oh, yes, they really are.

I hate whingeing about the job because I do enjoy it, and deep down, although a lot of us want to get out, it's not because of the kids, but because there's no thanks for it. Most of the teachers I know are really great people. Some are pains, definitely, but then again they probably think the same about me. There are some incredibly dedicated teachers, far more than I am. They live and die school. When we were told we were less professional than we were ten years ago, that was devastating. I think Sir Keith Joseph said that. Maybe not him. Probably the *Daily Mail* . . .

9

A Roomful of Animals

In the back of my mind, I have this idea that I've got a roomful of animals. I think of their awareness of me in animal terms, so that they can be whatever I make of them. If they were a bunch of horses, I could whip them up in such a way that they'd be useless. They could be fierce, as fierce as I make them. I remember that middle school where the kids went over the top about two years ago and were pulling down the ceilings. It's only their subconscious idea of what behaviour should be that stops them running riot. But I can also imagine that if I had the same horses and could evolve the right atmosphere we could do anything we wanted to together, and it would be a pleasure for all concerned.

George Finley, who is in his early forties, teaches at a middle school in the Midlands. There were long pauses in the conversation as he turned away shyly, lost in isolated thought, before he turned back again with a frank, engaging smile. He worked in industry before he became a teacher and it has taken him much time and effort to adjust to his new role and to learn how to cope with the complex interactions which go on in the classroom. He would like to have the chance to see other teachers at work far more and to discuss common problems.

I went into teaching for all the wrong reasons – short hours, long holidays and the idea that I'd have enough time to set up my own business. It didn't work out at all. I ought to have known better, as my father was a teacher, but he worked in a grammar school. Although he brought marking home, his job was very different from mine, much more settled. It was easier for him to know what he was doing. If he saw my classroom, I'm sure he would be absolutely horrified. He just can't envisage what my school is like.

Before I became a teacher, I worked as a designer in industry. It was a dead-end job with no chance of making progress unless you were brilliant. So I went on a post-graduate teaching course for a year, which I enjoyed. It was much better than sitting in a factory working out pattern designs. I liked the academic side, but the practical side wasn't very useful, though I understand it's much better now. The present students do far more observation in schools in a sort of apprentice fashion, which is the only way you can learn any sort of art.

My first job was at a small primary school in an expensive dormitory village, very different from my present school. All the children were smartly dressed in uniform. They were expected to move quietly from one classroom to another and to eat their lunch in total silence except for a short period of quiet chatting at the end. In assembly, the head stood behind a sort of lectern, in traditional fashion, with his staff ranged on either side. He once told the female staff, 'I like my ladies to wear skirts', and I seem to remember that I was obliged to wear a collar and tie. In many ways he was running a nice little preparatory school which was what the parents wanted.

Although I liked the head personally, he reminded me of my father; I didn't feel that working in a school like that was doing a lot for society. I wouldn't call myself a political – capital P – person, but I'd developed a bit of a social conscience by that time. So I left after two years and got a post in a middle school for three years.

When my first marriage began to break up, I left teaching and got a job mending holes in vinyl furniture. That was a dreadful job, terribly solitary. I was working in holiday camps in the middle of the winter in huge ballrooms which were bitterly cold and dark, not seeing another person for hours and hours at a time. After a while, I met up with a chap I'd worked with before, who was setting up a handicraft workshop. It seemed a good idea so I threw in my lot with him, lost a lot of money and just avoided being made a bankrupt. When the business collapsed, I just wanted to get away. I'd met my present wife by then and we went abroad for four months. When we returned, I needed money desperately, so I went back to teaching.

I've been at this school for four years now. We have about three hundred pupils. The catchment area includes quite a large number of council houses and terraced houses like mine. The teaching is mainly informal, but staff are allowed to use their own methods. Unless things are going badly wrong, no one interferes. We try to bring the children progressively towards a more secondary way of working. In the first year, they are with the class teacher almost constantly; but by the time they leave us at the age of twelve, they're moving around in groups from teacher to teacher.

I don't think the concept of middle schools has yet been sorted out. Like everyone else I have only hazy ideas about it. The middle school age range is considered to be a distinct era in children's emotional and psychological development. The first school was developed as a separate entity, dealing with . . . I don't know much about Piaget . . . but dealing with the sort of concrete, operational type, leaving the middle schools to deal with the transition to higher thought processes at twelve or thirteen.

The first two or three years in this school were very difficult for me, even though I'd already done quite a bit of teaching. The children didn't know how to act in a classroom situation: their socialisation wasn't complete. They couldn't sit at their desks and work, but wanted to make friends with the children around them. There was a lot of talking and moving about. They weren't actually destroying the ceilings, but the relationship deteriorated to such an extent that there was no way in which I liked them and some of them disliked me.

It needs a lot of work to recover from that situation. A teacher is very isolated. You can go to a colleague and say, 'They're a hell of a bunch', and get a sympathetic hearing, but you've got to work it out for yourself ultimately. I overcame it by trial and error. There's no prescription for getting control. Maybe it's a shout or a threat or just waiting there with the right expression on your face. There were times when none of these worked. Teaching is an art, having an eye for the types of movements and an ear for the sounds that indicate the machine is not running properly.

Teachers need much more time to discuss common problems and to evolve a sense of purpose between themselves. I went on a one-week course a couple of years ago – the only residential in-service training I've had in nine years of teaching – and what we all appreciated most was getting together, talking and comparing notes. It was so useful that some of us decided to meet every month as we still do. I would like to spend much more time seeing what other teachers are doing. That would be the best form of in-service training. It's just an extension of the apprenticeship idea really. I wouldn't mind people coming into my classroom so long as I could include them in what was going on. It's different if someone comes in to observe in a critical way. There are lots of complex relationships going on in a classroom. You can imagine what it would be like if someone looked at one of your relationships critically. It would alter it completely.

I like teaching much better now and I want to stay in this school because I'm reaping the benefits of all the hard work I've put into the relationship. I still have a yearning to set up another business, though that will probably remain a dream. A lot of teachers see their work as a vocation, but I could never feel that. In some ways, I see myself as a performer, an entertainer, setting up activities for the children at their level. If they enjoy them, then the job is done.

IV

COMPREHENSIVE – I

10

All Paper Tigers

Jane Rymell is a tall, strikingly attractive blonde with a trim figure in her early forties, who was smartly dressed in an expensive-looking frock and high heels. She teaches in a large comprehensive in the north with a socially mixed intake, which lives under the threat of closure. There has been some vandalism in the school, so that classrooms containing valuable equipment are locked at lunchtime. The staff have to go and find the key if they want to work in them. Her biggest problems are lack of time, conflicting demands and poor communications.

What did I do yesterday? Just let me get my diary. I shan't be a minute . . . Ah, yes, here it is. Well, I'd cleared everything the previous night – all my marking and preparation – so that the day would be absolutely clear. My head of year had been away ill for a month and I'd had to cope with all the pastoral and discipline problems.

When I got to school, I found that she'd returned. She told me that a visiting speaker was coming in to address the fifth-year assembly about religion. It was arranged that I would fetch her from the headmaster's study and show her off the premises. That immediately made me worry, because I knew that while I was showing her out, an unruly class of fourth-years would be waiting for me outside the classroom.

Anyway, when the bell went at five to nine, I dashed up to my classroom and took the register. I was also telling lads to put their blazers on, ticking off girls for wearing the wrong coloured shoes, taking an absence note, talking to other children who wanted to see the welfare officer about tetanus jabs and arranging to have the books for my fourth-year class sent up to the room from the main store. I was literally trying to do ten jobs at once. I was also thinking about the four notes I'd found in my pigeon-hole when I arrived at school, one from a social worker about a problem girl, another about someone who had been truanting, which would all need following up that day.

When I'd finished registration, I went to the head's office and met the speaker. She was a wispy little woman who looked very ineffectual and I thought 'Oh, dear, this is going to be a shambles!' I knew from past experience that if a speaker isn't very good, the atmosphere in assembly can soon deteriorate. But she proved to be a very good speaker and, even though she wasn't a teacher, she stopped when the bell went at nine twenty-five. On the way out, she started to get into a deep discussion about the lack of religion in assemblies, and though I would have liked to talk about it, I was getting increasingly worried about my fourth-year class. So I had, more or less, to push her out of the door and say, 'Thanks very much! Bye!' – without even offering her a cup of coffee. I felt guilty about that.

I dashed up the stairs to my fourth-year class and got them settled down. We did half an hour of a class reader, which is hard work, because the book is actually beyond them, but I'd chosen it deliberately, because I thought it would stretch their vocabulary and their imagination. For the next half hour, they were copying out and decorating work which I'd marked previously so that it could be displayed on the walls for a parents' evening. They love doing that and seeing their work on the walls, so I don't think that side of it is bad, but I was doing it mainly to sell the school to parents – to say, 'Look, this is what we're capable of producing.' Therefore I questioned my own motives. With falling rolls, however, it's a question of keeping the school open.

Towards the end of the lesson, I sent four children around the school with notes for children I wanted to see at break. I was concerned about this, because teachers don't like to be interrupted while they're teaching, and quite rightly so, but how else do you contact pupils in such a big school, when a situation suddenly crops up? It's all right if you've had time to get a message into the notices.

During break I was on duty as a wanderer, when you're free to go to any part of the playground. If you're in a bad mood or tired, you can make your way to the easy places where nothing is likely to be happening. If you're full of enthusiasm and zeal, you can go to the trouble spots, like the lavatories, where other teachers are likely to need support. In fact, it was a very pleasant duty and nothing dreadful happened, though I picked up one or two school uniform problems. Our school is very hot on uniforms. Personally, I think the whole business is ridiculous. All we're really trying to do is to say to the rest of the world that this is a good, well-organised school – and we need more pupils to keep open. That's what it's all about. If parents see children beautifully dressed in the same smart uniform, they'll imagine, quite wrongly, that it must be better than another school where the children wear a hotch-potch of untidy clothes.

Then I had a second-year, who were also copying out work for the parents' evening. That was easy, because they're a very, very pleasant class. They enjoyed the work and it gave me time to follow up on some pastoral stuff and have a look into absentees who might be truanting. At the back of my mind, I was very concerned about what was going on in the class, because these second-years need a lot of stretching. It worries me a lot how you stretch the brighter child as it's almost impossible in a class of thirty, particularly if you're teaching mixed ability.

So, out of guilt, I stopped them copying out work and spent the last twenty minutes setting up quite a lot of academic home work to make up for the time they'd lost in class. This was the only way I could justify the wasted time to myself.

I had lunch in the dining room, which I've only started doing recently, as it gives me a chance to discover what is going on in other departments. Although there's lots of paper being shuffled round the school all the time, some exciting projects in other departments just don't become generally known. For instance, I found out during lunch that the maths department had just started this fantastic project with their first-years of an individual-ised programme for each child, which I've seen in junior schools but never at the secondary level. The only way I found out was by chatting to a man in the maths department. It's just the same with in-service courses. The head is quite keen to send people off and the teachers come back all enthused, but we don't get the full benefits as there's not sufficient feedback.

After lunch, I had a fifth-year class. It was difficult with this class at first, because there was a new syllabus, which I didn't even know I was going to teach, called Communications. At the beginning I was frightened, but now I find it very good. Half-way through the lesson, when they'd settled down to some written work, I was very tempted to leave them to make some official phone calls. I resisted the temptation, however, because I'd come back on two previous occasions to find that they weren't working. It's not fair on them.

I then did another break duty which was fairly quiet. Finally, I had a first-year class that I'm not very happy with. Generally, I feel better with the upper end of the school – the fifth and sixth years. And I feel particularly uncomfortable with this class, because I'm teaching a method that doesn't suit me. My new head of department has a trendy 1960s approach. Her idea is that the children should all sit round in a group and do work on a theme she has chosen. When she discusses it with me, I'm very enthused. When I get in the classroom, however, I find it doesn't work. So I backtracked and did a very formal lesson on how to set out a letter, which bored them to tears. They complained that they'd already done it in junior school. Either they'd forgotten, or they'd been badly taught.

I wanted to leave school fairly quickly so that I could get on with my marking. I was giving two other members of staff a lift and I had to wait a quarter of an hour for one of them because he had a discipline problem.

My main worry is that there's never time to do anything properly. We're constantly being bombarded with so much paperwork, so much change. Just to mark, prepare and teach is too big a work-load for most people. You either dash through things and do half a job, or you cut out whole areas you can't keep up with. No sooner are you competent to do one thing than the

Whitehall people come along, or the headmaster, or the head of the department, and change the whole damn thing so that you're floundering again.

Yet information we *do* need is often not provided. For example, I agree with the new 16+ exam which I'm going to be expected to teach, but the only way I know anything about it has been by going out and buying the report. No one has come along and put it in my pigeon-hole. Why haven't they? Why haven't we teachers been informed? And other changes are happening in the sixth form. Next year the CPVE is being introduced. The only way I know anything about it is because I made the effort to find out for myself. It's all happening, but nobody knows.

Some teachers get very lazy, because they've become cynical about what can be achieved. Once they're on a Scale 3, they sit back and do less and less until they're doing next to nothing. There's one particular teacher who's been in the school for about fifteen years. He irritates me and other people tremendously. He doesn't mark much and seems very lazy indeed; but I've never actually been in his classroom and who am I to say that he isn't doing a better job there than I am?

It's very difficult to tell a good teacher from appearance. I've met some teachers and thought, 'Good heavens, they can't possibly cope.' In their classrooms, however, they've got instant discipline, instant organisation. I remember a chap who used to travel with me to school in my first job. He was a very shy man and had a terrible stutter, but in the classroom he had what it takes.

To do the job properly – I know some teachers would disagree with me – you have to preserve a certain remoteness. The older I get, the more remote I become. I feel sad about that. If you start being too friendly, all sorts of situations arise in the classroom – you know, jokes, a little bit of trouble-making. I've made the mistake in the past of letting sixth-formers chat as they work in a group of nine or ten, and I found it very difficult to get them down to work straight away in the next lesson. Keeping good discipline is the foundation on which you build everything else. It's not something you can learn. There are teachers who have been in the job for years who still have children hanging out of the windows.

With a new class, I give myself a fortnight to weigh them up, teaching very simple, well-structured stuff, before I start pushing them in the direction I want them to go. I like to sort out the personalities so that I know the likely trouble-makers who might disturb the rest of the class. Not that I don't think they're worthy in their own right of having my attention, but I don't want them to have too much. Once I've pinpointed them, I separate them.

We don't have many sanctions: we're all paper tigers really. The head of year and the deputy head can put kids on report, which means that they have to carry a card around with them which each teacher signs at the end of a lesson. That works well, if the head of year follows it up. If he doesn't, they can get away with almost anything. Detention is another sanction. It's not encouraged for classroom offences, only school abuse. Then there's referral to the senior master or mistress, who might give them a strict warning. Letters home. Bringing in parents to discuss whether the child will conform to the school rules. If they don't, they can be excluded for one or two days. And ultimately, I suppose, expulsion. A structured system helps younger teachers, but a good teacher can cope without it, while a poor teacher will always make a mess of the classroom situation.

I suppose a good teacher is one who encourages children to become complete, autonomous, decision-making human beings. But how do you do that in an authoritarian set-up? That's the conflict. And it's one I don't know the answer to, because all the time I'm imposing my discipline, I'm not encouraging their self-motivation. How do you have a child-based education with thirty secondary children in the class? I can't do it. I'm trying to get into lessons to observe teachers who say they can, because I would like to know the answer. I would dearly love to watch and learn. Unfortunately, I can't fit it into my timetable.

11

Don't Ask Me How I See Myself

Teaching hasn't been the radical profession I thought it would be. I'm a feminist, so sexism in schools is very, very important to me. Most of the teachers at my school would tell you they'd done their best to eradicate it, but the school is still riddled with prejudice, really.

Iris Leafold, who is twenty-four, teaches in a suburban comprehensive in the north-east. The sitting room of her detached house on a small estate was comfortably furnished with deep sofas and armchairs, a heavy-pile white carpet and velvet curtains. There was an impressive hi-fi system playing classical music when I arrived. Her surprisingly luxurious life-style was financed more by the pay of her husband who works in industry than her Scale 1 salary. This is her first job and she is still adjusting her idealistic views to those of the workaday world; but she believes it is important for the new generation of teachers to introduce their own values into the rather closed and conservative institutes of education.

Not long after I arrived at this school, I went to an exhibition of teaching materials. I picked up a book and the very first sentence was: 'In the beginning, man did not dominate the world as he does now.' That was the first sentence! So I cried out, 'Oh, look at this!' When the other teachers read it, they looked at me as if to say, 'What's she making such a fuss about? Everybody knows that by "man" we mean men and women.' Okay, I know that. But I don't think we ought to be telling children 'man this' and 'man that' when we could so easily use another word: 'humankind'. Those things may be insignificant in themselves, but they do have a cumulative effect.

Feminists may seem humourless at times – that's the classic criticism, isn't it? – but if you get involved in the women's movement, you get very angry, really angry, about what's happening to women. There are four deputy heads, three male and one female. The men are responsible for discipline, curriculum development and timetabling, while the woman is responsible for the pastoral side, the caring. That's an absolute stereotype. It's really, really wrong. Before we had a nurse, kids would be sent to her if they needed a finger bandaged. It's just awful, really.

Another teacher and I wanted to start a self-defence group for girls. There was a lot of opposition. One of the teachers actually made negative comments about us. 'I don't know what you want a self-defence group for, *girls*. Ho! Ho! Ho!' That sort of thing. Eventually we obtained the head's support and got the group going; but it was a shock to come up against such strong opposition. I'd never expected that. It was just my naivety, really.

As far as the subjects are concerned, the most obvious things have been dealt with. There's nothing like all the boys doing metalwork and woodwork and the girls doing cookery. But there's still a distinction. It's very subtle, but then it's the subtle things which are the most insidious.

You're right to ask me for specific examples, but it's hard to think of them offhand. Well, for instance, if there's some event in the school, it's always the girls who are taken out of class to help with the tea-trolley. It's partly a question of proselytising the boys, really. They demand your attention and energy all the time, whereas on the whole the girls don't. I've actually had boys saying to me 'You're giving the girls too much attention. You're always favourine them.' In actual fact, all I'm trying to do is to give them an equal amount.

I belong to a women's support group which meets every week to talk about how we're feeling and what's been happening to us. It's a consciousness-raising group, really. If it hadn't been for the other women, I would have given up. They've given me tremendous support by saying, 'Yes, you are right to make a fuss about that – you are right to say you don't think that's right.'

Curiously, I only got interested in the women's movement after I got married while I was still a student. I met an Italian woman at university, who was very involved in politics in her own country, and it was through talking to her that I became interested. My experiences since then have made me an even stronger feminist.

When I started teaching, I thought my youth would be a difficulty, but it's been a positive advantage. The kids don't like teachers who consciously try to be one of them, part of their culture; but I haven't had to try. I still listen to their kind of music and watch the same television programmes as them. I'm not all that much older than the sixth-formers, so I can chat to them about being a student, going to university, things like that. I look very young for my age. People often come to the front door and ask, 'Is your mum in?' It's been a great link.

The kids were a bit suspicious of me at first. They thought I was being a bit too matey, really. I was just being myself. It sounds a cliché, but it's true. I dress in jeans and tee-shirts to please myself. So, after a while, the girls started asking 'Where did you get those jeans?' or 'Oh, I do like your earrings: where did you buy them?'

I've been reprimanded by older teachers for getting emotionally involved with the kids too much in what they say and do. They were horrified that I actually had sixth-formers round to my house. It does mean that I get hurt and upset sometimes, but I've had immense rewards from my involvement, far greater than if I'd kept myself detached. It comes down to whether you can handle that kind of situation or not. A lot of teachers can't. Whether that's what teaching should be all about, I don't know.

Most of the kids come from prosperous working class homes. They've all got computers, videos and BMX bikes. None of the parents is really, really well-off, but there's plenty of money about. A lot of them work in local shops. Others are employed in service or manufacturing industries or at the local airport. There's a handful of coloured children, whose parents are mainly doctors or shopkeepers. In the town centre, there's much more unemployment and the schools are much more difficult, but I really don't know much about them.

The kids are so conservative, it's horrifying, really. They just repeat their parents' views. Anything I say to redress the balance has very little effect at all. Lots of parents worry about left-wing teachers subverting the natural order of things, but they don't need to worry about their children being turned into communists, certainly not in my school. It's hard enough to get the kids to question any of their own views. I'm not in any political party myself, though I do vote Labour.

Although it's stressful working with children, you can get a lot back if you invest enough of yourself. They're not so two-faced as adults. Although they sometimes try to talk about other people behind their backs, they haven't yet developed the kind of sophisticated back-biting which goes on in the staffroom, under the surface, for weeks and weeks and weeks. That's very nasty.

Honesty is very important to me. When I was a student, all my friends were really honest with each other. It was okay to say, 'I feel really bad or really awful about that.' When I started work, I hoped that people would be able to say what they really felt. It wasn't like that at all. I've had great difficulty in explaining what I wanted out of the job. There were a series of misunderstandings with my head of department about my needs as a person as well as a teacher.

I think I was naïve, really. It was partly a result of never having worked before. I went straight from grammar school to university, which isn't necessarily a good idea. Even on teaching practice, we were still relatively protected. We couldn't have coped with a tough school at all. We were very cut off from the outside world. During the Falklands war, a little isolated group of us on teaching practice were sitting around, drinking coffee, and criticising the media for trumpeting about the 'Argies'. I still wouldn't support a war of that kind politically, but I guess I'm much more in touch with other people's points of view now.

So when a little pip-squeak like me came into this school and started criticising things, I can see how other teachers resented it. A lot of them had been at the school since it opened and had put in an enormous amount of work to build it up. Academically, it's not brilliant, though it does offer a really rounded education, which is very, very good. I've had to learn to come to terms with what is going on outside myself and what effect I'm having on other people, though I still want to be myself and do what I want to do. I think teachers should be consulted far more about changes because it's only when you're involved in what is going on in the classroom that you can make sound judgments. We get edicts from the head, but he does very, very little classroom teaching. Schools aren't as democratic as they should be. That's what I've been trying to say, really.

Actually, I never wanted to be a teacher. Practically everyone who reads English at university wants to work in television, radio or journalism. That ambition was again the result of my incredible innocence and ignorance – and bad careers advice as well. I have to say that. It was an impossible dream. Like many other people, I'd applied for a teaching course as a fail-safe measure. So that is what I did.

The training course was very good. We did a basic core of English studies and another option. The teaching practice lasted six or seven weeks. The supervisor was excellent and kept a very low profile, because everyone gets paranoid about being supervised on TP. He was extremely helpful and supportive and made a lot of positive suggestions and wasn't critical at all.

In my first lesson, I'd put a simple, straightforward piece of work on the blackboard. The kids had to copy it down and put in the punctuation. Afterwards, the supervisor asked, 'Are you sure that was really worthwhile?' I had to admit that it wasn't, really. I'd felt that if there was any noise in the classroom, it would look as if I couldn't control the kids. I'd never do anything like that now, because I know there is such a thing as productive noise. Some teachers insist on absolute silence, but a lot of my teaching is based on group work and discussion. There are always kids who want to chat to their friends, but as you get more experienced, you begin to . . . I don't know how it happens . . . you begin to tune into things. You can be at the front of the class and know what's going on at a table in the far corner, whether they're working or chatting.

The school where I did my TP was on a split site, about three miles apart, really dreadful. As a student I didn't have a car, so I had to rely on lifts from other teachers or taxis, which sometimes didn't turn up. It was an extra strain, particularly as I like being punctual. Although it wasn't a tough school and I didn't have difficult classes there were times when I just broke down in tears in the staffroom. Oh, yes, I did that a lot. I can't remember what it was about. Probably a kid or a situation I hadn't dealt with properly. The staff were very sympathetic. They'd say, 'We've all been here before.' And then we'd just talk through what had happened and how I could avoid it in the future.

I've been teaching for two years now. My mum, who also teaches, says she thinks I'm a natural teacher. I don't believe her, really. There are lots of teachers who are competent and capable, but very few who have a real vocation. The thought that I might is quite worrying, really. It's not my own self-image. But don't ask me how I see myself.

12

Getting Me Green Bananas

She is black, attractive, bouncing with energy, laughter, enthusiasm. After working in industry for four years, Selma Thomson trained as a teacher and is now head of department in a Midlands comprehensive. She is only thirty. Her school, which is situated in an area which has seen better days, has a socially mixed intake with about forty per cent of the pupils from ethnic minorities. Selma was born in London, where her father worked on the buses, and has been to the West Indies only once for a childhood holiday, though she would like to go again. She is opposed to positive discrimination for blacks and appalled by the alienation from education of many black and white children – and their parents.

Being black means a lot of headaches, strife, struggle, proving yourself the whole time, proving that you're not like the parody on television, proving that you've got a brain, which may not be true in my case. [She laughs uproariously.] There again, I say I haven't got a brain, but that might be the result of what people have told me all along the line. That's a whole big argument we could get into.

I've always felt that as a black, you've got to be that little bit better. If somebody puts ninety per cent into a job, you've got to put a hundred and one per cent, you know what I mean? It's fighting against the system the whole time, making sure that you're getting your fair share, bracing yourself, hardening yourself. Even in this day and age, you're still expecting knocks. And it's being on the defensive, too: 'Well, I can't help what I am.' For me that's the hard bit.

The positive aspect is that there's a certain solidarity with other black teachers. Not so much with Asians, but if I come across a black teacher, we've got a united front straight away, even though, later, there may be things we don't like about each other. That is very powerful. I suppose there are so few black people in the professions that whenever you come into contact with one, you're brethren and sistren straight away, you know what I mean? At my school, there's a black probationer, whom I hardly ever see because of the timetable. We make a point of contacting each other – just a smile or an acknowledgement. 'We're in this together, huh!' I suppose it must have been the same for whites in India.

Racial prejudice isn't so overt as it used to be. No one calls me a black bastard now. I notice it most from white, middle-class parents who are absolutely shocked when they discover that I'm black. A mother came into the classroom after school yesterday to see me. She asked if she could speak to Miss Thomson and I replied, 'She's here.' Apparently the child hadn't even mentioned that I was black. The mother was shocked but quickly covered up her feelings by saying, 'Oh, really, I hadn't expected you to be so young.'

I've never come across a child who's resented me because I'm black. They treat me like any other teacher. If you take up your position in front of the class, holding that bit of chalk, you're in charge, well, as much as they will allow you to be! The black children test me more than the white ones. They want to know more about my life, where I'm from, which island, what I'm going to buy when I go shopping, because that tells them a lot about where you're at. They ask me, 'Are you going shopping, miss?' and I reply, 'Oh, yes, I'm getting me yams and me green bananas.' That's what they want to hear. When they speak in patois, Creole, or whatever you want to call it, I know what's going on, I can join in their jokes. Sometimes I use little terms of endearment that their mother might use, that my mother said to me. When they get a bit uptight, I can say, 'Co-oool it, baby!' and they'll do what I say. They see me as a mother figure in a lot of ways, do you know what I mean? As long as it's seen that I'm not pushing either the blacks or the whites it's fine.

White teachers treat me in one of two ways. Either I'm 'the lovely black whom the children adore' or there's a certain jealousy, 'How can *she* get away with that?' Some of them envy my relationship with the black children. We've only got one or two liberal white teachers in the school, or who think they are, or try to be. I have very little to do with them. They're more of a threat in many ways, because they're only expounding all those trendy ideas, which don't work anyway, for the furtherance of their own careers.

I remember reading a report about four years ago which said that one in seven hundred teachers was black. I wouldn't imagine that it's much better now. There are access courses – I know of one in London – which are trying to improve the situation, but I don't like positive discrimination. If you need two A levels then you damn well go out and get them, even if it takes you ten years. Otherwise, they're always going to have it over you that you just got there by going on an access course. I feel you've got to meet the whites on their own terms, you know what I mean?

I've got a very close male friend from a white, very middle-class background. It's got to the point where I dread meeting his parents, because I'm a bit of an oddity to them. They'll say to me, 'I'm sure you must find it easier with the black children than with the white.' I'm on guard all the time. When I go to their home out in the country, people in the street actually stop and stare at me. Isn't that awful?

A lot of the kids in the school, both black and white, think they've got a raw deal. Many of them think, 'Just let's get out of here as quick as possible.' There's a lack of vision about what they're going to do. 'Oh, well,' they say, 'I'll get a job or go on a YTS scheme, maybe.' Very few have an ambition to forge ahead and do the best they can. It's almost an acceptance of the inevitable. I say to them, 'Don't you want to do anything *more* than that?' and they reply, 'No, just want to leave school, can't wait to leave.' They're fourth-years, third-years even. A lot of them are just going through the system because they have to. Their attitude is, 'Let's get this thing over and done with and then get on with the rest of our life.'

We once had a discussion, well, a little chat really, about being at school. A lot of them were there for social reasons. It was boring at home and it was pleasant to come to school and have a muck-about with your mates: it's a nine to half past three club for many of them. It's almost impossible to motivate them. The only way is to give them easy work. Read a passage. Answer ten questions. If you ask them what they think about something, they'll say, 'I don't know. Where's the answer?' There's no feeling of inquiry. The girls are only interested in boy-friends, pop groups, hair-dos, fashion. They've got a school uniform, but they twist it any way they can. They're supposed to wear a navy-blue jumper and a white open-neck blouse, so they wear white blouses with ties, or light blue jumpers, or white boots instead of black shoes.

Sometimes we have real trouble. Three years ago, there was fighting between our school and another. It was mainly the girls getting their teeth into each other. They were nicking hockey sticks and rampaging down the main road, ready to bash people over the head. We had helicopters whirring overhead. It was all over in an hour or so. After school, the police, who were supposed to be keeping a low profile, parked a minibus full of burly policemen right outside the school gates. I don't know if it's all the fault of the school, or society, or their homes.

We now have the children of the disaffected couples of the 1960s in the school. These children . . . how can I put it? . . . there's nothing else in life but them. It's just what they can get, when they can get it. Me! Me! Me! That's something I've come up against time and time again, and it's sad.

Take Gloria, for example. She's a big fat girl and a very aggressive individual. She's got long hair which will be an attribute later as that's a sign of beauty if you're black, and she's what we call a fair skin. Teachers are frightened by Gloria, really frightened. She's threatened one teacher and the other girls had to hold her off. She's beaten up numerous children and even put a knife to one child. Luckily, she respects me. She sees me as a straight person. The reason is that I say to her, 'Look, this is what I think of you today. You're getting on my nerves.' So she realises that I've got limits too. If it was left to me, I'd spend every waking minute of my day dealing with her. I've recommended that she needs help, psychiatric or counselling, but no one wants to know. I don't like to prophesy, but within five years that girl's going to be inside for grievous bodily harm or something worse. I'm not exaggerating.

There are only three or four teachers on the whole staff who are really in tune with the kids. A head of year who was organising a day trip said to me, 'All the children on free dinners are going and they all seem to have plenty of money to spend.' I tried to explain that it might be their only holiday of the year and that their mothers wanted to make sure they had a good time, even if it meant not paying the rent that week. Having lived through that situation myself, I know what it's like, but I don't think she understood.

I'm sure some of the teachers see the children as animals, real beasts. I can't explain it much more than that. Some of them feel very sorry for the kids, so they're full of missionary zeal, but others say: 'I don't know what's going to happen to her. She just won't sit still. She looks so messy. And that jumper! Her mother's just as bad.' They just don't see that there might be other factors.

We run life experience courses, but too many of the teachers don't know about real life themselves. Let's say they're talking about going to a family planning clinic. They just photocopy something from a textbook. The kids really resent it when they're being taught about birth control by some wizened old spinster. 'Nah, you don't do that!' they say. These kids know more than she does, because they have to. You can't fool them. They're too sophisticated. Life experience courses have a certain relevance, but we only slot them in because they look good on the curriculum analysis, do you see what I mean?

I've always supported State education, but this last year or two, I've begun to question its value. Recently, I've talked to a couple of people who are working in the private sector. And they're able to teach. They can go into a classroom and do what they've prepared, but I'm spending a good half to three-quarters of my time acting like a policewoman.

Schools ought to get away from a rigid timetable and give the children a certain amount of work to do within the week. I don't know if it would work, but, just to illustrate the point, I've been doing a very simple thing this year. I'm hopeless at keeping records, so I got some ordinary eight-by-five cards and gave them out to the class, so that they could keep a record of the work they've done. If I forget to give them out, someone will call out, 'Where's those cards, miss?' They are their cards, their record and they want to keep them up-to-date for miss. It's just a simple thing, but they like that kind of involvement. We spoon-feed them far too much.

Effectively, education as we know it could stop at twelve or thirteen, once they're literate and numerate. Education in that sense would stop and real education as far as I'm concerned, of wanting to find out for yourself, could begin. They could opt for a whole range of things they'd like to do. For example, one might say, 'We've learnt something about the Romans and I want to know more about them.' So they could go and learn Latin. I'm not saying they'd do that all the time but for a large part of the day. Some might want to tinker about with cars. If they merely wanted to be acquainted with the basics, they could do it for a term. Some of them might say, 'Oh, I quite like this, I could get into this.' And before you know it, they'd be on an eighteen-month or two-year course. There are people who are bookish and they could go away in a corner and read. Entrance to universities or polytechnics wouldn't be decided on A level results, but by presenting a project. You're always going to have the disaffected. Quite what you do with them, I don't know. You could give them a voucher and say, 'Okay, when you're ready, you can come back.' And that might not be until they're forty-five. Economically, it might not work, but that would be my dream.

13

The Wrong Priorities

The problems of deprivation and alienation were already apparent in secondary modern schools as Valerie Ramsley discovered when she started work in a northern industrial city twenty-five years ago. The amalgamation of these schools with grammar schools to form comprehensives frequently intensified the problems as the grammar school staff (with their different experience, attitudes and aims) could scarcely be expected to provide solutions. Apart from a break while her children were growing up, Valerie has spent most of her career in secondary schools teaching domestic science.

The secondary modern school was in a poor area of the city and sometimes only five of the twenty children in the class could afford to bring ingredients. So, if they were going to make a cheese and potato pie, they had to make a potato pie instead. That didn't happen every lesson, but ingredients always seem to have been a problem, particularly with younger children, throughout my career. Sometimes, a number would say their family didn't like fish, so you could never cook that. It seems a great pity. In other subjects, the materials are all provided, even if they have to buy what they've made, as in woodwork.

I tried selling some of the cakes they'd made in school, but honestly you wouldn't have wanted to buy them. No, they weren't burnt. Some children came from very poor homes and weren't too clean in their person. Even though I always made them wash their hands at the beginning of a lesson, I wouldn't have trusted them not to dip their fingers in while my back was turned.

The lessons lasted the whole morning or afternoon, so I had time to deal with children individually; but when I moved to a girls' high school, which became a co-educational comprehensive within a few years, the lessons were much shorter. You'd got to get those cakes finished so that the next class could use the ovens. You were literally pushing one lot of children into the room, pushing them out, and pushing the next lot in, all day long.

Occasionally, the children made some terrible mistakes. I remember one child who was supposed to have put something in the oven on a baking sheet. After a while, I noticed a very odd smell, rather like mushrooms, which I couldn't make out at all. I went to the oven and found a white plastic tray which was dissolving and running down the rungs of the shelves. You needed eyes in the back of your head.

To save time, I sometimes used convenience foods, though I always taught them how to use natural foods first. I'd have liked to use more whole foods, but the changes in eating habits in the last ten years don't seem to have been reflected in schools as much as they should have been. It was partly owing to the exam syllabus, or maybe it was my particular head of department. You can't go very far beyond what the head of department or parents will accept. A parent once wrote in to say that she didn't think her daughter ought to be making salads in the winter. I went to the head of department and asked if she would answer it and she replied, 'No, because I agree with what the mother says.' Another problem with whole foods is that they take much longer to cook. It takes three-quarters of an hour to cook brown rice, while white rice takes ten minutes.

The Asian children were delightful and very hard-working. They used to ask me if they could have the recipes to take home to mum. Some of the West Indians weren't quite as biddable. None of them ever asked me if they could cook their own food. Not a single one. They were all quite keen on our cakes and puddings.

Some of the boys were very keen on cookery. One boy, who was a real devil in other classes, really liked cookery and always rolled up his sleeves and got cracking straight away. He came from a very large family. I don't think they had much money, but the parents were very keen for him to learn cookery. They'd always praise the dishes he took home. Food was more immediate to them than an essay. They could eat it! Eventually that boy went into the navy as a cook.

Education cuts made an enormous difference in my last few years at that school. There were only two vegetable knives for a class of twenty-five. I mean you can't have children cutting up vegetables with great big cook's knives. Somehow, the priorities were all wrong. We had a child-care flat, which was scarcely used, filled with expensive equipment like playpens, pushchairs, and Lord knows what, while we were scratching around for tea-towels, dishcloths and vegetable knives.

Domestic science had a pretty low status there, anyway. As it was originally a high school, all of the staff, apart from domestic science and PE teachers, had degrees. They'd all wear their gowns at speech day. I don't think that helped our status much. Oh, yes, they went on wearing them after it became a comprehensive.

14

Co-operation, Not Competition

Some secondary modern schools tried to provide a more open, flexible, child-centred education, but these experiments were often defeated by parental opposition, especially during their transformation into comprehensives. John Tapsell is one teacher who experienced such a traumatic change which has left its mark on his rather pinched and haunted-looking face. As he talked, he frequently clutched his brow and closed his eyes in intensity of thought, of feeling, as he pondered on the destruction of his dreams. From time to time he rifled through his large file, bulging with letters, newspaper cuttings and documents, to produce some evidence. He is in his fifties and teaches in a comprehensive south of London.

I've worked in this school since it opened as a secondary modern and I've seen it swing from one extreme to the other. Have you heard of Michael Duane? Right! Well, the first headmaster was very much in that mould.

The school was open, relaxed, innovative in its curriculum. The head wanted to teach the boys, not subjects, so he instituted a system called 'inter-disciplinary inquiry', which broke down the barriers between subjects. There were teams of teachers acting as consultants and sources of knowledge rather than givers-out of facts. The art department, the science department, the library became resources that the children could use for their research, you see. The kids no longer sat in rows but wandered about the school. They might be sent into town as part of their task. We had a fleet of twenty old bikes we'd repaired which they could borrow to cycle into town.

The head encouraged the children to treat you as a friend, to talk to you in a fairly familiar way. He deliberately appointed young teachers in the hope they'd be more open-minded.

Naturally, as anybody who has tried to introduce these more open, flexible methods will tell you, the kids were quite wild at first. 'We can go anywhere in this school? No locked doors? Go into the library at break! Wee-hee!!' It was a very strenuous and demanding time. The school wasn't entirely free – nothing like A. S. Neill's. Some people in the town thought that kids were no longer having proper maths lessons, English, French, history, geography, which of course they were, because you had to cover basic skills. It was much more structured than they thought – and extremely successful. When our first small intake reached exam level, we had quite staggering results for secondary modern boys. One has now got a fine arts degree, another a commercial art degree, another has a PhD, five more have got other degrees, and one became a doctor – not to mention others who became telephone engineers or plumbers and the one or two who ended up in gaol. Right?

An even greater success was a boy called Robbie who came to us at the age of eleven having been to no less than twelve primary schools. He was wild, he really was, completely unsocialised. The head called his year group together one day when Robbie was away. He told them: 'Look, Robbie's difficult. You know this and I know it. And I'm going to tell you what's wrong with him. He's been to twelve different schools. In every school, he's been beaten. And you can see that it hasn't worked. So I'm not going to beat him. The only thing we can do with Robbie is to let him run around the corridors and get it out of his system.'

And it worked. It wasn't a miracle, overnight cure, but gradually the lad settled down. He was still a bit mad because there were other mad kids in the class as well. The marvellous thing is that the other kids responded to the head's appeal, saw what the problem was and helped. That boy has grown up now. He's still not very bright, but he's got a beautiful wife and two small children. We just about managed to teach him English, but we could never teach him much else. What is most remarkable and rewarding is that he's just gone into an adult group to learn maths.

After a number of years, it was proposed that the school should merge with a girls' secondary modern and become an all-ability mixed school. There was great opposition from the parents at the girls' school. A scandalous series of letters was published in the local paper vilifying our school, saying there was no discipline, that the boys didn't take exams, that they were always in the town. It really was appalling.

Anyway, the proposed merger never came about and our school became a mixed comprehensive. A new head and a new board of governors were appointed, and there was a completely new policy. The school swung right the other way. The new head tried to run it like a grammar school. He even wore a gown. Within two weeks the kids were walking quietly in the corridors and standing in lines in assembly. Once, on a blazing hot summer day, the boys were told that they could remove their ties so long as they put their shirt-collars outside their blazers. The whole philosophy was, 'You don't ask any questions. You do as you're told. You toe the line.' One of the other teachers said, 'When are they going to tell them which hand to use when they go to the toilet?' I was miserably unhappy in that period. It was a diabolical time. It made me anti-authoritarian . . . Excuse me . . .

I'm sorry about that. When I was evacuated as a child during the war, I became a chronic bed-wetter. The stress of that period at school brought it back. It's left me with a weak bladder. I get little leaks, really. I keep thinking that I've got over it, but some things stir it up again and I'm just having to be very, very patient . . .

Now, where was I? Oh, yes. There are two ways of running a school: the Michael Duane, A. S. Neill – Whoosh! – Black Paper spectrum. Either you can open the doors, let the kids in, get to know them, find out what they know and what they want to know, and discover what their real needs are and try to provide for them; or, you can shut the doors first, draw up a scheme, then open the doors, let the kids come in, and force them to fit into pigeon-holes. Right? Naturally, if you do the latter, conflicts arise, because for a large number of children what happens in school is irrelevant to their needs. Much of what goes on has less to do with bringing out their latent abilities, or giving them an atmosphere in which they can grow, but far more with forcing them to conform to pre-ordained patterns. You've heard of the hidden curriculum? Right! The school prospectus says we do O and A levels and get people into universities, but what it doesn't state is that we also teach children to conform and toe the line generally by means of various ploys and sanctions: to walk quietly, to wear uniforms, to say, 'Yes, sir, no sir, three bags full, sir.' Another part of the hidden curriculum is what goes on in the playground: how the children learn to relate socially to their peers and to the generation above and below, be it in a civilised way or not, and how to deal with bullying, either as a bully or as a victim. Games! That's another part. Everybody does games. It's all based on the irrelevant anachronism of the old public school system as a criterion against which we measure everything we do in schools. The house system! Competitiveness! Don't get me on to the subject of competitiveness. Yes, it's all quite irrelevant and in some ways a lot of it is dangerous. Getting back to competitiveness, I think all this harping on winning and beating other people, which you get with exams, games and competitions, is evil, positively evil. We should be teaching co-operation, not competition. Sponsored events, where children compete against themselves, are much better . . .

Where was I? Oh, yes! Children who have academic ability, even if they come from a working class background like mine, can fit into this situation and get their eight O levels and their three A levels and go on to university. The reason is that although the home may be working class, the parents are potentially academic. They aspire, you see, to certain things. Right? That's one bit of it. Another bit is that they are well-integrated, well-balanced people, so that they provide a secure home which is very important for a child. A secure and loving home can be dirty, disorganised, illiterate. A secure home is a good foundation for kids to follow any path that suits them best. Kids who are not academic, but have domestic security, will still achieve well, which might mean five CSEs and a bricklaying apprenticeship or no CSEs and a builder's labourer. Right? What bothers me are the others for whom school seems inappropriate. To me that twenty per cent, or more, is just as important as the other twenty per cent of bright kids who need stretching.

Many teachers dismiss these disaffected children as dimwits, because schools are run by people who like studying and passing exams. Many of these 'dim' kids are streetwise: they can listen, remember, put two and two together, come to logical conclusions. It's just that they're not interested in what goes on in school; or, very often, all their psychological energies are tangled up in their domestic situation. I'm thinking of one particular boy who was capable of getting six O levels, but didn't get one. A teacher condemned him for being bone idle and wasting his talents. All the boy's energies, however, were centred on helping his mother to cope with five younger children and a drunkard father, you see. That's where you've got to find out what their real need is and, if it's for security and a loving relationship with understanding adults, maybe that's what we should provide – as this school did for Robbie.

In passing, I think this is one of the reasons that secondary moderns failed. The grammar schools were good – I was at one myself and was perfectly happy – because they knew what they were about: they had narrow parameters. So did the old elementary all-age schools. The Education Act of 1944 divided the elementary schools horizontally, putting all the elevens to fourteens in a secondary modern, which was the first step towards giving the pupils the same status as those who had passed the 11+ exam. Then the school-leaving age was raised to fifteen, and later sixteen, to end the business of you going to work in your clogs and overalls, while clever Johnnie round the corner was still going to a posh school with his cap and tie and satchel. Instead of trying to cope with the real needs of the non-academic child, many secondary moderns envied the grammar schools and tried to ape them, which made them feel even more inferior. In that situation, the comprehensive school was the best solution, but comprehensives continued the grammar school ethos and also incorporated the secondary modern's envy. If you were to quote me verbatim, you'd have every bloody comprehensive headmaster in the country saying, 'Rubbish! That's not what happens in my school.' But it does.

So, you've got this kind of unnatural situation stunting in many ways the growth of certain children. There's another bit that bothers me. You've got more and more people saying, 'Well, of course, you mustn't use the cane, it's uncivilised' and all the things that STOPP says. So what do you do with the little buggers when they won't do their homework? You mustn't cane them, so we make them stand out in the corridor, which they treat as a joke, or we put them in detention after school, and when they don't turn up, we put them in detention again. The headmaster wastes hours lecturing them ineffectively because he doesn't know anything about counselling techniques. He just nags them and they're bored to tears. Eventually, you write to the parents and they don't want to do anything about it, because they hated school, too.

In the present situation, I consider that I'm *in loco parentis*. I've always taken that principle as my guide. Therefore I object to someone telling me that I can't touch the kids, because I think I'm mature, intelligent and professional enough to control that situation. I'm not going to touch the girls and I'm not going to beat the boys black and blue. Right? I want to be friendly with them, but I also want to be free to express my anger in a way that is appropriate to our relationship. That relationship is being negotiated by people outside the classroom; it is being controlled by statute, which seems inappropriate to a human relationship, which is what teaching is all about. I recognise that my position is peculiar, but I resent the fact that someone in fucking Strasbourg is telling me that I can't grab a kid by the arm and say, 'Come on, you! Out!' which is what a father or an uncle does. It's insulting that someone over there, a bunch of bloody foreigners to boot, are trying to control this rapport which I have established with my kids. Right?

My ideal, though, is that the anger part need hardly arise if their being in school was completely voluntary. The reason you get beatings, violence and anger is because schools are unnatural situations. The local authority tells parents they must send their children into this institution, whether they like it or not, and that when they're there, they must do what they're told to do. Corporal punishment is a symptom of this situation, which is unhappy because it's unnatural, false and *forced*. My kind of day-dream is that education would be compulsory only until the child could read and write, say up to twelve. From then on, it would be voluntary for everyone, whether they were intelligent or not. I used to say there should be free education up to the age of twenty-five, then thirty-five and now I say, why not for ever? It's unrealistic, but how does progress come about except through idealists dreaming openly?

I don't know how you'd do it. It's just me trying to think out the problems that I'm faced with. Right? I'm not a Marxist or a socialist extremist, though, frankly, I am a socialist, but not left-wing. You'd really need to get a group of people together, who believed that school is unnatural and nasty and does a lot of bad things to the teachers and the taught.

There would have to be a lot of changes both inside and outside the school, a new teacher-pupil-family relationship. At the moment, if a teacher slots into the system, it turns him or her into an authoritarian person, not necessarily an unpleasant authoritarian, but one who is always talking down, a besetting sin of teachers. So you'd need teachers who didn't feel threatened if their long-established assumptions about their status as givers-out of knowledge and arbiters of values were questioned, ones who would be willing to sacrifice the idea that they're repositories of knowledge and culture which they are passing on to serried ranks of willing recipients.

They would need a completely different approach to learning. You couldn't simply transfer primary methods to the secondary age group. The children would resent it, because they'd see it as doing kids' stuff. That's very important to adolescents. It's why most of them don't sing in assembly after the third year. There would also need to be other changes in the schools. When I think of some of the headmasters I've known, they'd really be better as bank clerks or civil servants, because they don't know anything about how to deal with people. Schools are, quintessentially, institutions based on human relations.

Parents' attitudes would also need to change. The whole question of volunteer parents is very dodgy. Some of these mums volunteer because it gives them a sort of status: they're in with the head, on Christian-name terms. They come into the staffroom for a cup of coffee, but teachers don't like it. They whisper: 'What's *she* doing in here?' I've known that happen more than once. It often destroys their child's relationship with its peers, particularly in a socially mixed comprehensive. 'Ah, your mum's come in, eh? Trying to turn you round the head and get a good report, is she?' For a similar reason I wouldn't like a majority of parents on the governing body, which was one of Sir Keith Joseph's ideas. The sort of people who would volunteer would have a vested interest not just in maintaining the *status quo*, but in actually making it more *status quo* than it is, if you see what I mean, by preserving what they feel made them so successful, or providing their kids with what they envied, but didn't get themselves.

I don't understand this Joseph bloke. I never have. All he's really doing with profiles and the 16+ is putting a rubber stamp on what other people have been saying for twenty years. A lot of what he says, which is pounced on as radical, is actually very boring and pedestrian. Take the core curriculum. That's what all schools have, you know, in my experience, anyway. They establish a basic curriculum – English, maths, a science, a creative subject, a book- or literary-based subject, RE, history – which everybody follows.

His 'super-teacher' idea was dangerous and divisive. It's true that good teachers are promoted out of the classroom into administration or other schools, and this would enable a good teacher to get the remuneration he deserves without having to move out of the classroom. But it would turn teaching into more of a rat-race than it is. The scheme for teacher assessments also has some points in its favour, but it's riddled with problems. In both cases, you've got to be able, implicitly and unreservedly, to trust the objective nature of the judgement.

I loathe the swing-back to authority and narrowness, which is a reaction to the 1950s and 60s, when sociology became the new science and the educational world was turned upside down. It might be just my experience in this particular school, but I think people are beginning to edge back to those ways of thought again. You hear people talking far more about pastoral methods. [He produces an *Education Guardian* from his file.]

There's an article here which I put on one side to read properly, as a quick scan told me that it's the sort of place where I'd like to work myself. It's about a comprehensive school in Dorset where the head of the individual learning unit tracked down a self-study course in Gaelic for a boy who'd started learning it in Ulster. Now he's looking for an Irish nun to act as a tutor. That's the kind of openness, flexibility and creative approach to education that I admire.

Maybe our whole concept of schools is wrong. Perhaps we should rethink the whole idea of schools as fixed institutions with the people in them concerned about their authority status . . . I know I'm beginning to sound like a de-schooler, but I've never read Illich, only heard of him . . . Someone who had done a bit of sociology once said to me that there's one thing people always forget about schools. They exist to provide a career structure for teachers. It's one of the bugbears. What we need to do is to bomb the bleeding lot and start again!

15

The Best Days of Your Life

Another attempt to forge new kinds of links between pupils, schools and homes has been made by community schools, which can succeed to an extent if they have a dynamic head and highly dedicated, if not charismatic, teachers. John Burnley, who is now head of drama in a large comprehensive in the West Country, previously worked for three years in a community school, which he found enormously exciting. He is in his mid-twenties.

I started teaching in 1979. It was a community school. Within the grounds there was a shopping centre so that the mums and dads were constantly passing by the school on their way to the stores and supermarkets. Some of the classrooms actually fronted on to the pavements, which was probably more disconcerting for the kids than for us. Parents could come in at any time; adults were welcome in classes; kids came back to the youth club at night; there was a big printing resource centre and a church. It was marvellous, amazing. There was a very dynamic head who had been appointed specifically to set up a forward-looking school.

To be honest, not many parents came in, but it was nice that they could do so if they wished. It was a symbolic gesture which was sufficient in itself. Parents didn't have to make appointments. They often came at lunchtime.

The intake was predominantly white, but there was a great social mixture, ranging from kids of intellectual, upper middle-class parents to those who had moved out of large cities to be rehoused in this new town, plus kids who had been expelled from other schools, some of whom settled in very quickly. There were two big differences from most other schools. All staff, right up to the headmaster, were called by their Christian names, and there was no school uniform, so two obvious barriers of resentment were knocked down straight away. The atmosphere was very friendly. There wasn't a group of staff and a group of kids with a wall in between. There was a united group of people in a building called school.

Social contact with parents was much closer and more frequent than in other schools. There was a magnificent leisure centre in the school complex, so in the evenings I could talk to the kids' parents informally and not just once a year at an open evening, when it would all be forgotten for another three terms. The kids also came there at night, so they spent their leisure hours in the school as well. That made a big difference.

I'm absolutely sold on the idea, but you need a school that's prepared to go out into the community and encourage people to come in. As a form teacher, I was expected to visit parents in their homes by appointment to talk about their kids. On parents' evenings, if some parents didn't come in, the sort who traditionally don't bother, I'd make an arrangement to go and see them. Once, I was greeted with a four-course meal. The parents, who were Chinese, hadn't come because they couldn't speak English. I had to use their daughter as an interpreter. Parents were always pleased that I'd found time to go and see them.

Drama was one of the big departments in the school. I learnt an awful lot from my head of department. The first time I ever saw him in action, he walked into a fifth-year group of skinheads who looked horrific to me. I thought, 'Now, how is this man going to control them?' He walked in, sat down, didn't say a word, and then the skinheads all broke up from what they were doing, brought their chairs over and sat around him. He was a very quiet teacher.

Once, when I was having trouble with a class, he came in to teach them, with me as an observer. His opening question was, 'Who are the kids in here who muck around?' The others all pointed at one boy and said 'Him.' So he just turned to him and asked, 'What do you do?' The kid said, 'I do this, this, this and this.' And he couldn't do them anymore, because he'd admitted what he'd done wrong. My head of department had great control immediately because he'd defused the problem immediately and was being dead open.

I really like teaching drama. It's exciting and absolutely classless. You don't need to be an extrovert. You can sit quietly at the side, enjoying the spectacle and be involved without actually saying a word. Everybody can take part. I've seen mentally handicapped people get involved in drama sessions. It works right across the ability range and breaks down the barriers that academic subjects put up.

It teaches kids group awareness. The old-style drama teachers used to teach children to be individuals. The new method teaches them that a lot of little individuals operating on their own are useless. You've got to learn to operate as an indvidual within the context of a group or society. It gives them opportunities to make decisions, to live through situations, to replay them, to say, 'Now what would have happened if . . .'

I want my kids to be sensitive to the needs of other people in the group, to learn, as I am learning all the time, how they can see personal truths about themselves through an issue like the miners' strike, and that life isn't a simple thing but full of complexities. Okay, you might say, the government or Scargill should back down, but it isn't as simple as that. You can tell kids it's not simple, but if you actually get them to reach that point in drama, they know it. They haven't been told by somebody: they've realised it themselves.

The other use of drama is as a service subject. A teacher can go into a classroom as a character like Galileo, dressed in costume. The class are willing to suspend disbelief and talk to him about his experiments, his life, his feelings. It's incredibly effective, but very slow. It takes me about four hours to deal with something that a stand-up teaching teacher could deal with in ten minutes as a series of facts; but I think it's a far stronger method of teaching.

I always wanted to be a teacher. When I was nine or ten, I wanted a blackboard and easel for my birthday. Mum and dad bought me one, and I used to take it into their bedroom early in the morning to give my dad a French lesson in bed. He's a teacher, too. I used to take his work away and mark it. I found it really exciting.

I'm a person who likes to be in charge, not in a nasty way, but in charge of something that perpetuates itself. There's an old phrase, 'School-days are the best days of your life.' I think teachers should make an effort to ensure that comes true for every child. For some kids, passing examinations is obviously important and that shouldn't be belittled. Those who aren't going to pass many, or any, shouldn't be pushed through the same curriculum just because it's convenient. Education is mostly about homing in on people's strengths and making them stronger. Positiveness!

V

HOME TUTORS AND SPECIAL SCHOOLS

16

Home Tuition Saves Money

When home tuition started, it was mainly for sick children. It was a nice little job for middle class ladies who could take their children along and arrange the hours to suit themselves. During the last ten years or so, the number of children needing home tuition has increased greatly. Ninety per cent of them have behavioural disorders resulting from emotional disturbances at home. The number of sick children is now minimal.

Pauline Kelland works as a home tutor in the north. Previously, she taught in a primary school and a school for maladjusted children when she returned to teaching after her family had grown up. Although the results of her work are sometimes rather intangible, she firmly believes that without home tuition the consequences for both the children and society would be far more disastrous and much more expensive in the long run.

The children I teach are mostly boys from fourteen to sixteen. There are very few girls. They seem more able to switch off from what is happening at home and get on with their lives. The majority are on probation, have been in care at some time, have probably been with foster parents for six months or a year, might even have been in a residential home, or occasionally be on a suspended sentence, which is going to be transformed into a custodial sentence for another misdemeanour which they've already committed. So, the future often looks pretty grim and the past has been just as bleak.

Many of them are illegitimate or the father has deserted them. The mother is usually a fairly feckless, ineffectual sort of person who has resorted to sleeping around, or drink, or drugs, because she wasn't able to cope. The mother of one West Indian boy I've got has been in prison as a drug pusher and has three of her illegitimate children in care. I think she keeps her only son at home just to have someone to yell at.

These mothers really do pile a hell of a lot on to their teenage sons. They treat them as the erring husband. If their own life isn't a bed of roses, which it isn't, they're looking for someone to nag at. The nearest person is this great big teenage boy, whose voice has already broken, who is probably doing the same sort of thing as the husband did, like staying out late at night or creating a lot of mess when he invites his noisy friends back home. So the mother starts the whole destructive nagging process, which the kid isn't mature enough to deal with. You often find that there's another boy or girl at home, an absolute angel, who's in collusion with the mother against the erring son.

Because I'm a mother, the mums immediately think that I'm their ally, which I'm not. They start ringing me up and telling tales on the child. 'Oh, he was out late again last night.' They're often jealous because I've got their child's confidence, so they're always pointing out his deficiencies. If I say, 'He worked really well today,' they'll reply, 'Oh, yes, but you should see the state of his room.'

Before I see a child, I read up all the reports, but when I see him for the first time, I try to put all of it out of my mind, because I don't want to feel sorry or prejudiced. I visit him at home first just to get the feel of the place and to find out what's happened. I start in a very low-key, conversational way, just asking what things have made him happy in the past. Usually, they're very much on the defensive as they've had a succession of what they call 'busybodies' – social workers, educational welfare officers, psycho-therapists, psychiatric social workers – dealing with them, and they see you as another one. I always make it quite clear that I'm simply a teacher.

I've never had any children where it's been impossible to break down the barriers, though it's sometimes taken quite a few months before I've had anything except a monosyllable out of them. You can often break through with a shared joke. I was in the home tuition centre one day with one of my boys who's very solemn, watching a procession of tutors and kids going past. I said: 'You know dogs and owners often get to resemble each other. Do you think tutors and pupils ever get to look like each other?' And he replied, 'Christ, I hope not!' And so, you're on their side and it's very friendly.

The main thing is being very, very positive, saying, 'All right, forget all that shit! That's happened. It's past. You don't rub your nose in shit. You move away from it.' You've got to bring the child to the point of not feeling sorry for himself and trying to take a more positive attitude to life by improving his self-image, which you can only do by letting him talk things through, finding out what his weaknesses are and whether he has any positive talents he can build on. Unfortunately, you don't often see the results of your work because they either go off at Her Majesty's pleasure or they're passed on to someone else or, in very lucky cases, they go back to school. It's not easy to get a boy of fifteen back into school because they've only got a year to integrate him into the system.

I think home tuition works, I really do. Some of my kids really settle down and enjoy their work. I've been in maladjusted schools, I've worked in one, where the results weren't nearly as good. A lot of these children's behavioural problems only appear when they're with a group of kids and they start to show off and compete to hide their own feelings of inadequacy.

If there was no home tuition, you'd be spending even more money in the long run, because they'd end up in even worse trouble. I don't begrudge the taxpayers' money at all. I think it's something these kids deserve, a little bit of space, someone on their own, before they get to the crucial age of sixteen, when they're going to have to start fending for themselves.

I did a course in counselling which taught me how to listen rather than swamp them with advice; but a home tutor now should be able to provide something more than just cossetting a child who temporarily can't go to school. There ought to be some sort of training.

17

His Face Was Pink With Pleasure

Vicki Morant is a home tutor in the West Country, who has previously taught in two comprehensive schools. There were many thoughtful pauses in our conversation at first, but as it went on a much warmer personality began to emerge.

Being a home tutor is rewarding work, but very demanding. I seem to be rather well-suited to it because I can offer an all-round timetable. I'm not really strong on maths, though I can manage CSE, just about. I'm also interested in reading difficulties. I hesitate to use the word 'dyslexia' now, but quite a few children with behavioural problems also have a reading difficulty.

I start by visiting the home. Most of the homes, though not all, are a bit rocky financially. They're poor in terms of basic equipment, but not always in terms of love. Once I get the official letter, I'm expected to make contact very quickly, because there's generally been a difficult set of circumstances, like an expulsion, and there's a lot of anger around. If they're not on the phone, I write a letter – not on official paper, just a scribbled note – giving them twenty-four hours' warning. I try to pick a time of the day when the whole family will be there. Six o'clock is a good time or, if the parents do shift work, I go in the afternoon.

I don't think I've ever had a hostile reception. The first meeting generally lasts about an hour. I throw out one or two questions and then just sit and listen. An enormous amount can be picked up intuitively from what people say to me and what they say to each other. I also pick up a lot of non-verbal clues. Those first meetings are crucial as to how I plan my work.

You've got to be incredibly adaptable to the whole family. If the mother, for instance, has failed in every male relationship, and derives all her emotional support and solace from her only son, she may expect far too much of him. He is now carrying all her hopes. She may ask the home tutor to really push the son academically or into the sort of job which would make her proud. You may see that it is not on. If you told the mother that, it would create a lot of anger and resentment, which would be reflected on to the son and that would come back to you, when you were teaching him.

My successes have not been in developing a child's academic potential, but in his gaining some measure of self-respect. One of my pupils had behaved very badly at school. There was a great deal of aggression and swearing. I had the benefit of teaching him there, before I became a home tutor. All the teachers loathed him and thought of him as scum. He was nearly sixteen when he was expelled for swearing at a very important member of staff – or that was the reason I was given.

Then I became his home tutor. He made very little progress in vocational maths and English. His handwriting was still very childlike and he was awkward with pen and paper. Eventually, he did understand how to run a bank account and a little about writing a letter, but it was pretty minimal progress.

The thing that really brought him out of himself was cooking. With these pupils you've got to find at least one thing that they really enjoy. He had very big hands which were always covered with grease, because he liked fiddling around with bikes. One day, about four weeks after I'd taken him on, I said, 'You're really good at fixing your bike. Those hands are not really suited for pen and paper. They're practical hands. I can't let you loose in the garage, but I could in the kitchen. You could make some biscuits.'

He didn't look at all put out, but quite interested. I was surprised. Then he told me that he'd enjoyed cooking and liked the teacher in his middle school. So we cleaned the grease off his hands, read the recipe together, and then I more or less left him to it. He was humming to himself. He was really happy. And, as luck would have it, the biscuits turned out very well. His face was quite pink with pleasure when I gave him the whole lot to take home. The next time I saw him, he said his dad had thought the biscuits were fantastic and his mum wanted the recipe. That was the start. Weekly, he did cooking: various types of biscuits, scones, cauliflower cheese, a flan. He even helped to cook our Christmas cake. Then, one week, he asked me for the recipe for macaroni cheese and went home and cooked it for his mum. His mum and dad both worked full time. And so the boy started to cook the evening meals. His self-respect grew and grew and the whole atmosphere of his home changed completely.

I didn't try to get him on a cookery course because I didn't think it was something he could do for a living; but I did think he might go into landscape gardening. We did explore it, but he couldn't quite make the break to be independent. He hadn't got quite enough confidence. Eventually, when the tuition stopped, he went to work with his dad. You can't really reverse the pattern of a whole life in six months.

18

The Third-Week Confrontation

One afternoon, it must have been about five o'clock, I had about twenty teenagers in my kitchen. It was raining. I said, 'Scott of the Antarctic is on television. You've got exactly five minutes to transform the living room into the Antarctic. You can use anything in the house on condition that you put it back again.' So, they rushed out to the garage and got the toboggans; they emptied the larder of tinned stuff; they sprayed the lamp bulbs blue; they got sheepskin rugs and opened the windows; they put a Union Jack on top of the telly; and we watched the programme in that authentic atmosphere. That happened long before I went into teaching. So that was the beginning. . . . It was also my need, wasn't it?

Diana Churchfield is an elegant woman in her early fifties. After her children had grown up, she trained as a mature student and went straight into a purpose-built special school, where she has worked for sixteen years. She believes that the expertise of teachers in special education would be of great benefit to the educational service as a whole if it were used as a model.

Our garden backed on to the grammar school playing-fields. We'd chosen the house because both of our boys were at the school. The house had a very large kitchen and I always did a lot of cooking so it became a sort of half-way house for the boys at the school. I could never work out whether they came because it was obvious that I enjoyed their company or for the food. It was a two-way thing, really.

I always had a blackboard in the kitchen. No, not for teaching. It was very useful with so many boys coming and going because they could leave messages or, if there was a party somewhere, they could draw a map. I got it originally because one of the boys was a marvellous cartoonist. If he'd been in for coffee at break time and there were crumbs left on the table, he would draw a cartoon in them. I said, 'It's a shame to wipe that away, John,' so I bought a blackboard.

I enjoyed their company so much that, when I thought about the future, I knew that teaching was what I wanted to do. In a way, I suppose, I'm a child who hasn't grown up. I don't mean in a childish sense: I just think the world is a very exciting place.

When I went to college it was an absolute dream. I didn't find it hard work at all because it was something I wanted to do. I loved the teaching practice. As a mature student, you're very centred, so if a child screams and shouts abuse, it doesn't bother you. You don't have a need for children to like you, though they do in the end, but in no way are you going to sacrifice discipline for popularity. Years ago, children were brought up through fear. As soon as you use fear to control a child, you're producing an authoritarian person who will be totally at the mercy of other authoritarian figures, and will want to kick his own minions around. Fear only works when it's there. You probably know children who have been treated like that and when a stranger walks into a classroom they give him hell. Reason, however, works all the time, whether you're there or not. So you've got to persuade the children to have faith in reason.

At the college, I chose to do literature, because I'd always been an avid reader. Long before I went there, I'd read a great deal about every school of psychology. I particularly wanted to work with children who had been rejected or excluded for one reason or another, so the more difficulties a child had, the more fascinated I became. With intelligent children, you just have to direct them; but with the children I teach, you've got a lot more challenges. I can never see them as limited in any way. Education for me is nothing to do with stuffing the head. What makes it exciting is getting what's inside to come out. So I went straight into special education. I didn't have any training for it, though you have to now.

There are many reasons why the children are at the school. Obviously, children who are in care. Children who through no fault of their own have disastrous backgrounds. Down's Syndrome children. Children with very slight brain damage which is enough to handicap them in a bigger class. Children suffering from epilepsy. Deaf children. Children with personality disorders. Children who have been excluded from comprehensives for being disruptive, as that seems more acceptable to them than being thought of as dim because they couldn't keep up with their work. It's just an attempt to retain their dignity, a big cover-up for their own inadequacies.

When I first went there, it was mainly boys, but now it's about equal. Years ago, you see, if a girl was difficult at school, she was usually withdrawn. Now we've got girls who are just as big a nuisance as boys. That's because of women's lib in a way. They're no longer playing the old passive role.

I teach the children of fourteen or fifteen. I have sixteen children in my class, though I've had as many as eighteen. If there's a cluster of very difficult children when they come to the school, it's broken up, so that there are only one or two in a class. The children who benefit most from the school are those who have been there longest.

The trouble-makers always come from the outside as it's difficult for them to break into a cohesive group. When they come in, there's usually a three-week pattern of behaviour. The first week, they sus out the other kids; the second week, the rules and regulations; and the third week – it's funny how it happens time and time again – there's a confrontation because these children need to know how far they can go.

A few weeks ago, we'd been making kites and there was one cane left over by the blackboard. A boy in his third week who had provoked and provoked and provoked, said to me, 'You're too chicken to use that stick.' The other children said, 'Mrs Churchfield doesn't use the stick.' So the boy asked me, 'What do you do then?' And I replied, 'I just rely on your common sense.'

You've always got to deal with them in such a way that they have a chance to come down with dignity. You're not there to destroy them, but to help them.

I use the rest of the class as a Greek chorus. If I have a child who is really difficult and has gone and sat in a corner, I'll say, 'You can go out if you like.' I always leave my classroom door open. 'You can go to the library, if you like.'

The boy will say, 'No, I'll stay here.'

Then the rest of the class will ask, 'What's he playing up like that for? Why don't you take him up to the library?' And I'll say, 'He doesn't need to go to the library. You know how you feel when you're in a bad temper and your heart is banging. Well, he's just sitting there quietly, and then he'll go and wash his face, and he'll come back and it will all be gone. Just the way you feel when you get very angry.'

In this way, you can talk to the boy through the rest of the class. And he will take his cue from that and go away and wash his face and come back. If I'd told him, he would have rejected it. If a child ever gets to the stage when he's in a screaming temper-tantrum, knocking chairs and tables over, one of the other teachers will quietly go and get the headmaster and they'll come in and gently take the child away.

With some children, we have to recognise that there is nothing more we can do for them and we have to send them on to a boarding school for disturbed children for their own sake. They're better off away from the aggro that is very often coming from their own home and need the peace of being contained and looked after.

The teachers are very alert for any signs of trouble at home. If a child has a bruise, it's noticed straight away and we go straight to the headmaster. They often develop a pattern of behaviour when they're having trouble at home. I had one girl who used to come in every morning very edgy and wanting to work hard all the time. By two o'clock, she'd blow up, because she couldn't contain her anxiety any longer, so I knew there was something seriously wrong at home. If you get a child who has developed avoidance technique, you can guarantee that they're being pressurised at home. There's always some mother, you see, who is very angry with her child for being relegated to a special school and has unrealistic ambitions for him or her. There's still a stigma about going to a special school. The other children taunt them when they get on to the special coach. I've actually had people saying to me, 'Are you still working with the dimmies?'

Some parents fight all the time to get their children back into an ordinary school. They can do that now, you see. With this new Act, the parents can say they want their child re-tested and, if they're academically able, they can go back. I'm totally for the integration of these children in ordinary schools so long as proper provision is made for them. But in comprehensives, remedial teachers are the scum of the earth, and the really good teachers are the ones taking the high-fliers, which is stupid, isn't it? Unless we change our attitudes to what learning is about, the victims are going to be the children who are integrated, aren't they? Oh, yes, I'm all for integration to get rid of the stigma, but I think that special schools should be kept as centres of expertise.

In the classroom, I always try to make democratic decisions. At the beginning of the term, I'll say, 'I wonder what we should do this term. Can we make a chart of what we did last term? And where do you think we should go from there?' This gives them a feeling that they have some say in what is happening to them. I've had some bright, useful suggestions. We have to do a lot of comprehension, spelling and reading, and one class suggested we had a little drama, where some people were commas, others full stops and so on. They really enjoyed that.

If I asked these children to write a story, they'd freak out. So we do a lot of story-making, always in groups, so that the timid ones are carried along. I pretend to be a postman and give each group a letter. In fact, it's a blank sheet of paper. I ask the first group who their letter was from. 'Oh, well,' they say, 'we've just won a lot of money.' I tell them to think about it and in this way, each group develops its own story. After they've done that for a term, they say they'd like to write plays, which is something I couldn't have imposed on them.

I've always enjoyed doing art with them, even though I've had no special training. One of the first things I noticed with these children was that they didn't have good memories in academic subjects but had staggering visual memories. I started reading about the left- and right-hand sides of the brain and developed techniques which produced most beautiful art. We've won prizes all over the country. Perhaps we go in too early on the left-hand side, so that by the time the children are nine or ten, they've become self-conscious, and lost touch with their creative side. Perhaps we're a bit unbalanced in what we do.

I'm glad in one way that education has become as difficult as it is, because people are really starting to think about it. As long as things are comfortable, people don't think. Now that it's got really uncomfortable for parents, teachers and children, we'll probably reassess what we're doing. I think there should be a tremendous concentration at an early level on social and emotional development. Special schools have probably got an expertise that the whole of the teaching profession could benefit from. The teachers love the children and are dedicated to them. But you can't love children unless you love yourself, not in a narcissistic way, but recognising your own vulnerability. I really do feel that part of a teacher's training should be a TP in a special school to see how they deal with difficult children, because they'll all have them, you know.

I have great faith in human beings. I do. I'm really fascinated by people. Yes! You could change the whole world, you see, with just one generation of children if you could only get it right.

19

Fuck Schools! They're Terrible!

We all have nice stories about why we went into this kind of school. Mine is that I was working in a private school for middle class, off-beat children, which was used by the local authority for some bright, not too screwed-up children. Gradually, the governors and parents started to feel that these children were disruptive influences; but I saw them as the yeast that leavened the middle-class grain. When the school decided that they wouldn't have these local authority children any more, I thought, 'I'm going with them, because I'm one of them.' I'm in the process of trying to look after my own inner child. And, really, I shall have done it soon. And maybe then, I should leave and do something else.

Jonathan Fereday is a fifty-year-old teacher who works in a boarding school for behaviour-disordered children – what used to be called a maladjusted school. He has great empathy with his pupils, even a kind of admiration, but beneath the pleasant, charming exterior, there is a much tougher, inner spirit which guides him exorably along a semi-mystical path which he would like his pupils to take also. I liked his engaging personality and his sense of humour and the liberal supplies of wine which had been thoughtfully provided. It was rather late at night when I sat down beside the recorder in a slightly befuddled state. When I saw the transcripts later, I discovered to my concern that, not only had some parts of the defective tape been inaudible, but that I had also intruded much more than usual. It was much easier to excise the latter than to restore the former, though enough of his words remained to reproduce the essence. He works in the West Country.

Teaching is a very complicated matter, but I tend to think that the children are in the same game as I am, trying to express their potential so that, like Gerard Manley Hopkins, they can say, 'This is me, because I came.' And that's all I'm really interested in. I don't know how you do it, but I do know that the only way to begin is not to have your own framework for a person, so that, to quote somebody else, you have 'a form proceeding, not a shape superimposed'.

Some people at my school think they can engineer circumstances to develop change. That's the one way in which I disagree with my school. I feel that when the children are centred and whole, they will work; before they're together, they won't. The school believes that by putting their noses to the grindstone and getting solid academic achievement, it will straighten them out.

The staff are all very strong people it seems to me, very powerful. I think it's really important to have a spectrum. Just imagine a world full of people all like me! I must say I am at an extreme.

Something really funny happened the other day. The head and another teacher had been giving one form a really hard time. While I was in the staffroom, I heard my name being mentioned in the connection with the form. So I asked what it was all about. 'We think we need someone to come in and be a good guy,' the head replied. 'That's why we mentioned your name.' I'm regarded as a softie; but, you see, I'm not. Actually, I'm quite tough. When I was walking along the corridors one day, I overheard a very tough boy say to another: 'He looks like a poof, but he ain't.' I cherish that.

I've got six boys in my class. One boy was expelled from nursery school for attacking the teachers. He was born when his mother was sixteen. His parents have split. He was living with his mother in his grandmother's house and they shared one room, so he was sleeping in his mother's bed. A really terrible situation. He was hard to hold in any school, so he came to us when he was eight.

He upsets everybody and has the most extreme talent for creating accidents, like knocking someone's work off their desk. He is a most talented games player, but he really puts people off by screaming out to his opponent, 'You fool!' whenever he wins. I was playing golf with him the other day. He won the first hole because I hit his ball, but I won after that. A few holes later, he said, 'Let's start again.' So we did. I think he won a couple of holes, but when I was taking my shots he was jumping up and down all the time, so I said, 'Look, I'm not going on, because you're so awful to play with.' And I just walked away.

I started playing swing ball with some of the other boys and he came over and said, 'Can I play with you?' I replied, 'All right! We're going to play so that you can improve your backhand.' He looked furious. 'My backhand's all right. I don't need any help from you.' He went on saying that sort of thing. So I asked, 'Shall we play a game?' 'Yeah', he said, because he wanted to thrash me.

I don't play this game very well, but I play better than him. I think he won one game. The last game was very much touch and go. I placed every shot as carefully as I could. I was telling him what I was doing. And in the end, I won. There was some sort of joy involved, because I had played with him; because he knew he couldn't beat me at this moment; and because I wasn't trying to beat him down. It was actually a very good thing, because he needs to admire and to realise that he needs help, which he doesn't accept very easily. There are times when they all have to express their supremacy. There are other boys, the real maladjusted, who are far more difficult. One boy is always hurting himself or breaking his legs; another just pokes his fingers in his eyes. The treatment there is to give him a rubber band. I honestly think that is really beyond us and not far beyond anybody. As I see it, the only magic ingredient is time.

The reason they get sent to boarding school is because their home is inadequate. They are referred here by a doctor or a school psychologist. It's quite a lengthy process, because there's a lot of tests and consultations with parents, and lots of paper flying around. We do see some of the parents and the current trend is to see them much more. I think that is a very good thing, absolutely. Their main reaction is aggression. 'What are you doing with my child?' They don't have a very good self-image of themselves, so they actually want to live through their children.

Some of the best work we do is in relation to parents. It must be. Making them take responsibility. The father of one boy and his separated wife and her boy-friend all came down to a conference at the school. The boy actually took over the meeting and said, 'Look, I don't want to have to choose between you. I care for both of you.' It was beautiful for a boy of twelve to have such sense and balance.

Ordinary schoolchildren allow lots of false assumptions to pass them by for an easy life; but these children won't take it. I think a bit of magic could change them. They have experienced so much difficulty in life, that when they have overcome it, their maturity and humanity is much greater than that of ordinary children. I'm not sure that the ones who become behaviour-disordered aren't right. I have a certain admiration for them, you know, as their protest has been so vigorous that the authority is willing to spend £9,000 or £10,000 a year on their education. I'd love you to come and see the school, Frank. You could, quite easily.

The other day I was with two friends of mine who are both teachers and they suddenly said, 'Jonathan, you actually hate teachers.' This placed me in a difficult position, you know, being one and hating them. The answer is that I actually do hate teaching-teachers for one reason or another. In ordinary schools, both pupils and staff are crucified, hurt beyond endurance really. Children are not recognised as individuals and unrealistic goals are set for them. That is particularly why I hate teachers. Children are asked to do and to be things that the people who are asking them are incapable of doing or being themselves. An example? Well, containing anger is one thing. Yeah. Well, that's enough. Anger in schools and violence. The children are recipients of inadequacy.

The staff are crucified because they're asked to do something which is impossible, to teach a syllabus which will probably entrance none of their pupils, unless they have a passion for the subject and a rapport with the

93

children which is, I think, an unusual combination; and by having such a multiple function, as social workers, carriers of the country's traditions, purveyors of information, enlightenment, creativity. It's just not possible. So, really, fuck schools! They're terrible!

But what are we going to do about these schools? Do you know, I was hearing about the Norwegian system the other day. No school has more than four hundred pupils. All their special-needs pupils are integrated in ordinary schools and a special allowance for an extra teacher is given. Every teacher is paid the same amount and the only way you can get extra money is by getting additional qualifications. Out of thirty teachers in one school, seventeen had special qualifications. And every child has a chance. That's the only way.

20

She Screamed and Screamed and Screamed

Josephine Braddell was out when I arrived, but her ten-year-old son let me in and made me a cup of tea. His mother, a brisk Welsh woman in her early forties, returned home a few minutes later. She works in a school for the severely disabled in the Midlands, and believes that there has never been any really genuine commitment to special education and that the money put into it is likely to diminish even further now. Just before I left, her only son presented me with a drawing of the house inscribed 'To the best reporter', a kind gesture but unfounded praise, as he had not heard the interview.

There are six children in my class from five to seven years of age. They're like a little infant group, but they're all in wheelchairs. Five of them are what you would call cerebral palsied children, who are severely handicapped mentally and physically.

One, who lives in a home, is severely handicapped with spina bifida and hydrocephalus. They often go together. John has spina bifida, hydrocephalus and is very poorly sighted, so you've got a multiple handicap. Their hearing or their vision is often impaired. I've got another little girl whose speech is impaired, but it's coming along nicely now and she's just about to move on to a physically handicapped school. We sometimes get children like that who seem to be mentally handicapped, and, occasionally, if you're observant enough, you realise that the child is only physically handicapped and shouldn't be with you at all.

One little boy was thought to be blind, but I discovered that he was using some sight. I consulted some teachers of the blind and we concluded that he might be taught to see. Some time or another he must have mentally blocked out visual things. I started showing him a very bright toy, which hasn't got a rattle or a bell, so that his enjoyment could only come from seeing it. It's got to be really, really bright. An ultra-violet light would be ideal, but we haven't got that kind of equipment.

I'm very interested in psychology. Do you know the work of B. F. Skinner with animals? Well, I'm a great believer in his theory of behaviour modification. The development of a mentally handicapped child is nothing as easy, you see, as that of a normal child. They don't develop unless you teach them to do so. If their handicap is very severe, you could be teaching something as simple as eye contact. You can't teach these children in the same way as normal children because they're not always highly motivated. Even ordinary children often aren't, but they will work for something like a tick in a book or a sign of the teacher's approval. For most of my children that wouldn't mean much. You've got to study each child and decide what he or she will work for. It may be something like a food or drink reward. That's a very strong motivation. If the child is blind, it might be a song. A child who is not so severely handicapped will enjoy a cuddle or an approving 'That's a good boy'. For a really profoundly handicapped child, who is not interested in something to eat or drink, or a song, you have to use a vibrator or a massager on the skin. You've got the whole gamut in the same class. That's the difficulty.

You need lots of special equipment of the right kind. If you're using a computer, you need a special attachment with a pad which will fill the screen with coloured lights, or make it play a tune if the pad is touched. You also need appropriate PE equipment, like tunnels. When they opened this school, they built a beautiful gym with wallbars and all sorts of equipment that these children can't possibly use. They also provided us with lots of sewing-machines.

I don't try to teach these children a set activity like putting shapes in a posting box. I consider the intrinsic value of the activity for their lives. Therefore, I don't think reading and writing are very important for them. How many people read books? To enjoy reading, you've got to be really proficient at it. It's the same with writing. Lots of children in ordinary schools learn to read and write and rarely do either again.

Communication is the topmost thing to work on. They have great difficulty in looking outside themselves and building relationships. Some of them appear to be aggressive, which comes out of frustration. That might be a response to a failure, not in themselves, but because others have asked too little or too much of them. If a mentally handicapped child isn't handled properly when he's young, he becomes maladjusted, too. Schools have made him like that. There are some autistic children who are not with you at all. You can't break through with them; but they're a small proportion.

We have the children until they're nineteen, and I'd like to teach each child to survive, whatever that might mean for him or her. I might be able to teach them to go out into the world, get on a bus, pay their fare, go into a supermarket and do their shopping. The tendency with the older children is to do a lot of home tasks and personal hygiene to prepare them for life outside on their own. Some of them will be alive for quite a time, living in sheltered accommodation, which the middle-of-the-road children will be capable of doing.

I've often wondered why I've never felt appalled by these kids, but relatively at home with them. When I was about eleven or twelve, I was in the Legion of Mary. We used to visit a hospital ward of mentally handicapped children who were sixteen years old or more chronically, but much younger developmentally, to teach them about God. I can remember going in and seeing one boy sitting in a corner like this. [She crosses her arms defensively in front of her screwed-up face.] Another child was sitting in a corner screaming. I can remember feeling a little bewildered, but I can't really remember being frightened. I think I was always a mature little girl. Some of the other members of the Legion refused to go back. But I had this fantasy that I wanted to be a helper in the world and later on in life, I went back to work on those wards in that same hospital. It was quite a progressive place. You could chat to the psychologists, who would sometimes work out little programmes for you to use with the patients. The programmes weren't firmly based on a reward system, but they were verging towards it. and that's where I first became interested in that kind of approach.

I don't want you to think that I'm an overly dedicated sort of person who is doing this wonderful job and deriving enormous personal satisfaction from it. Actually, I feel quite detached. People often come to my school and say, 'You're really wonderful', but I always find that embarrassing. I don't feel at all emotionally involved. The job has a lot of interest for me from the psychological point of view, because I'm particularly interested in the abnormal.

Not all special teachers think the way I do. There's a great division in our school. A small nucleus of younger teachers are willing to learn new approaches, but the majority are older teachers who are trying to apply ordinary methods. What happened was that, when the educational service took over responsibility for these children from the health service in 1971, they started by putting up lovely buildings without giving any thought as to who was going to teach these children or how they were to be taught. The authorities more or less said to ordinary teachers if you come into special education, we'll give you more money, Scale posts. We've got PE teachers, women who have come back to education after bringing up a family. Out of the whole staff there is only one who is specially trained. It's a fallacy to think that we're very skilled people. Even the adviser isn't quite sure what we should be doing.

We have a situation which, in my experience, is typical of many special schools. The young staff, like me, get the most difficult children, whom you couldn't pretend to be teaching in an ordinary way. Then you have the other group who pretend that their class contains ordinary little infants. If they spot an able child, they'll do everything possible to get him in their group. To some extent, they can go through the motions of teaching them to read and write. They can do certain limited number work and so on. Whether it's effective or not is another question, but it looks as though it is. The parents like to see their children in a class like that. They feel good. If you're dealing with the most difficult children, the parents don't think much of you, because they can't imagine what you're doing educationally.

The barriers between the two kinds of teachers are appallingly high in our school, and very obvious. We all do assessments of each child. Sometimes when you get an assessment from the class below, you stare at it in amazement because you feel sure that the child definitely cannot do the things that are claimed. You couldn't possibly go to the other teacher and ask 'How on earth can you get him to do that?'

Not so long ago we had an afternoon disco for the kids. The teacher of the top class is a middle-aged bachelor who has devoted his whole life to this kind of teaching and takes any form of criticism personally. The boys were giving out drinks and you had to pay with pretend money. So I went up and said, 'Right, Sam, I'm having two cups of juice and they're three pence each.' The boy had to tell me how much to pay. I could hear the other teacher whispering 'Six pence'. When Sam repeated it, the teacher said, 'Very good, Sam, very good!'

I like being involved in the psychological part more, the testing and that sort of thing. It's more of an experimental area, but it can be very frustrating. You might work with them for a whole month, with a rigid routine and in the end there's no measurable change. That happens nearly all the time. So you could end up by saying, 'Well, it's nearly Christmas. I won't bother. I'll put up the decorations.' You could spend the whole day doing that and if you did, you'd have fallen into the trap of being a child-minder. That's why teamwork is so much more effective, because one teacher might notice a response which you had missed. I want to make the job more clinical, though still caring. I'd be quite happy for the assistants to sing the little songs, say the little rhymes and do the classroom decorations, if I was left to do the specifically educational work.

The doctors aren't very helpful either. We have a lot to do with them, because they do medicals on the children. Even when you've worked very hard with a child and recorded its behaviour on a video tape to show some skill that it's learnt in six months, the doctor only says, 'It's amazing how these little brains mature.'

With improvements in medicine and technology, we're keeping more and more children of this kind alive. There's a little girl in the school who has a lot of involuntary movement. She's quite a happy girl and the quality of her life is reasonable, though not great. A ward sister came round from the local hospital the other day and said, 'I remember that child. I delivered her. She was a twenty-seven-week birth, but the young doctor was determined to save her.' The child had an epileptic fit when it was born and went on having fits and fits which was what caused the brain damage. When the sister went back on duty the next day, the doctor was very pleased with himself and said, 'Come along and look at this. I saved her.' The sister told him, 'You've saved her for nothing, for the rest of her life.' She was disgusted. The child was in hospital for months and when she first came to the school she screamed and screamed and screamed.

It's all a great strain for the parents. Most of them feel guilty. The mother of one child had German measles; another child was the result of a road traffic accident. Even when the child's brain has been damaged by chance, the parents, particularly the mother, always think, 'Why me?' Quite often you don't know why the brain was damaged. And quite frankly, it doesn't matter why, because it is! The parents feel guilty and embarrassed. It's strange that a lot of them are middle class. I don't know why.

The relationship with parents is often very difficult. Because they're under such great stress, they will send their hyperactive child to school even when he's ill, because they can't really cope with him. The parents are very pressurised because the whole emphasis has shifted to looking after these children in the community. The authorities say they will back them up, but the support isn't always there. I had a mother phone me up to say that she was going to be violent to her child and asking for it to be taken away. I tried to get a social worker sent round straight away, but when I saw the child again it had been bruised and battered. The strain takes its toll on the parents. As the children get bigger, we can see the marriage going to pot.

As a result of the Warnock Report, the latest idea is to integrate handicapped children into ordinary schools. The only reasons the physically handicapped aren't integrated is because they're in wheelchairs, so the only changes you might have to make is building ramps. With modern drugs, epileptic children could also be accommodated. The same with the visually and hearing-impaired. The mildly mentally handicapped will also go in – or the best of them will. You might think that the severely handicapped could never be accommodated, but some of the best ones might, if they built small units for them on the ends of schools. That's the idea anyway. Some authorities will introduce these changes, but others will only pay lip-service to them for ten or twenty years.

There'll be great problems with integration. We already segregate the children in special schools, with the most severely handicapped older children in one class and the more able in another. If you have a child who is very, very quiet and a hyperactive child who is always tugging at your skirts, the latter is always going to get the most attention. Teachers in ordinary schools are already hard pressed and won't be able to cope with this additional burden, but the authorities will try to do it on the cheap.

Some of the teachers in my school, and the assistants, are disgusted by the large amounts of money being spent on these children. All I can say is that if you've committed yourself to educate them to the best of your ability, then you must do it. And if you can't afford it, then you must be honest and let it be known. They aren't really committed; they're only pretending that they are. A lot of money has been put in to keep up a front, but it's going to dry up now.

VI

COMPREHENSIVE – II

21

When the Bell Goes, You Jump

When the bell goes, you jump. For the first period you're a patient teacher of children with special needs, a small group of ten. Three-quarters of an hour later, the bell goes again, and you dash off to a class of A level kids who are going to university. You can ignore the next bell because they have a double period. The bell again! You rush off to grab a cup of coffee in the staffroom, which is smoky, dirty and untidy. There aren't enough chairs, so you have to stand unless you get there early. If you've had to wait for your coffee, you gulp it down in the hope of finishing it before the bell goes again. By then, you've got two or three people who want to speak to you. It might be to do with one of the kids in your class, a responsibility you have for the whole school, or a dinner invitation for next week. It could be anything, but you can be sure that someone will want to talk to you about something. The bell goes again, and this time you've got a class of horrendously naughty third-years. They don't want to learn and you don't want to teach them, but you've bent over backwards to find a way of creating a climate in which they can learn something without either you or them getting too excited about it. Another bell and off you go again. You don't decide when you're going to change your activity or your *persona*. It's decided for you.

I arrived excessively early for my Saturday morning interview with Jan Vicars, who appeared at the door in her dressing gown. She accepted my apologies graciously and quickly presented me with *The Times* and a cup of coffee before she went off again. The sitting-room of her small flat in a northern city was comfortably furnished. There were some intriguing paintings and drawings on the wall, a music stand in one corner and the usual teacher's bookcase in another, which revealed her catholic tastes. Her flat was in one of the few surviving traditional buildings in the area. The window gave a view of the huge concrete slabs of linear houses and high-rise flats, a crumbling memorial to Sir Keith Joseph's tenure of the Ministry of Housing in the 1960s. The streets of the nearby estates were curiously, ominously, quiet and deserted and there was a general air of desolation, which made the cosy flat seem even more of an oasis of culture in the surrounding post-industrial desert.

Right on time, Jan reappeared for the interview. She is an extremely attractive mathematician in her thirties, a dedicated teacher whose personal and professional lives were linked for many years in an intense love-hate relationship, from which she finally broke free by withdrawing part of herself for her own activities, which allowed her to become more dispassionate and professional in her role as a teacher.

Bright and frustrated at school, I was. Successful up to a point. I find it very difficult to talk about my school-days, as I feel quite angry about them. I went to a girls' direct grant grammar school which force-fed people with an academic bias and was very keen to get its brightest pupils to do maths or science at Oxford or Cambridge. I resented being pushed into maths, having a label hung round my neck, saying, 'You're going that way', because I quite enjoyed English, I liked music and I was particularly excited by art. Many years later I realised that I didn't actually like maths at all. My little piece of rebellion at the time was to refuse to try for Oxford or Cambridge as I thought they were elitist. I'm sure I was wrong. It was a silly thing to do from a personal point of view.

When I went to university, I crashed. I'd gone from a school which had encouraged me positively to an institution which couldn't care less, where no one took any interest in how I was getting on. And I couldn't cope. I was very angry with my school for forcing me to go there. I didn't go to lectures or tutorials and I didn't do any work, and because I wasn't participating in what was on offer, I had all those dreadful feelings of guilt, of failure. I was a drop-out. My friends were a bunch of middle-class people who were disillusioned with the technological, money-oriented world. We were all conventionally educated, but were curious – because our natures were curious – not about academic things, but about spirituality. None of us had had a classical education so we couldn't context it at all. We found out a lot through drink, religion, politics. Our only gratitude to the educational system was that it had given us three years to sit and do nothing but talk.

I left university very disillusioned. I knew that I wanted to work with people. I knew that I had this wretched maths degree. In the state of the nation then, people thought of teaching as an Okay thing to do, a way of earning a living without compromising yourself too much. You could limp up the steps and be put on the pay-roll, particularly if your subject was maths. So I did a PGCE, basically because it was only a one-year course. I didn't see myself as teaching for ever, but thought that it would provide a breathing space in which I could sort myself out and think about what I'd actually like to do. How many people have said that to you? A million, I should think.

The first school I went to in the early 1970s was a boys' secondary school. The fifth-formers were huge, much taller than me. They set up situations to see how you would cope. There was a big black boy – I can't remember his name – who had a white friend. Usually they were very nice, but on occasions they could be really mischievous, wicked. One day, they had a row in class, which became much more serious and ugly, when the white boy called his friend a 'jungle bunny'. The black boy grabbed a chair and advanced on his friend, while I thought, 'Oh, my God! What shall I do?'

I was too proud to go and call for help because I knew it was a test of myself which I had to win somehow. Acting on an instinctive level almost, I went and stood between these huge boys. I fixed the black boy in the eye and told him to go and put the chair down. To my astonishment, after a lot of glaring, he did. And then we carried on with the lesson as if nothing had happened. Fortunately, it wasn't very long before the bell went. When I got to the staffroom, I found that I was shaking. Anyway, half an hour later, the boys came along and apologised. I didn't know if I'd handled the situation well, but I knew that I'd passed some sort of initiation test. And at that point, I thought, 'Yeah, I can do this. It's hard work, but I can do it.'

A couple of years later I went to teach in France for a year, because I'd always wanted to learn another language. The excitement of living in another country also attracted me. It was a British school, a so-called revolutionary school, which had no head, but was run by a parents' committee, a staff committee composed of all the teachers, and a student council. It was all terribly progressive, or so they thought, and a lesson in how excessive liberalism can easily degenerate into something else.

The school was housed in a beautiful old villa with very limited facilities. There were only two loos. One of the liberal traditions of the school was that both lavatories were used by all the boys and girls and all the staff, male and female. The girls were terribly sensitive about their periods. They asked if they could have the exclusive use of the upstairs loo, the only one which had an incinerator, to spare them the embarrassment of the boys knowing when they had a period. It seemed a reasonable request to the female staff, but we had an academic council meeting, which lasted four hours, to debate all the philosophical implications. No one recognised the inherent sexism of the debate and neither did I at the time. In the end, it was decided that for the best liberal reasons, the girls' request could not be granted, which seemed to me grossly unfair.

That kind of thing happened all the time. A practical issue would be transformed into philosophical argument. The pupils wanted to make it optional to attend lessons. There was another long debate about that. Ultimately, it was decided that lessons must remain compulsory, because there were O level exams to be taken at the end of the course. Some of the children didn't support the decision and didn't come to lessons. As it was a liberal school, there were no punishments, so it was difficult to make them attend. The idea was that you should make the lessons so interesting that they would want to. It was an interesting place to work in and I learnt a lot, but I couldn't wait to leave. The light of one's ideals had been tarnished slightly.

So I came back home and married a fellow mathematician. I was twenty-five or twenty-six and it seemed the right thing to do. I was very immature in not realising that you could be good friends with somebody, a man, and not marry him. It seemed the only consequence then. Don and I had been going with each other for a long time. Before I went to France, we'd lived together, squabbled, lived apart and then got together again. We should have known better.

I didn't go straight back into teaching, but got a job on a newspaper, selling space by phone, trying to convince customers that they needed five times more column inches than they actually wanted. We were all girls together. There was no responsibility except to make as much money as you could. The more space we sold, the more money we earned. It was a real carrot and stick job, really diabolical. I stood it for three months, but when I saw all my teacher friends breaking up for the Easter holidays, I threw it in and went back to teaching.

Don was a musician as well as a teacher and was very involved in doing his own thing. We both got more and more entrenched in our own ways. I felt very frustrated in my own life, uncreative, unfulfilled. I didn't want to be categorised as a typical maths teacher, but I saw myself as becoming narrower and narrower. So I compounded it, by becoming more and more involved in my work, spending extra time at school, making costumes for plays, organising things that had nothing to do with maths, which resulted in even more stress. I was clearly getting better at my job and I was promoted. People were saying that Jan was a good maths teacher which I liked. I was very busy, so busy that I didn't have time to see things clearly at all. It was like being bounced from one set of needs to another. I was disappointed about the marriage and myself. And then it all went nuclear and we split up after four years. We liked each other and still do. I assume Don likes me. I like him still. But I don't think either of us made much effort marriage-wise. It was during that period that I began to feel thoughtful, properly thoughtful, about the effects teaching was having on me.

I used to feel embarrassed – not embarrassed – cross, when I told people I was a teacher and they replied coldly, 'Oh, yes', thinking to themselves, 'Well! Move on! Next question!' I expect if you tell people you're a writer, they'll ask more questions. They'll want to know what kind of writing you do, I should think. I don't know. Do they? Teachers never feel valued in that sense or that their work is interesting to people.

Teachers would like a few more pats on the head instead of being constantly knocked. Even simple things in teaching are enormously stressful. If you're five or ten minutes late for work, it wouldn't matter in a lot of jobs. You'd just apologise and the only thing which would be affected would be the structure of your own day. In a school, the consequences are immeasurable compared with that small amount of time, in that the deputy head has to set the wheels in motion for someone else to cover for you. When you arrive, you have to pacify the person who has reluctantly sacrificed his or her own time, and the class of thirty individuals will be slightly bumpy because they've missed you, they've been wondering what has happened, they feel a bit threatened. And things like that go on all day, every day.

From nine to four, you are constantly being bombarded with other people's needs and demands. There's no time to think of yourself, no time to acknowledge that you're inevitably hurt. From the moment you walk into a classroom until you walk out again, you are a caring person who simulates every feeling from pleasure to rage which you may or may not really feel. It's a controlled reaction all the time and very wearing.

Of course, there are bad teachers, people who are really lazy, who don't care if they push things on to other people, don't do any extra work, won't take any responsibility, expect other people to pick up the pieces when they're in difficulty. They're the ones Keith Joseph is talking about. And, in my experience, they are in an infinitely small minority. In my school, there is no one like that. In the last school there was one, possibly two. I expect you've had other people tell you the same thing.

You have to give an enormous amount of yourself. And if you feel, as I did for many years, that you're giving your all, it makes you think, 'What the hell am I? Take teaching away, and I'm nothing. I'm not a person of my own.' Mercifully, I don't feel that any more. Shortly after my marriage broke up, I was seconded to do a post-graduate diploma for a year. Going back to university was extremely good for me as it unblocked me. I'd had these feelings that perhaps I wasn't as clever as I thought; but I did very well on the course and redeemed myself academically in my own eyes. Compared to teaching it was a piece of cake, even though you had to do four hours' private study a day as well as attending lectures.

While I was on the course, I took up with somebody else, an artist. It was an extremely tempestuous affair which lasted a long time, until early this year, in fact. As an affair, I don't really want to talk about it because it was distressing in many ways; but it was extremely good for me in that here was a person, a poor but dedicated artist, who was committed to a higher order of things really, something which I'd always admired and aspired to myself. The affair forced me to do something more creative. I discovered a great love of drawing and painting, which I still do and enjoy immensely.

That has freed me to see my maths in perspective. For years, I felt so very cross and frustrated about why I'd done maths. For a long time I felt that to be a mathematician was to be a socially unacceptable pariah. In a social situation, it's very difficult to have a deep conversation about mathematics, though it's perfectly acceptable to have one about music or religion or politics. There are mathematical processes involved in logical planning, spatial awareness, in probabilities and all that sort of thing; but mathematicians aren't allowed to hold court because other people are frightened of it as a subject. People think that mathematicians must be frightfully clever. And it isn't true, but the only people who know are other mathematicians.

Now I don't care; I'm not a brilliant mathematician but competent, and I see teaching maths as a perfectly honourable way of earning my living. I do care about it now, I do enjoy it, because I've got this other private facility which means a lot to me as a person.

When I was young I was idealistic. I saw teaching as a way of not betraying my ideals. Now I think that it's an immensely hard job and that teachers put an enormous amount of themselves into it, often with little encouragement from others and very limited resources. Your professional skills aren't recognised. In the past the way to teach was an academic thing handed down from universities, colleges and other institutions, which philosophised about the ways in which people learn, the content of education and so on. That worked in the grammar schools, because the children negotiated a contract with the teacher – 'Yeah! Okay, we want to learn something, so we will.' It also worked to a certain extent in the secondary moderns because they aped the grammar schools. It didn't work in comprehensives at all, because for many of the children there was no carrot at the end, no job. So when a new teacher went into a comprehensive, the first thing the other teachers said was, 'Forget everything you've learnt at college. I'll tell you what to do. You've got to learn discipline, how to establish class control, then you can relax.' That's all very well if you're born charismatic, but most people aren't, so they found it immensely difficult to cope.

What's been happening over the last ten years or so is that some teachers have been finding out by action-research how children learn, and developing new styles of teaching. For the first time as far as I'm aware – I'm no historian, but you may be able to tell me – some teachers are moving ahead of the received knowledge coming from the universities by introducing collaborative learning – speaking and thinking at the same time. In a science lesson, for example, the assessment of how much a child has learnt depended on how successfully he or she wrote up the experiment. Some children, however, may know perfectly well what has gone on, understand the concept involved, be able to repeat or transfer it, but be incapable of writing it up because they lack the necessary writing skills. Teachers are having to discover other methods of assessment and talking is one of them.

Teachers have to create an environment where people feel comfortable, where they can securely fail. To succeed in maths, for example, you have to take risks, to commit yourself to an idea. Teachers have to make it comfortable enough for you to take these risks without damaging your self-esteem. We have to relate to specific people in front of us, not from our point of view, but theirs. If it isn't accurate, they will resent it. What's more, it then becomes your problem, because if they resent it, you know it. You have to recognise and understand the dynamics going on in a group.

For example, your friend who sits next to you uses you all the time as a prop to his own ego. He is not very good at maths – not as good as you are – but has a bigger, more fragile, more vulnerable ego, and so in no circumstances can he appear to be less able than you. So what does he do? When you start doing any work, your friend will disrupt you. It might be a serious disruption, but it probably won't be, as your friend is quite simple. So when you're just getting into a problem, he will lean across and help himself to your pencil or your rubber. That dynamic means that the teacher has to find a way for you to work so that you can increase your self-esteem. There's an even bigger problem with your friend, as he won't admit he's got a problem, and will use avoidance tactics to stop himself getting down to any actual work which would set him up as a failure in front of you, or the teacher, or anyone else in the class. Or you may find that another child, who is very bright but also kind, will set himself up as a class clown in order that other people won't be the worst. Do you see what I mean? Teachers have to recognise these interactions and try to make as many people feel comfortable and put the right person in the position of being a facilitator. You can be trained to recognise the dynamics in a group, but the ability to deal with them only comes with experience. As I said, you can be trained and we aren't, but it's coming.

Another new development is for children to assess themselves. As adults, we know that we're different at different hours of the day, let alone days of the week or months of the year. You go through phases in your life when you develop a creative interest in or a scientific curiosity about things which you're not going to be particularly good at. Because someone once said you weren't good at chemistry, it may have repercussions fifteen, twenty, thirty years later. Exams are cruel statements which make judgments which remain with people for ever. With self-assessment, you learn automatically that you change over time in your peer group. The reason that assessments are restricted mainly to lower-ability people is that they're expendable. The bright kids can't be risked.

22

Exams Don't Tell You Everything

When they've left school, some boys write to thank me if they got good exam results, but last week I received a letter from a boy who hadn't done very well in his A level at all. It was a very sweet letter, in which he said, 'Sorry I didn't get a better grade, but I do love literature and I read more novels than I ever did before.' I felt much more chuffed by that from a teaching point of view than by somebody getting an A or B.

Mike Broadberry teaches English in a comprehensive school, formerly a traditional grammar school in a mixed, but highly middle class, suburb in south London. The school has a very large sixth form and, usually, excellent examination results. As a consequence, it is so greatly over-subscribed by parents in the catchment area that it is sometimes the number of the house and not the street itself, which decides whether a child will be admitted. Mike, who has recently been recording some of his lessons to check up on his performance, has been teaching for twenty years. Although he sees much of value in traditional examinations, he has some serious reservations about them and also believes that they don't necessarily tell the whole truth about a school.

Examinations work on a practical level in two ways. They provide a motivation for a large number of pupils and they standardise a lot of teaching. I do get a little uneasy, however, when I see some question being repeated again and again so that the majority of answers will follow a formula. In examinations, so much depends on the aptness of the task that is set. A lot of examinations show what people can't do under certain circumstances. Your heart bleeds for some pupils. They are thinking people, conscientious, well-motivated, but don't do very well in exams. Bad examinees deserve more consideration: they might be given a term to do the longer essay.

The most distressing thing, however, is when the general results don't tally with your own or your colleagues' expectations and assessments. The injustice of the system really got up my nose last year. Over 60 per cent of the pupils we entered for O level English Language got D, E or U, and others, who were expected to get As, got Ds. When I wrote to the board, I didn't get any satisfaction. Not one grade was changed. I thought it was a bad paper. I've been an examiner myself and know the system from the inside. In one section, 84 per cent of the people failed. It's a bad examination if that happens. So I switched boards and the results were much more closely in line with the views of the pupils' teachers, with nearly 70 per cent gaining As, Bs or Cs.

I remember doing the same thing many years ago at A level, when boys who were really pedestrian were getting As, while a boy who was really excellent, a brilliant scholar who went on to get a double first at Cambridge, only got a B.

I suppose the answer is for teachers to have more control over the exams, with the board setting one half, so that it has control over what we do, a sort of hurdle, and the teachers setting the other half, doing the kind of work which ties in with their interests and enthusiasms. In other words, a Mode 2 exam. You can get O levels of this kind by negotiation with some boards, but it's much more common in CSE.

I've always felt that CSE was a good, imaginative exam, but there was a gap between the teachers' and the public's expectations of it. Among the public, there was a mixture of ignorance and knowingness: an ignorance of the actual system so that many employers didn't even know that a Grade 1 CSE was equivalent to O level, and a knowingness in that people asked, 'How many people who can do O levels actually do CSES?' It was caused partly by bad public relations, partly by academic snobbery.

The new GCSE will affect classroom arrangements quite a bit, although there's still a lot of argument about the actual papers that will be set. It could lead to more mixed ability classes otherwise it would run counter to the idea of all pupils doing the same work, or you might have some boys and girls set into different classes on the pretext that they were studying the subject more intensely.

Examinations tell you something about a school, but not the whole story. Good results tell you that the school is organised, but there are other questions to ask. Now that schools' results are published, you have to ask whether a school is giving the benefit of the doubt to marginal candidates or excluding them to keep up the pass rate. Reputations may also be out of date by the time they're made, as you're always looking at last year's results. When parents choose a school, they have to remember that their children won't be sitting the exams for five years. They can get some indications from what has happened in the past, but reading examination results remains a tricky business.

23

What Vocation?

I've had to teach five new pre-vocational courses in the last ten years or so, all of which were started in great haste. One by one they've been replaced or abandoned so that employers and parents don't know which is of any value. Certainly most teachers don't because they're in a fog. One course was called 365. The children didn't know why and neither did I, so they'd no idea what the aim of the course was. In fact, only the other day, some teachers were saying that one of the reasons it hadn't been successful was its name.

Joan Dulwich, a short matronly woman in her early fifties, teaches commercial subjects in a mixed comprehensive in the Midlands. She has been teaching in secondary moderns, comprehensives, and further education for nearly thirty years and believes that the current confusion in schools has been even more compounded by the introduction of hastily conceived courses.

Currently, we're into a new scheme, the CPVE. Like all the other courses its aim is to give what they call an all-round education to less able pupils. As there are ten core areas, the kids will just finish up with a hotchpotch of bits of information. It's supposed to be pre-vocational, but what will it train them for, what vocation?

I still believe in comprehensives. I believe in justice, equality and fairness and the kids certainly get more of those things now than they did with the old system of grammar schools and secondary moderns, but like many other teachers I have become increasingly disenchanted in the last five years. The main reason is the total chaos. There are two main reasons. The administration of all schools I've been in, which is quite a number, always seems to have been pretty disorganised. The people who run the schools – the heads, second and deputy heads and so on – don't generally reach those positions because they know anything about administration, but simply because they've been promoted up the career ladder for some reason, which is very often because they're creeps who never disagree with the head. In the last few years we've had the added horror of government intervention which has certainly added precisely nothing to education or the ability to organise each school better. The prevailing inefficiency has simply been concealed by chaotic change.

The aims of education need to be redefined by people who know what goes on in the actual classrooms, not by Whitehall mandarins or by heads, who increasingly spend more and more of their time out of school meeting other people who are equally remote from the real classroom situation. Both vocational and academic education seem to be out of touch with the realities of life in the western world. The less able kids, as we call them, are being taught skills and vocations when most of them are never going to get jobs or certainly not reasonable ones which can provide the way of life they want: while the brighter ones are being taught academic subjects which have little relevance to their imagination or to the real world in which they're going to live.

For example, politics isn't taught in many schools. In fact, it's become rather a nasty word as far as education is concerned, a danger area. Nothing is taught, or very little, about the genuine responsibilities of scientists and technologists or about social and moral responsibilities. Curiously, you do get a little bit of those with less able kids, things like community care, which is only taught to them, because it's deemed that they can't cope with more intellectual matters. So, the less able are dumped in this despised area of looking after other people and considering what their responsibilities should be to those even less able or less fortunate than themselves. They learn how to look after old people in homes, how to deal with handicapped people, and then go out and help with meals on wheels, that sort of thing. The thinking kids, in my experience anyway, are kept right away from such things and never consider the moral and spiritual aspects of life, except marginally in some religious education classes. The main reason is that they've got no value, as far as their parents are concerned, in getting a job. So, increasingly, in the last five years or so, there's been more and more of a division in the kinds of education we're providing for the different classes of kids in our State schools. It's ironic, really, that some public school boys and girls probably do far more social work of this kind than many bright children in State schools and also have much greater opportunities to consider controversial and even left-wing views than many bright children do in some comprehensives.

24

The 16+ Market-Place

Owing to unemployment, the non-academic sixth form is a growing market and everyone wants to get in on it. There's intense competition for this 16+ age group. The secondary schools want to keep them because there aren't enough children coming in at the bottom. Further education wants to attract them into its colleges. The government wants to get them on courses so that it can hold down the unemployment figures. And examining boards are only too happy to provide new exams because there's money to be made in it. City and Guilds is a commercial enterprise and so is the RSA. I'm not saying they want to make a profit, but they do want to break even. That's why there is such a bewildering array of courses and examinations for this age group now.

Mary Dunmow is head of English in a suburban comprehensive in the West Country. The school is situated in a select area of the city, where she lives herself, with large detached houses well spaced out along leafy roads. There are few problems of deprivation in the catchment area and the intake leans towards the middle class, though it also includes the children of operatives and artisans and a small minority of coloured pupils.

Before we sat down at the dining table in her spacious, well-furnished home, she thoughtfully provided me with a whisky which was three times as large as hers. (I had come a long way and it was a bitterly cold night.) I felt relaxed and comfortable from the start. She was obviously a sympathetic, caring person and dedicated to her pupils, particularly the lower ability groups, whom she liked teaching most. Although she welcomes the new courses which have recently been introduced for pupils of this kind, she has some serious reservations and misgivings about the way in which education seems to be going in comprehensive schools.

Behavioural objectives, to use the jargon, are increasingly being used in these new courses, such as the City and Guilds' 365, the CPVE and, I think, the TVEI. The theory is that teaching should change their behaviour in some way. For instance, children come into your classroom not knowing where to put speech marks and by the end of the lesson, they have this knowledge. So you could have as your behavioural objective, 'Can understand and use speech marks.' Now that of course is a fairly mechanical function. Unfortunately, these objectives are also being used in circumstances which seem to me inappropriate. I've already mentioned 'can distinguish fact from opinion' in the DES booklet, English 5 to 16, and 'can understand non-verbal language'. In other words, you're going to teach them body language. Now that seems to me an invalid objective.

Behavioural objectives are a fashion. They're neat, simple, mechanical, you see. They provide a checklist and also to a certain extent a syllabus, so that teachers feel 'I can tick this off and that off.' They do have the effect perhaps of appearing to reduce teaching to something simple, whereas, really, of course, it's a very complex interchange of all kinds of ideas.

I'm not decrying behavioural objectives. Some of the new courses, like 365, can be very useful. No, I don't know why it's called 365, except perhaps that it would be of benefit to you every day of the year. That's my interpretation. It's a kind of low-level City and Guilds pre-vocational course for CSE Grades 4 and 5.

It's given our boys and girls a great deal of confidence. In communications and subjects of that kind, you don't set them an essay and give them a mark which might be low or medium but never perfect. Instead, you teach for mastery which is a very different thing, so that you're saying, 'Look, you come in here and you don't know how to set out a letter, but we'll keep on till you do.' The tasks tend to be broken down into easy stages so that all the time you're saying 'Now you can'. The whole emphasis is on 'Now you can', though I must say a lot of my teaching of low ability groups has always been based on that anyway. One of the aims of the course is to alter their low self-image, to show them how to search out things for themselves. That's how it differs from a CSE or an O level.

The 365 is a precursor of the CPVE which is not a subject-based course like O level. What they've done is to identify ten core studies, you see. For instance, you don't teach communications as a separate subject as it can be covered by projects in other areas. Say you had a project like running a school tuck-shop. They would sit down first and work out what they were going to do, which would be communication, you see. You would listen to them and try to identify the people who had positive contributions, though I don't know whether they've thought this out well enough, as it's notoriously difficult to assess things like that. Then they might go on to finance and that would cover numeracy. After that they might come up against a difficulty, which would be problem-solving. That's how it's broken up. You do need very clear objectives, of course. The teachers have to meet and work them out, which is team teaching really, so the amount of time needed is enormous.

It's going to take a very long time for parents and children to understand these new courses because they're so jargon-laden. There are core studies, vocational families, three different modules – introductory, exploratory and preparatory. Would you know immediately the difference between 'introductory' and 'preparatory'? Yet they represent entirely different levels of skills. Even teachers find all this jargon difficult. I had a meeting of my department today and they found it very hard going. If you've already had a long hard day and you've still got your marking to do, it does require a great deal of effort.

They haven't really worked out the assessment of CPVE, except that it's going to be profile-based; but I don't know yet what form the certificate will take or whether they can fail it. And not enough attention has been paid to bridging, whether CPVE can lead to O level. They haven't given enough thought to that.

Although I've no real grounds for my fears, intuition tells me that there are going to be increasing divisions in comprehensives between boys and girls who are judged academic and can go on through O and A levels to universities, and those who are deemed non-academic – they wouldn't use that phrase, but invent some jargon – who would be put into a more technical and supposedly vocational-orientated education. Training rather than education. And that worries me. Although I welcome this interest in the lower half of the ability range who have been neglected in the past, I don't know whether it's based on a desire to keep them quiescent or on a genuine interest in their education. When I look at the people who have composed these new courses, I become a little suspicious, because they're mainly from further education and business, who often aren't fully aware of the school situation and are frequently anti-intellectual. Although I feel it's good for schools and industry to co-operate, I'm a little worried by the denial of the creative arts in all these courses. You want people who are working in an office or a factory to be able to work as a team, to be tolerant, to be aware of one another's needs. English literature has just as great a role to play in making people sensitive and aware as learning to use a typewriter. We should be teaching boys and girls crafts, creativity, story writing, poetry. They love writing poetry, but that's not included in these new courses, though it would be considered quite suitable for anybody taking A levels, so why should they alone be taught creative skills?

It also worries me, which I'm sure has been voiced to you before, why there is such an emphasis on vocations and careers now that the world of work is fading. We should really be disabusing people of the idea that status is linked to work. But the government has this bee in its bonnet that education is no use to industry and what you really need is training. So they're trying to loosen the teacher's hold on education. What these new courses are doing, by laying down everything so minutely, is removing the autonomy of the teacher, which has been one of the glories of the British educational system. With the CSE, teachers were very free to explore their interests; the whole course was much more open-ended. CSE gave teachers much greater autonomy, too. If I'd been tied down to a very tightly prescribed series of behavioural objectives, I could never have had such a stimulating project with my fourth-year CSE class as I did last week.

It started as a simple comprehension. I took an article from the newspaper about the pound coin, the way the Royal Mint introduces new coins, the tests they do, and so on. I'd built up a comprehension test on my word processor with marks for each question. After that, we started to talk about coins. Suddenly, it occurred to me that some of the boys did milk rounds, others helped their fathers in their small businesses, one boy helped his father, who is a taxi-driver, to sort out his money each evening. I thought, 'These boys know much more about handling coins than I do.' So I asked them to write about coins they found useful, those which were fiddly, which could be easily mistaken. They wrote about that very well. To build on it, I took in all my husband's foreign coins which he throws into a box when he comes back from foreign business trips. I gave each child three coins and asked them to describe them, which led on to a very interesting lesson.

'Who's this on the back of this coin, miss?' – Well, that's Marianne.
'This is a Chinese coin, miss, but it's got a British king on it' – That's from Hong Kong.
'What these words around this coin?' – That's Latin . . .

It was a good lesson. It was child-centred you see, finding out what they could do and leading out from that, an extension of primary methods into secondary education.

With lower ability groups you have to coax them all the time. It's a fairly slow process and you need a lot of sympathy. In the past, a teacher would go in and bellow at his class, but you wouldn't get very far with that now. The whole concept of authority has changed so dramatically that you can't expect immediate respect because of your position. You have to earn it. It's a negotiated contract, really, so that you're saying or implying, 'Look how carefully I mark your work . . . Look how well you've got on since you've been in my class.' All teachers negotiate a contract, either implicitly or explicitly, though a lot don't realise they're doing it.

The official, the legal contract of *in loco parentis* is hopelessly out of date. It puts the teacher in a very, very difficult position because it's based on what an old-fashioned, not a modern, relaxed, parent would do. So schools have to stop near-adult boys from smoking, going into pubs at lunchtime, going home outside normal school hours without first inquiring if the mother will be there, or even playing snowballs because they might hurt one another. You, as a parent, would never be so protective of your own children. It would nullify their initiative. Yet when I'm in the classroom I'm responsible for the health and safety of thirty adolescents. If a boy throws a little bottle of erasing fluid across the room, I have to stop everything and say, 'Now, suppose it had hit that boy in the eye.' And the boy who threw it, says, 'It wouldn't, miss. I threw it straight into his hands and he's only three yards away.'

I wouldn't recommend anyone to enter teaching now, I really wouldn't, not if they wanted a fulfilling or a well-paid career, or any kind of excitement. My husband feels teaching is very underpaid because he knows what someone with a master's degree like myself would be paid in industry. Pay has a lot to do with the low status of teachers. People talk a lot about the way in which some teachers dress, but I know young men, with wives and families to support and mortgages to pay, who have to dress in cords and out-at-elbow jackets because they can't afford to spend money on themselves, even though they might like better clothes. They have old bangers or bicycles because, again, that's all they can afford.

Although many pupils and parents look with gratitude on what we've done and tell us so, you never hear about that in the newspapers, only about teachers' alleged faults. Everybody thinks they know about teachers because they've all been to school. A lot of people criticise us to get their own back for what happened to them years ago. Now they're no longer small, they can cry, 'Yaboo, I'm free of you! I can say what I like now.'

25

Alienated Pupils

Bill Foard was something of a puzzle. He is a tall man of thirty-three with the charming smile, the social ease and the assured manners of a Sloane Ranger. So what, I wondered, was he doing hanging out his young child's clothes on the balcony of an inner-city council flat in the Midlands and speaking in a faintly working class accent, which sounded more assumed than natural to me? The mystery was never fully solved, as he seemed somewhat confused about his own motivations; but he is certain that education as we knew it is finished and that the plethora of vocational-based courses offer no valid alternative.

Haven't you got a schedule of questions? Oh! . . . You see, I don't know where to begin . . .

Well, I've been working on a link course with a few alienated pupils in their last year at school. They attend the local FE college one day a week, have one day's work experience and spend the rest of the time in the school workshops or having a kind of social education. Initially, it looked a nice idea. You've got these kids who don't really want to be at school and you've got the college with its workshops and wonderful practical things like a vast, unused mock television studio. In the end, however, the course seemed to be symptomatic of what is wrong with education.

Basically, the college was trying to recruit people, so it tried to get them for half a term of this or half a term of that instead of one day a week. The work experience was sometimes very dodgy. Most of the firms were pretty helpful. They sometimes paid the kids, though we weren't supposed to know about that. Or they'd give a girl a bottle of sherry at Christmas. It was all right if you got a person to take the kids under his wing, but occasionally some fellow would just use them to stamp his boxes or sweep his floors. You couldn't blame the kids for not liking that – or force them to go back. We tried to sell it to them by saying, 'Well at least you'll get a reference.'

At school, they had a sort of social education. We'd get people to come in and talk to them. The most popular speaker was the one who told them about their legal rights, what to do if they were arrested and things like that. A local trade unionist used to come in. Yeah, they were quite interested in him. We also used to do things about housing; but very often the kids were already well informed about that.

Most of them had dropped out of CSE to come on the course, because they weren't getting on very well. The other teachers used to moan and say, 'It's not fair. They've sodded about all this time and got on this course which might get them a job, while poor so-and-so has worked really hard at his CSES.' A few of the kids did get jobs, but they didn't usually last long. A lot of them leave their first job after two or three months anyway.

So, after a time I got a bit disillusioned. It was like a pre-YTS course. The kids don't like that much either. They say, 'What's the point of going on YTS for a year when you're not going to get a job at the end? What are you training for?' YTS doesn't approximate to an apprenticeship. In this area there are still quite a few apprenticeships, because there are a lot of small firms which prefer to go on doing things in a traditional way. Apprenticeships are supposed to have ended in the building industry, but I heard from a kid today who claims to have got one. Mind you, whether it's a proper apprenticeship, I don't know. The parents put the kids off YTS by saying that it's slave labour. Some prefer to keep their kids at home rather than let them work for £25 a week. I tend to agree with them. What parents want is a skilled job for sons and a good office job for daughters.

I can't see how TVEI will work either. They're training people from fourteen to eighteen in these so-called new technology skills, but they don't know if the jobs are going to be there when they come to the end of the course. The first lot haven't finished their course yet. All these work-related courses are just an attempt to put some meaning back into education. Maybe TVEI's a way of bringing back the technical element, which got lost in the tripartite system, for 20 or 25 per cent, but that still leaves 75 per cent. What are they supposed to do? Do CPVE or the bottom grade of GCSE? Do their two years' YTS and then go on a community programme? To make that work, they've got to cut people's benefits, haven't they?

In the past, schools had a top 20 per cent who were going on to higher education and would become teachers and things like that. Below them, there was another 40 per cent. Teachers could tell them that if they studied hard for their exams, they'd get a good job. The girls could go into banks or offices and the boys could get apprenticeships. There was a bottom 40 per cent who could be sent on link courses or jollied along in some way.

That's all collapsed now, which is why the schools are in such a mess. A lot of kids who could have gone on to higher education wouldn't think of doing so now, because they know of students who are unemployed when they come out. Apprenticeships aren't available for the next 40 per cent and office jobs aren't so easy to get around here. And the bottom 40 per cent are alienated from link courses and YTS.

Teachers like to think that kids are studying for the sake of knowledge, but most of them are looking for a better job. The people who used to go into the sixth form try to get jobs at sixteen, if they've got good CSES or O levels. The sixth forms . . . Were you teaching recently? No! I imagined you had been at one time . . . The sixth forms around here have collapsed except in a few schools like a Church of England school, the girls' Catholic school maybe, and perhaps another girls' school. There's a new sixth form of non-academic kids, you see. I wouldn't advise anyone to stay on at school. There's a college for any academic sort of kid.

At my school, the official priorities still tend to be: stay at school; go to college; get on a YTS course. For the kids these priorities are reversed. Get a job; go on a topped-up YTS course which looks like a job; go to college; and, last, stay on at school. And I think they're all headed by a fifth priority, which is to sign on and get a part-time job, or go on with some Saturday job that you've been doing anyway, or help your family who runs a stall down in the market. In that way, you're going to get more money. The kids don't seem to be downhearted. There are still little fiddles, jobs you can do here and there, even crime. That's interesting in a way. People call crime 'doing a job'.

Education has been emptied of any value for the majority of these kids. It's no use to them. It wasn't ever much use anyway. Only to some of them. And that's gone. That's the long-term problem really, especially in secondary schools. In primary schools, I don't know . . . Are you doing primary schools? Oh, good! . . . Apart from visits, I don't know much about them, but I would imagine there's a consensus about what they're doing. Basically, you want your child to read and write by the time he leaves. There may be disagreement about how you go about it, but I would have thought that the kids, the teachers and parents accept that. Increasingly, that kind of consensus doesn't exist in secondary schools.

What may happen in the medium/short term is that the MSC may throw money at the schools, which is one way of buying off the teacher, because it will create a new career route for those who go into TVEI. That's what has happened in colleges. I can't see any solution. I think it's going to get worse and worse in terms of political options. I saw one of the Labour party people on television the other night and he was talking about a three-year YTS. I'm a bit disillusioned, but I don't feel demoralised myself, not really, because I never had much illusion about it anyway. Teachers who see it as their life work, who are really committed to comprehensive schools, must be very demoralised.

When I left Oxford, I didn't go straight into teaching. Oxford would strike me now as a ridiculous place, the way everyone behaves there. Unless it's changed. I can't imagine that it has. I was watching a Russell Harty programme the other night. Did you see it? Do you remember that chap from Liverpool, the one with braces. He was quite nice. Most of the people at Oxford aren't like him. Mind you, I wasn't like him myself. I don't know what I was like. I was pretty confused actually. It was all at the beginning of the 1970s.

When I left Oxford, I started doing social work. I didn't know what it was, you know, but I wanted to do something social. I worked for a charity for a while after that. Then teaching seemed to be one way in which you could keep in touch with people. I think it's good for that. And help people? No, I don't think I do much of that. Lately, I feel I've been learning much more than I was ever able to teach. If you really wanted to teach people, you'd probably work in a primary school, but I don't know if I'm committed enough for that.

I've been a great disappointment to my father. He used to be in the Navy actually. I suppose it may have all been a reaction against my home. They were rather conservative. They still are. We've got to go and visit them next weekend. It's not so serious now.

Politically, I suppose I'm towards the left, but I can't see any party that's going to do anything. I'm not in any party myself, and there's not likely to be one I'd want to join. I think the situation in schools will get a lot worse, before it gets any better.

26

A Totally Professional Approach

The trouble with education at the moment is that there's too much incomplete analysis. Each person is looking at it from his own point of view. The industrialist, whom I shall parody for a moment, is saying, 'The system is not turning out people with the skills I need to operate my machines. Something is wrong!' The shopkeeper is saying, 'These kids who come along can't count the change in the till. Something is wrong!' Yet the professional in the classroom doesn't seem to be standing back and looking at the educational process analytically. It's no good teachers saying that they are locked into the system and their job is merely to operate it. Our job as professionals is to look overall at what we expect from the educational system, to decide whether the ways in which we are doing things are appropriate and, if they aren't, to change them.

Brian Westward was involved in a long telephone conversation about his school when I arrived at his modern detached house early one wintry morning, when the ground was covered with snow. More than any other person I met, he provided the most convincing and cogent analysis of what schools are at present, and what they might be. He believes there is a great need for more analysis, curriculum development and professionalism of which his own career provides a paradigm. After working for a year in a grammar school, he spent four years in a well-known independent school, before he moved as head of science to a recently opened comprehensive school, where he had the chance to put some of his ideas on curriculum development into practice. He stayed there for nine years before he went on to his present school in an outer London suburb, where he is deputy head. Meanwhile, he has carried out part-time research for an MEd and a PhD based on classroom experiences. He is only thirty-seven.

We've got to decide what we want our priorities to be. If you define a skill as the ability to do something that you couldn't do before, then education is about skills. A fair number of those are intellectual, but quite a number are to do with attitudes and relationships. I could, for example, say that the educational system which has produced Arthur Scargill, to say nothing of the people on the Coal Board side, has failed in something which is vital to our industrial survival, because it doesn't seem to have done much about personal relationships. So, the way in which a school sets about organising its relationships, the discipline system for example, is an extremely important part of a child's education.

In practical terms it means that whenever you are disciplining children, you must be aware that your actions are a model of the way in which you hope children will be able to cope with conflict situations in the future. Now, that doesn't mean to say that you have to be soft and wishy-washy, because that isn't going to get you anywhere, or that you have to be incredibly hard and dismissive. In fact, hopefully, what you will do is to show children that there are two sides to an issue and if you finally pronounce in favour of one, you've got to be dispassionate and honest in your judgment, which means that sometimes you'll support the child.

Attitudes are just as important as relationships. I was brought up to do physics, chemistry, maths and so on, yet when it comes to considering a current international problem, like acid rain, I'm not well-equipped to do so, because I was never taught to look at the moral connotations of scientific development. There are many other social problems, like the animal rights people, Molesworth protesters and so on, where we do not seem to have the apparatus that we need to make reasonable decisions. Education has produced people who think in compartments, instead of people who look at the whole spectrum.

One of the things we need is curriculum balance. A person who specialises in science and doesn't look at the wider issues of life has had a very unbalanced education. Equally, the person who specialises in arts and knows nothing about science may, Heaven help us, end up in management in a technological company and be ill-equipped to make the right decisions. We need to produce people who understand the nature of their discipline, whether they're doing science or history, and are not simply learning a series of unrelated, obsolescent facts as they do with current O level examinations. If you're not careful, education can easily become a series of uncoordinated experiences of what you happened to learn in English, maths, chemistry, physics, biology and all the rest.

New courses, like the CPVE, are designed to be more relevant by using the world of work as a focus for education and concentrating on those areas which seem to be important, such as numeracy, communication skills and so on. The idea is that the package should be integrated in the minds of the children; but the possible disadvantage is that the experiences will occur in a way which cannot be usefully assimilated. If you take an integrated course, relevant to modern life, which covers transport, food, water and so on, there's a good chance that the subject structure will be lost in the process. I suspect that in ten years' time, if we're not careful, we shall find that the new integrated system is no better than the old differentiated system. So, it seems to me that we need to know far more about the structures of individual school subjects and the way in which children learn.

If I want to teach you something, it makes very good sense for me to structure the teaching to provide a bridge between what you know and what it is I want you to learn. If I simply start talking about a topic of which you know nothing, you'll be faced with the choice of learning it by rote or dismissing what I say. If you are used to receiving that kind of information and you're a reasonably submissive person, you'll probably be prepared to store some of the information and, later on, if you're lucky, make some sense of it. On the other hand, if education isn't particularly important to you, the information will probably go in one ear and out of the other, and you'll say that it's totally irrelevant. So, one has to know the structure of a subject to communicate it and one also has to know how children progress through learning structures.

Yet, strangely enough, if you look at current curriculum projects, you'll find an awful lot about what children ought to learn and all the marvellous experiences we want to give them, but an amazing lack of any understanding of how children can be put in a position where they can make any sense of what they've been provided with. My own work at the moment is analysing structures to produce what I call knowledge-maps, which enable me to identify the points through which children need to pass to build up an understanding of the subject. Very interestingly, a number of the points are the very ones which would be glossed over in traditional teaching.

Let's suppose O level chemistry could be put together with a network of two hundred rather general concepts. If you give a teacher the knowledge map, he can pick his own route through it in a way that suits him and his pupils best. This would not take away the teacher's autonomy, but would enhance his professionalism. You would need to give teachers much more time for planning this work. As I found out in my first comprehensive school, curriculum development can take up a very high proportion of a teacher's time and probably equals the teaching load. Even when you'd devoted every evening and all the weekends and holidays to it for several years, the effort still required to service the system was far greater than the average teacher would ever dream of putting in.

Teachers have got to go in for a totally professional approach to their work. This means (dare I say it?) that teachers should have the same kind of salary negotiations as doctors and forget this silly kind of industrial approach, which hasn't got us very far at all. If they take industrial action, they harm their public image, they hurt the people they are most concerned with, and thus send themselves into a downward spiral. We've had about ten years of this kind of approach and as salaries have declined by some thirty per cent over that period, I don't think it works successfully. Admittedly, you might argue that if the NUT hadn't taken that line, salaries

125

would be even lower; but then the Prime Minister argues that if she hadn't taken action, unemployment would be even higher, and I tend to treat both claims with equal scepticism.

We do need some mechanism for teacher appraisal, but I have grave doubts whether it should be tied directly to salary as in the latest management proposals, because it might mean that the sycophantic got on best. I'd rather like to separate appraisal, which is a management technique, from the salary issue.

There's plenty of room in education for management training. To put a head in charge of fifty staff, several millions pounds' worth of plant, and just tell him to get on with it, without telling him how, is wicked. There's also plenty of room for thinking about what the educational system is setting out to do. Teachers have got to be prepared to do this and to make changes, otherwise the MSC will come along and remove another element of education from the DES. This could mean that we returned to an academic or a practical curriculum for different types of children by a back-door approach. It wouldn't surprise me if we were heading in that direction.

27

Teachers, Not Baby-Sitters

In this school, with a staff of just under sixty, we've got six unfilled vacancies and about four people away this week through normal January sickness. So, we've got ten people out any day this week, but only four supply teachers, which means that six timetables are not being covered daily. Those classes are just being sent home or left in the playground. And this is an EPA, a social priority, school.

John Saint teaches in an inner-city comprehensive in east London, with a 50/50 mix of black and white pupils. He is a tall, well-built man of thirty, slow of speech and thoughtful in manner, who feels deeply that the whole of the educational service is threatened by present government policies. He is the NUT representative in the school.

Normally, if a teacher is away, another member of the staff will look after his class. If you're covering, however, you're just baby-sitting really, and we are not paid to do that, but to teach, to educate. The teacher who is covering has to give up his or her 'free' periods, which are used for marking and preparation; but they can't be done efficiently if you're covering.

So, at the moment, we're taking no-cover action. We've got union backing for one-day cover which means that we don't cover after the first day of absence. We continue to cover, however, where people are away on courses to do with all these new ILEA initiatives, which we see as a benefit to the children, or when they are out on curriculum-related trips. Basically, all we want is more supply teachers. The authority has said that they've employed three hundred more, but we've got fewer supply teachers here this year, when the situation is worse, than in years gone by.

We've been forced to take this action through a combination of factors. It's the whole uncertainty that is so stressful. There's not only the stress of the actual job, but also the additional strain of teaching in a social priority school. Fifteen years ago, this was a real sink school, but the previous head pulled it up for all the wrong reasons. He would only employ men who were tall, young and strong-looking. It was very much a macho environment. Primary school heads from all around would say, 'We've got a bit of a bubbly character, so we'll send him there. They'll know how to deal with him.' We're still suffering from that legacy. We've also got stress from all the ILEA initiatives – Hargreaves, multi-ethnic, sexist. I mean, I agree with all of them, but they need resources, time, staff, money to do them properly. The staff here want to do those things, but we feel we're being asked to do them on a shoestring.

There's also uncertainty over falling rolls, education cuts, job prospects, redeployment. Our intake has been halved, so redeployment was an issue here for the first time last year and suddenly the whole staff joined together to oppose it. We were set to lose nine teachers, but because a number left through promotion, we only lost three. They were redeployed. Now there's talk of fifteen redeployments this year. I've heard that by 1988, there'll be only enough secondary children in this division to fill either the voluntary-aided or the county schools, so there's a lot of uncertainty about what will happen. Then there's the abolition of the GLC, the changes in ILEA and rate-capping. I think many NUT members see rate-capping as the government's way of destroying education in a school like this.

The majority of teachers have never been raving left-wing militants, but conservatives, with a small 'c'. I think that if the public understands that, they'll begin to ask, 'What has moved this type of person to protest, to strike, to take to the streets? There must be something wrong. Their conditions of employment and their pay must have deteriorated so much that they've been forced to take this action.'

VII

GRAMMAR SCHOOLS

28

A Minimum of Eight O Levels

Mike Hildrich's experiences as an English teacher span the three main types of State secondary schools. He has worked for long periods in a northern grammar school, a secondary modern in the south and an inner-city comprehensive in London. He finds the grammar school, where he is currently employed, far too snobbish and narrow in its ethos, old-fashioned in its teaching methods, and casual in its treatment of the less able; but the comprehensive, which was fraught with social problems, was even worse. He is forty-seven years of age.

I preferred the secondary modern in many ways. The youngsters were keener and had a much wider breadth of experience. It was a mixed school, so a number of the boys had girl-friends at the school. In my present school, which is an all-boys' academic school, a lot of the boys are very narrow and snobbish in their attitudes. For example, if the miners' strike were being discussed every boy would be pro-Thatcher and would feel that Scargill should be shot.

The secondary modern youngsters were much franker and more open in their attitudes. You could ask a boy, 'Were you smoking in the woods this morning?' and he'd immediately admit it, if he was. In the grammar school, the boys are clever and sly enough to cover things up. The other day a boy called out 'Liar' in the corridor. He was obviously referring to me. When I challenged him, he said, 'Oh, no, sir, I was talking about a Beatles record called "Flyer".'

The teachers in my present school are all highly academic. It's an all-graduate staff and quite a few have Oxford or Cambridge degrees. There's a very slow turnover of staff. Many of them have been here twenty or twenty-five years. The boys tend to take ten to fourteen subjects at O level which, I feel, is far too many. The minimum number they can take is eight. The school is very science-orientated, which means that it's very difficult to change the curriculum. There's no innovation in any field really. The library, for example, has books going back to wartime. Some of them are even pre-war. In third-year history, before they start O level, they do one term on the industrial revolution, one term on Russian history, and one term on American history. They're still using the same textbooks as they did when I came here years ago. Oh, no, that's not strictly true. They've just bought new books, but they're merely revisions of the old text.

In some ways, the teacher's work-load is smaller than in other schools. Preparation is simpler. The work is bookish, which means that you can have boys reading quietly, or writing essays, in a way which would be impossible in a secondary modern, because you've got to interest pupils there, which means far more preparation. Some teachers still use their old university notes. There is a lot of marking, particularly in subjects like history and English, and a terrific number of exams, twice a year for each class.

Participation in out-of-school activities is very high. There are musical and drama productions which the staff are expected to attend and quite a lot of matches, football, hockey and so on. Then there are the speech days, when the head says the school is even better than it was last year, and eight parents' evenings a year. A large proportion of the parents of bright boys in the top sets attend, but the parents of children in the bottom set, who are probably going to fail exams anyway, don't often come. About 20 per cent don't get the minimal number of O levels. There are no remedial classes. If a boy doesn't make it, he's had it.

The comprehensive school was very unpleasant, particularly as I'd been used to well-behaved youngsters at the secondary modern. We had two or three members of staff attacked. One boy pulled a knife on a teacher and although she wasn't hurt, she had to go on tranquilisers. I got involved in two incidents with boys myself. One boy hit me three times after I'd asked him to move in assembly, so I knocked him to the floor. The boy ran off home to his parents but no action was taken. On another occasion, a boy threatened me with a chisel and stopped me from leaving the room. I reasoned with him and managed to get away. Funnily enough, as a result of these two incidents and the fact that I'd kept my cool, I was promoted to head of year, a role that I enjoyed.

Many of the youngsters had only one parent or lived in homes. There were some really tragic cases. For example, there was one girl who refused to do PE. I asked the lady PE teacher to do something about it. She made the girl change and to her horror found that the poor girl had about fifteen scars on her back where her father had hit her with a belt buckle. We informed the police about it, but I don't know what happened.

There was another case where a father had been imprisoned for sexually assaulting his daughter. She was put into care. When the father died, the mother wanted to have the child back home; but the social services objected, because they thought the mother was inadequate. However, they had no ground for keeping the child in care once the father had died. So she went back to her mother who was living in one room with only one bed.

29
Discipline Must Come From Within

Although I've had some super headmistresses and headmasters, I really had my eyes opened at that grammar school. I think the headmistress must have had some unhappiness in her life. How can I describe her without being discourteous? Perhaps one could say strait-laced. I don't know what sort of school she'd been to, but I imagine that she'd had a rather sheltered existence. She hadn't come to terms with the changes that were going on in the outside world. She seemed to have no sense of humour and if you haven't got that in teaching, you might as well walk out of the back door.

Now in her mid-fifties, Heather Foxhall taught in secondary and independent schools before she obtained a post in a girls' grammar school in the West Country in the 1960s. Partly as a result of her experiences there, she realised that she was far more interested in the education of the whole child than in merely passing on knowledge and therefore transferred to the primary sector.

The headmistress found it very difficult to relate to the children and the staff and wanted to keep them both under her control. There's something I can tell you about that in a minute. I went there mainly to teach religious education and that resulted in a terrible battle, because she probably thought at the beginning, though she did change while I was there, that religious education did not necessarily extend beyond the Bible. By then I'd realised that the Jewish and Christian teaching embraced the whole of living.

Religious education is a tough subject to teach. My faith means a great deal to me, but in every school it's taken at least a year for the children to see that what we were talking about was our lives and how we lived them. It wasn't just words. So, to the headmistress's horror, I drew up a new syllabus and talked about what the girls wanted to hear. We went into all sorts of religions; they were just coming in then. We also discussed all sorts of other things. Drugs had started. Abortion was just about coming in. Whether you should sleep with your boy-friend. All that sort of thing. They were super lessons after the first year and by the time I left, five years later, I had lovely, trustworthy links with the girls.

The girls were often very difficult, especially the older ones, because many thought they were sophisticated and went around with self-opinionated airs. It was the place to live; quite a fashionable town. And school was a bit of a bore, you know. That was the attitude of some of them. The headmistress tried to keep discipline by imposing her beliefs on the staff and children, whereas discipline, as I think you'd agree, must come from within. She was strict about uniforms. The mini had just come in and, of course, the girls wanted to wear it. Their skirts got shorter and shorter, so a rule came out that they could only be a certain number of inches above the ground. It didn't end there. The head had told us that we must set a good example to the girls. Fashion didn't bother me particularly then; but we had one or two young teachers, just out of college, who were very fashion-conscious. They started wearing mini-skirts. If you remember, Frank, they went right up here. Some of the younger teachers' skirts had almost reached that point and the head had them in individually and measured their skirts with a tape or a ruler and told them they must wear longer skirts. She lost her battle there because they wore even shorter skirts.

That was her sort of approach. At staff meetings we all had to stand up when she swept in. Well, you don't really do that, do you? After she'd greeted us, we could all sit down again. I think the head must have felt that if she had this kind of hold over her staff it would encompass the children too.

The children, of course, reacted against this strict discipline. On one occasion, stink bombs went off. The worst thing happened at the end of one term. Some of the girls, who were about fourteen or fifteen, a difficult age then, had smuggled in some bottles of alcohol, all different varieties. After they'd imbibed all the different kinds, they staggered into the school, drunk. They were violently sick in the corridors. The head was horrified. All the staff were shut in the staffroom and not allowed to leave, except for the few who had to go out and clean up the mess. I'd never smelt so much disinfectant. It was like a hospital. Our poor headmistress thought the end of the world had come, but it was just a high-spirited rebellion. The girls hadn't realised that mixing liquor was going to have such disastrous effects.

Academically, the school had a very high standard. It was very geared to the syllabus, which is necessary to a point, though not to the extremes it was taken there. We had exams almost every term. All of your examination papers had to be tied up with pieces of string of exactly the same length. The returns had to be done in different colour inks for pass and fail. If you made the slightest mistake they had to be redone. And, I've never come across this in any other school, all your reports had to be vetted by the head who would quibble about little words like 'could' or 'would' or even full stops. As a result, the report-writing took weeks, because we all had to go in and show the head every one.

It was so restrictive there that I felt I couldn't go on. It was driving me insane. Much as I loved teaching, I started thinking, 'Have I got to do this all the rest of my life?' I wanted to get married, but I hadn't found the right one yet. So, I thought, why not go into primary teaching? I'd already worked in an independent school, where I'd had a lot to do with the prep department and that's where my idea of teaching younger children originated. Oh yes, I'm sure it was also because I wasn't married. I'd always wanted children of my own.

Anyway, I'd made friends with a super person in the education department who told me that the only way I'd get into primary work was by making myself familiar with modern maths, which was just coming in then. That set me back, because I'd been taught abominably at school and maths was a real terror to me. When I was at school, you just didn't go out to play if you couldn't get the right answer. You were looked on as a dud. So when he told me this, I said, 'Oh, I'll never be able to cope.' And he replied, 'You'll have to, otherwise you'll never get taken in.'

So I went to the education authority and poured out my heart. They must have taken pity on me, as I was given a place on a course in modern maths. I learnt more on that course than I did in the whole of my life. It took away my fear of maths. I'm still not very good at the actual mechanics, but I know what should be done.

Since then, I've worked in some very tough primary schools, doing mainly remedial work. One church school, with a super staff, in a town in the Midlands, brought a great deal into my life. There was a little boy there called Rob who was about five years old. He was a lovely-looking child, just like a little prince, the sort of child who would be whipped away in a fairy story and taken to the castle and brought up as a young lord. He had an angelic face and curly hair, rather like Bubbles.

Rob came from a terrible background. Mother and father had never married, and father was an alcoholic. They used to burn the furniture to keep warm. Rob used to come to school in filthy, ragged clothes, which seemed extraordinary in the seventies. The first day at the school, I couldn't understand why I smelt so awful when I got home, but it was poor little unwashed Rob. Oh, it's terrible, the smell of neglected children. So aprons came on then: we used to wash him at the school. He was the worst case, but there were other children with parents in prison, mothers who were prostitutes.

I think this was one of my happiest times in teaching, because I discovered without any doubt that it was the child I had always been interested in. Rob was a completely emotionally disturbed child, so I frequently had him on his own. All he wanted very often was cuddles. Gradually, I taught him to play, because he didn't even know what that was. I remember taking him out once with his parents' permission, to an outdoor swimming-pool. I thought that would be best because he was so dirty. The towel they gave me was almost black. Another time we had a picnic in a park and he asked me, 'Are you going to love me all your life?' He was so deprived of love and I had masses to give which all came out with children.

I understood what Rob was feeling because love had got lost in my own family. My father set up a business which failed. He ran into debt, went to sea, and eventually found a job in Africa. He wanted us to go over there, but mother declined, and finally the money and the letters stopped coming. I have no knowledge where he is now, though there are no bitter feelings.

Nowadays, it's not at all strange for a parent to walk out, but then it was a terrible disgrace, you scarcely liked to mention it. So, in later years, whenever another member of staff has said that a child has just got to adjust to a parent going off, I've always been inwardly angered. It does have a very strange effect and we were a happy household. It put me off men when I was at college. I wouldn't even sit by them on the bus because they represented something disloyal. And I know it made me terribly wary of marriage. In one sense that's probably why I got married so much later in life. I've always felt very akin to children when anything like that has happened to them.

That's what I've liked most about teaching – being with children. I do love them, perhaps because I've never had any of my own. Teaching was always something I wanted to do from the age of seven – never anything else.

30

The Captain of the Ship

I see a headmaster's role as rather like that of the captain of a ship. He needs to be able to delegate responsibility. The best head I've ever known actually said on one occasion that he liked to step back a little and let the school run itself.

Brian Shortland, who is forty-seven, has had seven headmasters in his career as a science teacher in four independent schools and a voluntary-aided grammar school in the south, where he is currently employed. He believes that some heads are too inclined to interfere in areas which they should leave alone, and weak and ineffectual in others which should be of central concern.

Some heads have a tendency to interfere in teaching, particularly those who have degrees in subjects other than science. The best head I ever had left the science department to flourish independently.

The most useful quality of a head is, perhaps, to be a judge of character. Some are quite unable, or unwilling, to admit that any boy can be basically bad and they will always listen sympathetically to what can only be described as a sob-story. Every headmaster I've known, with one possible exception, has been extremely reluctant, for one reason or another, to pitch boys out of school. Whilst one does not wish to be harsh, a number of my schools would have been better off morally without certain boys. Even though they might have suffered personally, they would perhaps have learnt something as a result of that fairly drastic treatment. Certainly, whenever it has happened, the effect on other boys has been salutary. The biggest change I would like to see in education would be more training of senior staff in the ability to handle almost everyone.

I went to a public school myself. What I most liked about it was the very high standard of teaching and the level of attainment which was expected and generally reached. The organisation was very efficient in that the senior boys virtually ran the school, particularly the houses. What I most disliked about it, looking back, though I was not personally involved, was the very considerable amount of petty bullying of boys who were unpopular for reasons which were never satisfactorily established. The discipline was certainly a great deal tighter than in any school I've been in since.

When I left, I did my National Service in the Navy. My views were very much coloured by that experience. The general standard of discipline and cleanliness was something that I've never forgotten. You learnt to get on with your own job. There was no interference providing you did it efficiently. A lot of people saw National Service as two years' training in how to shirk, but when I went to university at the age of twenty, I felt I was a man. One had seen more of the world. The things I liked most at Oxford were the opportunities to train one's mind and to organise one's life in a way which I had never previously had. The amount of work you did was very largely a matter of personal choice. In my last year, I did a large amount.

I decided to become a teacher in my last year. There were teachers on both sides of my family. I didn't do a teacher's training course, which wasn't compulsory then, though if I had, I think I would have learnt a lot about the maintenance of law and order in the classroom. A lot of teachers with my kind of background tended to have difficulties in maintaining discipline, especially in their first year or so.

I had no particular axe to grind in going to teach in an independent rather than a State school. The reason was very simple. I'd heard some fairly nasty stories about landladies and lodgings, and it was possible to live in.

A lot of independent schools are much cheaper to run than State schools, because they don't spend so much on administration. The only independent school comparable in size to my present school was run just as efficiently without the interference of LEAs and area education officers. One of the things I like least about my present school is the tendency of bureaucrats to interfere with the running of the school and to give instructions which are extremely difficult to comply with. There has also been an enormous increase lately in what I believe is called management in State schools, whereas in most independent schools all the staff are expected to teach a full timetable, and extra pay is given for extra responsibilities such as headships of departments. The standards of discipline and achievement were also much higher; but then, of course, when parents are paying, they expect, and get, much more out of their children.

I don't think all the Conservative praise of grammar schools is justified, but some certainly is. The features that could be usefully incorporated into comprehensives are above all the standards of organisation and discipline. The vast majority of grammar schools are too closely geared to exams. Most examination syllabuses have progressively become overloaded so that they leave too little time for other things. There is still a good deal of learning by rote. If the new GCSE exam can diminish that, it would help. A few boys get forced along an academic path which they don't want to travel. Part of the trouble is that we do not have the facilities for less academic subjects such as craft work, and even if we did, they would be used by a very small number of boys. Education cuts have tended to narrow the curriculum further, especially in the sixth form, where a number of subjects which were studied by only two or three boys have had to be cut out altogether. We have only a few visiting speakers, mainly on careers or religion. The public transport system is so bad, that most activities have to take place in the dinner hour.

One impressive feature of my present school is the tradition of coming to school even if one is feeling far from well. One simply does not take time off just because one has a cold. Teaching is not a nine to four activity. One night earlier this week, I was working upstairs until it was almost time to go to bed. Recently a very considerable part of my allegedly leisure time has been spent working out a new scheme of work for my department.

Although I would certainly feel that my salary has fallen behind, I am very alarmed about the current strikes, which may harden the minds of those who hold the purse-strings. Speaking personally, I do not think that I am particularly badly paid, but then I am fortunate in having a good graded post.

31

I'm Still a Chalk and Talk

Jill Manderfield, who has been head of biology for thirty-five years, first in a girls' grammar school and more recently in a sixth-form college, represents the best traditions of the old-style grammar school teacher. Although she is a strong supporter of educational standards, she has never wanted to produce mere academics, but well-rounded characters who are able to cope with the exigencies of life. She is a short, bespectacled woman, with a friendly smile and alert eyes, who obviously does not find it easy to tolerate stupidity or pretension in herself or others; hard-working; and dedicated to her students and her subject. When I arrived early one morning at her spacious house some thirty miles north of London, she was marking essays in her well-appointed study whose windows gave a restful view of the garden and an adjacent copse. She has gone on working to the age of sixty-five not so much through financial necessity as her love of teaching, and was due to retire in a few weeks time. She has no regrets about her life as a teacher, only a certain sadness about the decline in standards and professionalism which she has seen in the State sector over the years. Although she has spent thirty-seven years in all as a teacher, her first job was very different – working on Enigma during the war.

I come from Yorkshire. I went to a council school – I go back a long way, you see – until I was eleven and then went on to grammar school. In 1938, I went to university on a teacher's scholarship. My father, who was a graduate of the same university, had agreed to keep me so long as I could get the money to pay the fees. The only thing I could get in those days was a teacher's scholarship. You had to agree to teach after you had graduated; but by the time that happened the war had started.

As a scientist I would have been registered and called up; but one of my lecturers was in cryptography at Bletchley Park. You know all about that. It was recruitment by word of mouth, so I went there to work on Enigma. When I arrived in 1942, we were simply clerks working in army huts. It was really a collection of individuals. There were mathematicians to cope with the machines, Oxford and Cambridge graduates, people from other universities like me, civil servants. I call it my post-graduate education.

They weren't all intellectuals by any means. In my team, taking the extremes, there was a buyer from Marks and Spencer; two American army men, one of whom had been a lecturer at Yale and the other at Harvard; and West End stage people, yes, they got those in, some of whom went on into ENSA. I suppose I did rather well there. By the age of twenty-three, I had a staff of fifty. Yes, it's true. It was ridiculous. I liked the work. It was an intellectual exercise in that, although the breaking of the thing was done, what I really developed, if you like, was where the codes were; if they were moving backwards or forwards; and what could be predicted. I also knew that you were messing about with people's lives. I never forgot that. If you made a mistake, you put lives at risk.

I could never tell anyone about the work, not for thirty years anyway, until all those books about Enigma started to appear. I got an MBE for my work, which was stolen later by a burglar. I suppose people who saw it on my records when I applied for jobs, must have wondered how I got it. It was put down as 'secret work for the Foreign Office'. I suppose they might have thought I'd been a spy. No, I don't think so, really. I could have stayed on in the Foreign Office, but I got married in 1944 and one of you had to follow the other. Two jobs, you see. My husband was an accountant, but he's retired now. We were living in the Midlands and nobody wanted me for anything else, so I wrote to the local Director of Education. I started teaching in a secondary modern school. When I arrived, I asked the head what he would like me to teach and he replied, 'Do what you like'. So I did. After I'd been there for a week, a poor lad came back from the army on his teaching practice. So the head said to me 'Write a criticism'. I protested, but he insisted that I write a report. All I can remember saying is that he'd drawn a caterpillar with the legs in the wrong place.

Then we came down here and for five years I didn't teach, and then I went to work in a girls' grammar school for twenty-seven years. That folded seven years ago and I moved to a sixth-form college. For twenty-five of those twenty-seven years at the grammar school, we had a headmistress, who is a very remarkable woman of the old-style, yes, a classicist, with the most wonderful command of written and spoken English. And in a way, you could say she was a dictator. We got on well though there were some points of disagreement. I can't really remember what they were. Over the girls' behaviour, I think. She was more authoritarian and concerned about uniforms than I was. But she was a wonderful woman. We're still good friends. She rang me only yesterday.

The school was very well-equipped. We had everything we needed. It had a very high reputation academically. I know that some people say grammar schools were too academic, too examination-orientated. It's true, but it's necessary. As a biologist, I say I train technicians. People don't always understand what I mean. To train as a doctor, you've jolly well got to know where all the bits and pieces are. And in a similar way, if I'm teaching someone O level who is going on to A level, they need to know all the details of, say, the enzymes in the digestive system, because they have to communicate. Biology has its own language. If somebody's going to follow biology as a career, they need to know the language. If they're not, and nowadays we have more mixed courses in which they do biology with every other subject under the sun, I agree it matters less.

I'm still a chalk and talk. I did try overhead projectors, but they were never big enough to get everything on. We make more use of videos now. At one time, we used to get, let's say, six frogs to demonstrate muscle twitch, but now we've got it on a video. We have a video of all the rat dissections, too. That's not the same as doing it yourself, is it? As long as it's put in practical exams, folk must still do it. You really have no choice. If anyone ever says they can't, I always try to cajole, but I would never force them.

You see, no proper biologist likes killing anything. We don't kill rats. I've never killed one. I wouldn't. We get them dead from the university. I don't even like killing worms. We cover them up. It's silly, but . . . You put them in a container with the ether, you see, and I put a cloth over the top so that I can't see them wriggling. I mean, it's childish, I know. We don't get any protests from the students about the use of animals – not yet. I was waiting for it this term, but nothing was said. We've got environmentalists and conservationists in the class, but no animal liberation people, no, not yet.

Animals are so beautiful when you look inside them, even the earthworm. Oh, it's wonderful how everything fits in. Then there are all those glorious colours. It's a beautiful subject, biology. There isn't any subject like it. I suppose I'm a teacher who wants to share that enthusiasm with others. You do it automatically. If you don't, you're in the wrong profession.

I was sorry when the grammar school closed, but I like being at the sixth-form college, though in a different way. The standards are down, because the feeder schools don't have sixth forms, so the students are less well-trained academically. And as it's open access, we've got a mixed bag. The motivation at A level is high for the majority, but the O levels are merely repeats, so if they do any work, they'll up their grade. We only have two years, so you have to put a quart in a pint pot. All we can do is to coerce: there's no threat except to say, 'Go somewhere else'. We do have that sanction, but people don't like to use it, because we want to keep the numbers up. We're in competition with other institutions, like the technical college, so our problem is getting enough students to remain viable.

I've got no regrets, I enjoy teaching. I shall miss the students. Every year, every two years, a new lot comes in, a new set of faces, and you look at them and wonder what their potential is and whether you can do anything about it. I think that's what I like. I have one lad who stands out in my memory, who's at Oxford now, the one you get in thirty years, with more than everything coming back to you in the classroom. The real pleasure is that

John had the potential and we were academically sound enough to deal with it, to get him where he wanted to go and where he should be. It's not reflected glory. You couldn't send some people to Oxford. Mentally, they'd be overpowered. There have only been two girls like that in all these years. I don't know whether we sent the wrong bods, or what happened.

What delighted me about John was that I couldn't find a weak spot in his character. He wasn't just academic, but well-rounded, conscious of the world outside him and of other people, including those who haven't got his ability.

To teach, you've got to be mentally alert. You've got to know your onions, because one half of your mind is on what you're saying and the other half is watching all the responses. You develop antennae. This last week, you know, I have gone on automatic pilot, because I've been tired and there have been so many other things going on. They appointed my replacement on Wednesday; we had the mock exams; and the lab technician fell down and broke a leg. So I got a bit behind. That's why I'm marking now. How much the students have noticed, I don't know. I hardly dare ask. But I go on.

That's one thing that I've noticed in the last thirty years. Teachers have become less professional, if you define professionalism as always putting your students first, before yourself. So, if you have a cold . . . Well, hard luck! You just get on with it. But morale is low. That's partly the reason. Academics have had to adapt to less academic students. I mean, I teach B Tec English. Fair enough! But I can't really get the same enthusiasm, because I haven't got the people who really want to learn. And so one copes with them as one must. Professionally, you must cope with whatever comes in, though I never did subscribe to this idea of education overall. I'm afraid the students I receive now are less well-instructed in factual information. The gap between the State schools and the independent schools is wider now, much wider, for academic ability, and I think it will continue to grow.

Oh, there's something else I should love you to put in. I'm fed up to the back teeth with 'educationists' and jargon. On that, I get very cross. After all these years, I think that no one has come out with anything new, but somebody, who is paid more than the working teacher, gets a new word and all the other young ones think, this must be it. When you look at it, how could there be anything new in education? Projects? They've been in for twenty years. And what's a project anyway? Just a chunk of original work by a student. I always objected to the word because I didn't think it meant anything.

I learnt from my *Times* yesterday – and I shall use this – 'weasel words'. Did you read that bit? There are lots of weasel words in education. Look, I can show you a bit. [She hands me an official report.] Read that! It's meant to be a summary. And frankly, it makes me sick!

143

VIII

SIXTH-FORM COLLEGES

32

It's Easy Relating to Computers

June and Brian, two highly-qualified young graduates have used teaching in a sixth-form college in the south-east as an escape route from the 'incredible boredom' of local government and banking respectively. Their small living-room was crammed with books which overflowed from the shelves on to the tables, the chairs, the floors. Their two collie dogs who had been banished from the interview expressed their resentment by barking almost continuously in the kitchen. June Carling, who has black hair and blue eyes, was casually dressed in a tee-shirt and harem trousers. Brian Laythorpe, who was dressed in an equally casual sweater and slacks, was tall, bespectacled and bearded. They both believe that their college provides great opportunities for students who would have once been labelled as failures in secondary moderns.

BRIAN: Before sixth-form colleges were set up as part of secondary education going comprehensive . . . some of my best A level students would have left secondary modern school with CSE Grades 3 or 4. One lad came to us with no CSES. He took CSE and a couple of O levels and then did A levels. He was twenty or twenty-one when he left, but he's now doing a degree course at a polytechnic. Under the old system he would have been *out*. There's a whole load of students who would have left secondary modern at sixteen who have a chance to do A levels now. On the other hand, some of the students who would have gone to grammar school, might have done slightly better in A levels than they do with us . . . might have done.

JUNE: Oh yes! I've got quite a few people doing A level who didn't get a good range of O levels or particularly good grades, or only got CSES.

BRIAN: We run courses for anyone who is sixteen to nineteen. You have to come in before you're nineteen. We have City and Guilds . . .

JUNE: Pre-vocational courses.

BRIAN: They're fairly small. It's a fraction. I'm doing a YTS course as well. It's quite interesting because the students are very different. We only have these sixteen-year-olds one day a week as they're working on the other days. They seem much more mature, more adult. You need a different approach to them as they're outside the institution.

JUNE: I think all the students believe we treat them differently from schoolteachers. They prefer a sixth-form college to a school. We tend to treat them far more like adults. They don't wear uniforms. There are fewer rules. We call them students . . .

BRIAN: That's when we're being polite . . .

JUNE: It's different from further education.

BRIAN: Technically, we're still a school.

JUNE: More regulations.

BRIAN: School rules, regulations, which means registration, mornings and afternoons. In FE, you're just there for your particular subjects, three A levels or whatever. Here, we're expected to do non-examination courses.

JUNE: There are lots of different courses from ceramics to electronic systems to give them experience in areas they're not studying and to widen their perspectives a bit; but most of the students hate them, don't they?

BRIAN: That's right!

JUNE: Quite often they don't turn up because there isn't an exam at the end of it.

BRIAN: The college isn't exam-orientated, but the students are. That's what they're there for. Unless of course, they have a particular interest in a course or they can become interested.

JUNE: We have a pastoral session once a week to talk about their problems, usually academic, occasionally personal. I've had people whose mothers have been terminally ill, but if they've got a real personal problem, they'd rather see you individually. Their main complaints are that they don't like a subject or a teacher. They have a moan, a general whinge, or they want a change. It doesn't happen very often. Usually they say, 'That teacher can't teach.' So I ask them what's a good teacher. And they don't know. They don't really like that question. We also use the sessions to give them advice about careers and how to fill in forms, which they also seem to find boring. Students come to us because the FE college has a reputation for being less academic. They seem to think FE is the place to go if you're doing a vocational course in hairdressing or something, or a government course, like YTS or that sort of thing; but if you're doing A levels it's better to go to a sixth-form college.

BRIAN: Parents prefer the college to FE. We get a wide social range of students, but with a middle class bias. Motivation isn't much of a problem. You can point out that (a) there's an exam at the end of the course, and (b) there's the door!

JUNE: We get quite a few students because, first, their parents wanted them to come and they've given in to domestic pressure, and, second, because it's better than being unemployed, having nothing to do. Some of them don't really go to many lessons. They're there for the social life. We have a social centre where students can meet, get food and coffee . . .

BRIAN: Very few.

148

JUNE: No, but . . .

BRIAN: There's almost a class difference between those doing A level subjects and those who are there for one year. It's in the one-year group you tend to get people who are there because they have to be. And their enthusiasm and attendance rate drifts off.

JUNE: Quite a few of the A level students lack great motivation, particularly in the first year. It's just another step after O levels.

BRIAN: Most of the A level students carry on when they leave.

JUNE: Universities, polytechnics. Teacher-training courses are quite popular.

BRIAN: Quite a few get jobs. In my A level group about eight have left and gone into employment, which is quite nice, as I've only got six left. That's another difference from schools: small groups. I think my largest is fourteen.

JUNE: Last year I had twenty-seven in my sociology group. At A level that's quite a lot. It's gradually come down to eighteen or nineteen, but it's still quite large. You can't give them the amount of time they need individually. Sociology is usually over-subscribed.

BRIAN: A wonderful teacher!

JUNE: That's it! I'm not sure. We do have a good pass rate and some of them do it because they've heard it's an easy option, like British government. I teach that as well. Others just want to do something different from what they did at school. You can make sociology sound interesting, even if it isn't. Most of the students tend to be conservative. They believe what their parents and the tabloids say, and don't even question it. We do have a few who are left-wing and rather trendy, but on the whole they're very pro-government, so you have to be careful what you say. I admit I'm left-wing, a healthy socialist. I'm prepared to criticise the government and praise them where praise is due. If you're teaching something like government and politics, bias does come into it, and you're not being honest if you say it doesn't. So I usually tell the students at the beginning, 'I am biased and it will come out in things I say. You've got to take that into account and come to your own conclusions.' The teacher I work with is pretty right-wing and I'm sure he's biased in the other direction, so we make a nice match. Most of the criticism, however, about bias in teaching seems to be an attack on the left rather than the right.

BRIAN: You can't stop political issues being discussed in classrooms. If you're teaching economics or business studies, one of the things you're going to talk about is unemployment.

JUNE: The same with sociology.

BRIAN: Some of our books are fairly new, but if you've got a ten-year-old economic textbook, which says that mass unemployment is a thing of the past and the government is now able to control it, what do you do?

JUNE: Students in my groups will argue with me and say that's not fair, that's biased, and then give you an equally biased account of what they think.

BRIAN: Even though they may be politically naive, they can distinguish between theory, fact and opinion, probably because of the way I put it. It's very obvious if it's an opinion. We had a Tory MP here the other week and I told them to make sure they went to listen to him, because it wasn't very often that they had a chance to hear a representative of the worst government the country's ever had. Somebody said, 'What do you mean? That's only your opinion.'

JUNE: My students are not so concerned about the big things like unemployment, or even students' grants, which are going to affect them directly, as things like violence on the picket lines. That's a big one! Whether we should have a queen or not . . .

BRIAN: Oh, yes!

JUNE: . . . which is interesting, but terribly irrelevant in some ways.

BRIAN: They're quite keen on hanging.

JUNE: Yes! Yes! Bring back hanging. That's always a good one. They're terribly uneducated about politics. Most of them don't know anything about the machinery of government, which I always think should be a compulsory subject in schools. They know very little about local government either, or how to complain if they think they've been badly treated by an administrator.

BRIAN: It's sometimes a hell of an effort to think of ways to put a subject across, when it's so obvious . . .

JUNE: To you!

BRIAN: Yes, to me – who's been doing it for years. Teaching is a strain. You've got a group of people who are all working at different rates. You've got to be aware of everything that's going on all the time. Sometimes, they'll start chatting to their neighbour about football, what happened at break. You can't jump on them every time. We were allowed to talk when I was at school.

JUNE: Good Lord, we weren't.

BRIAN: It was a direct-grant school. In maths lessons we even used to play bridge, which was quite difficult because we had to lay out dummy somewhere. It's all right for them to talk, so long as they're getting on with their work at the same time. Ninety per cent is about the work they're doing.

JUNE: They learn a lot from discussion. Quite often, they'll talk about their own experiences which mirrors what we've been discussing. For example, we might be talking about divorce rates, and quite a few will chat about their divorced parents, which isn't strictly sociology, but relevant. Education isn't just learning academic subjects. If I stood there, just writing on the board and talking at them, I'd get very bored. It makes it more interesting for teachers to get some feedback.

BRIAN: My teaching tends to be much more one-way. At the moment, I'm doing a lot about mathematical techniques for solving problems. I tell them about it, make sure they've got something in their notes they can refer to, do an example for them and then give them a question. Things like: there are four factories producing so much, and four warehouses around the country, your transport costs are so much, which is the cheapest way of moving the goods? It's the sort of thing that could easily be done on a computer, a typical problem, but I don't use them. The object of an A level course is to give students the ability to think in abstract terms, conceptually. We're interested not so much in getting the answer, but in formulating the problem, finding the appropriate technique, and understanding what the solution means. If, eventually, they're going to have senior positions as managers in education, industry, even the civil service, they've got to be able to think about things they haven't had first-hand experience of. The government goes on and on about the need for everyone to be computer-literate, but I'm not really sure they know what they mean. The trouble about computers in schools is that they're taught as something special. Students are taught about hardware, software, core memory and things like that, but when they use a computer, they're going to treat it as you or I treat a car. They get in and drive. It doesn't matter what goes on beyond the dashboard.

JUNE: You just have to press the right button.

BRIAN: It's a tool. Computers are going to affect everybody, but I've got a washing-machine, I press a button and it works. That's what computers are about. I don't really see it as different from any other piece of machinery or equipment, though it can be made to look clever and it's very fast.

JUNE: I've never used computers here, but I tried a history programme when I was on teaching practice which told you whether you were right or wrong, but didn't really explain why.

BRIAN: If you have a specific teaching objective and a suitable programme, it's a useful technique. It allows a child to work at his own speed. Recently, however, I went to look at a package for business studies, developed by a government-funded body, which didn't do what it was supposed to do as far as I could see. One of the elements in the package was cash flow and I thought you would be able to see how it changed in various circumstances; but all it really did was to shuffle records around. It was a file-handling routine for computers. I'm sure a lot of little children suffer through having a home computer, when they'd be much better off hanging round the street corners talking to their friends.

JUNE: Yes, we know some people who have two children. The boy sits in the corner of his bedroom, playing with his computer, programming it. He's considered to be incredibly brilliant. His younger sister, who is very pleasant and charming and can talk easily to people, is seen as the less intelligent of the two. I think she's probably far better adjusted. It's easy relating to computers, but much more difficult with people.

33
Like a Miniature University

Suddenly it went dark down there in the water. I looked up, frightened, at the silhouettes of three huge manta rays, gliding like Delta bombers overhead, which had temporarily blotted out the rays of the sun. As they passed, I could see the coral reefs of the Red Sea again, which were just as magnificent as they had seemed in films. There were quite a few dangerous fish on the reefs – stone-fish, scorpion-fish with poisonous spikes, and sharks about five, six or seven feet long. In films, you're always told that you've got to be terribly careful with scorpion-fish, but when you're down there, you can swim right up to them and feed them. The sharks didn't bother me either. I knew that Red Sea sharks exhibit territorial behaviour before an attack by swimming with wide, undulating movements; but they were keeping their distance, swimming peacefully above the coral reefs, so I was not afraid.

Colin Shore started work as a marine biologist in Africa and now works in a sixth-form college in the north-west. He is thirty-two, a short, dark-haired man, who sat erect and almost motionless as we were talking, at attention while he was sitting down, which is a common characteristic, I discovered later, of people who are involved in the growth movement. He was very pleasant, honest and direct and extremely idealistic in his aims of introducing some of the most beneficial aspects of the personal growth movement into education.

That experience of sub-aqua diving was probably one of the few things in my life which was as good as I thought it would be. Ever since I'd seen Jacques Cousteau's films, I'd always dreamed of being a marine biologist, travelling about the world, diving, leading a romantic exciting life. The reality was different. That trip to the Red Sea was only a short holiday, a break from flogging my guts out for twelve or more hours every day, month after month, on a fisheries project in Africa. For hours at a time I didn't have any contact with English-speaking people and I found the cultural isolation very difficult to bear. The other people I met doing similar work were like characters out of a Graham Greene novel – very cynical, always on the move from one project to the next, homeless, rootless. I didn't want to end up like that and I quite missed Britain. So I came back home to London.

I was pretty much in a mess because my life-dream had been shattered. For a year or so, I did freelance writing, parts of wildlife books and magazine articles, but even though I was interviewing people and meeting publishers, there came the time when I had to settle down to writing and I felt just as isolated as I had been in Africa. So that's how I got into teaching.

I moved out of London and taught science in tutorial colleges in various parts of the country for a couple of years or so. It was intensive work, but fairly easy, because you're dealing with only one, or a few people, at a time and there was no problem about classroom management or control. The students were all fairly adult. There were a lot of foreign students and British students whose education had been disrupted by their parents moving from one country to another or by a divorce or separation. Most of the students came from wealthy homes, but there were some one-parent mothers who were really struggling financially and the more reputable colleges would sometimes reduce their fees. The tutors were mainly in their thirties or younger and many had dropped out in some way or were just passing through. You were paid about £7 an hour then, but only for the hours you taught. In the holidays, you could go on social security, but it was difficult to get it in the short holidays. One college was very lax in paying you, so that you sometimes got your cheque a fortnight after it was due. Some tutorial colleges are reputable, but others are primarily money-making concerns.

When I realised that tutoring wasn't going to lead anywhere, I went on a post-graduate teaching course. I really enjoyed it and got a lot out of it, because I'd had some experience of teaching already and I wasn't too concerned about my subject, so that I could look beyond to broader issues underlying what actually goes on in schools – what are we trying to do when we teach, what schools and educational institutes are about. It was there that I was introduced to action-research which tied in very much with what I sensed should be happening in the classroom.

Most people would agree that a good teacher, whatever they might mean by that, should be preparing, doing, evaluating and modifying. There should be a loop feedback so that when they've monitored their perform-ance, they modify what they do in future, otherwise they're in danger of just repeating their errors year after year. Action-research is just a formal description of that loop which makes it easier to identify the individual parts. One method of evaluation which we did at university was to video ourselves, not only for what we said or did, but also for what we were saying with our body, whom we addressed in class and whom we didn't and so on. I found that very interesting.

By this time I'd become deeply involved in the growth movement. On my return from Africa, I hadn't known what I was or what I was going to do. My family was quite distressed because I'd thrown my career away. My ideals were not given much credence in society at large, which measured success in terms of money and careers and the very English way of life of people in boxes competing with people in other boxes. I felt that the only way in which I could succeed in my self-search was by finding other like-minded people. I went on an EST course – very American – an experiential course, very difficult to describe, which is basically concerned with freeing yourself from behaviour patterns of the past so that you react spontaneously to situations as they arise. It was a very intensive course lasting eighteen hours a day in which you and about two hundred other people were being pounded about the things you held dear. In other words, the foundations of your day-to-day experience were under attack.

I then moved on to co-counselling, in which you play the roles of client and counsellor alternately with another person. One of the main aims is to discharge emotions linked to past situations, which frees you of the hold that pattern of behaviour has on you. There's so much else you can do – life-planning, acting out situations that concern you, like job interviews or possible confrontations, in a safe situation, which gives you a lot more confidence. Later on, I joined a support group, half businessmen, half professionals. We had to state what we were going to achieve in the next month and report back at the next meeting. It was a source of advice, too, as you had all this great wealth of experience to draw on.

The growth movement helped me so much that I'd like to introduce some of its ideas into schools; but I find it very difficult to reconcile the values I hold with what I actually do, or see, going on in classrooms. I'm still a probationer, so I'm wary about what I do and I'm also finding it much more difficult than I thought to keep up with the day-to-day work, the preparation and the marking.

I deliberately chose to train for FE or a sixth-form college as I thought that the discipline problems and the demands in comprehensives would be so great that I'd never get around to introducing these innovations. I'm sure they're going to come from the top, sixth-form colleges, and move downwards. My college, which has a very high reputation, includes a lot of rough districts in its catchment area. In theory, students come because they want to, but there are quite a few who are there because they couldn't find jobs. It's an open access college with over a thousand students, doing everything from CPVE to A levels. There's a strong emphasis on the pastoral side, as there is in many sixth-form colleges, in contrast to most colleges of further education. Normally, every subject tutor is also a personal tutor. Although we don't have any full lessons with the tutor group, it meets once a day to take the register for a quarter of an hour, which gives the chance to sort out any personal problems. There is also a pastoral vice-principal. The college has a policy of having as little middle management as possible, particularly on the pastoral side, so that students can go direct to their personal tutor or the pastoral vice-principal. There's a very relaxed atmosphere in the college.

The range of courses is quite phenomenal. It's like a miniature university. There are over a hundred additional studies courses on all sorts of subjects, including photography, the role of women in society, jewellery-making, genealogy, catastrophe theory, local history – over a hundred and twenty if you include games. In the college where I did my teaching practice there was a much narrower range of options and, because of the timetabling, people often didn't get their first choice, which had a very negative effect. The timetabling at my present college is much more flexible so that students can usually do the subject they have chosen. As the staff are genuinely interested in their subjects, the classes tend to be well-attended.

One of the courses I teach is Personal Relations which is part of the core curriculum. It's assessed on a profiling system, which is less artificial than an exam and which covers a much greater range of attributes and abilities. One defect of profiling is that it has no place for positive criticisms like 'this person really needs to get here on time' or 'this person needs to organise his file'. If profiling is done properly and you really do negotiate about what goes into it, the students appreciate it, but I wonder if everyone does that.

The Personal Relations course was built up from one on child development which still makes up too big a chunk of it. We get a good response from the students because they find the topics interesting. We cover the roles of men and women, marriage, birth control and so on. We've had some excellent discussions and blown a few old wives' tales out of the window. I was amazed that some of these sixteen-year-old boys had got birth control all wrong. One thought that a woman only took the pill on the day after she'd had intercourse. I was going to say there are a lot of misconceptions. Yes, it's been interesting talking about things like that.

I'd like education to focus far more on feelings. I'm sure some teachers are good at that, but on the whole we tend to steer clear of feelings and emotions in schools. They bubble up occasionally and are dealt with by the pastoral system, but they're not often integrated into lessons. People don't feel safe to show emotions about subject matter and other people in the classroom. It would be really healthy if you could have a situation where people were able to do that without fearing that others would take advantage of them or put them down. Some people might object that it's got nothing to do with education, but we place far too much emphasis on academic subjects, writing and communication skills. I'd like to see each person being given a chance as part of their education to explore the emotional aspects of their personality, the things that are really important to them. Some of the methods used in other caring professions could be introduced into teaching: role-playing, simulation, support groups for teachers, perhaps teachers and parents, or teachers and society at large, and even, maybe, co-counselling among members of staff.

Basically, I'd like to get far more involved in life-skills teaching, preparing people for employment – or unemployment – and if possible acting as a facilitator who provides a safe framework for people to explore their own feelings and, I suppose, the old cliché, to help them to help themselves. It's all connected with relating to other people. That's the ideal I'd like to achieve.

A few days later, Colin sent me the following statement of his values or concerns:

i) Concern to look upon/deal with people/pupils as individual persons with their own interests, points of view, etc.
    Also, we as teachers wish to be seen as individuals, wish to:
        treat everyone as an individual
        allow the pupils to express their own ideas
        treat the pupils' ideas as valid
        not act as the source of all knowledge
        treat pupils in a civil manner
Teacher provides a framework in which young people learn for themselves from their own and shared experiences.
Teacher's own experience should *not* be the overriding influence.

ii) Concern to adapt/relate 'subject matter' to needs and interests of children,
or (perhaps more strongly) to use children's experiences or background as a basis for learning.
Work/learning *must* be related to child's experience, interests, attitudes.
Child/pupil is seen as:
        active not passive
        creative, not just 'accepting'
        equal, not subordinate

iii) Need (as teachers) to be enthusiastic about what we have to offer (or clear about what we have to offer).
Need to:
        interact ⎤ ⎡ feelings
        encourage ⎬ ⎨ situations
        explore ⎦ ⎣ creative opportunities
Emphasise 'good' relationships; taking one's time, *not* harassing or hustling; asking important, open-ended questions, *not* trivial or uninteresting; being gentle and relaxed.

IX

INDIVIDUAL RETREATS

34

Not a Clean Slate

Marie Eltringham, who is in her early fifties, is an energetic, forceful woman of medium height with a serious, rather careworn, face. After having a variety of jobs, she trained as a mature student some twenty-five years ago. She wanted to do drama and movement but had to be satisfied with PE. After a couple of unsatisfactory years in secondary schools, during which time her marriage broke up, she left teaching for a number of years, until the sudden demand for primary teachers persuaded her to return to teach infants, which had always been her original intention. In the last few years, however, she has become increasingly disillusioned by the growing alienation of even five-year-olds from school.

My first job was in a little secondary modern in the north, a mixed school. They had an enormous turnover of staff, about eighty per cent a year. I only stayed there for a year, because I was having trouble with my husband and I wanted to get away from that part of the country. The school was very, very tough indeed, but I must have done all right there, because I had people fighting to get into the three netball teams, although there were only a couple of hundred girls in the school. When I told my class I was leaving, they said, 'All the best teachers leave, miss.'

There were different kinds of problems at my next school, a large girls' comprehensive on the south-east coast which had just changed over from being a grammar school. Almost all the staff had stayed on and most of them seemed to resent the change. They had all the headships of departments, taught all the top streams and the sixth form. Generally, they didn't seem to care about the bottom end of the school – or that was my impression – and naturally the kids in the lower streams felt it, and were very difficult. With the older girls one had to spend about three-quarters of the lesson persuading them to change for PE. That was their physical way of demonstrating their resentment. In a classroom, they could sit around and do no work; but in PE they could demonstrate their refusal to co-operate with authority more pointedly by bringing in notes, claiming that they were feeling unwell, saying there was something wrong with them.

They also had a genuine dislike of PE, but that was probably because of our department's attitude. In winter, the playing fields were like Siberia. I had no intention of freezing to death, so I used to dress up in a track suit, a jumper, scarf, sheepskin-lined mittens, the lot. And I allowed the girls to wear tights, scarves, gloves, all that sort of thing. Very often, when we came out of the door, the head of department would be waiting to monitor the girls and saying, 'Take this off; take that off.' As a result, the kids would just stand round moaning that they were cold. It was very difficult to get them into the netball teams, because we were still playing grammar schools which invariably won.

Like many comprehensives, the school didn't get the right start. Huts were just put up in the playground to accommodate the new pupils. And like other comprehensives, it was far too big. They could have been viable in terms of subject and finance on a smaller scale, so that more attention could have been given to the individual child. The children became alienated because they didn't feel they had an identity, a part to play, or that if they played a negative role, no one would ever notice. Comprehensives usually had house or form systems, but the teachers were fighting so many difficulties, that they came low in their priorities. Perhaps the biggest problem was the need to prove that comprehensives could work academically because there had been so much political opposition to them. Teachers concentrated on academic results so that they could turn round to opponents and say, 'Look, comprehensives do work.' Although I'm in favour of the comprehensive system by and large, they were always underfunded and never got a fair run.

At that time, there was still some glimmer in secondary pupils of what I find attractive in young children, but it was fast disappearing. You couldn't love them as readily. I felt that if they formed a love of school at the primary stage, they would not suffer this sea change when they went into secondary, so that's why I went into infant teaching in 1970.

A love of school is based on a personal relationship, building up children's confidence early on and making them feel loved, wanted and important. Almost every child, I think, is capable of something. Even then some children had very aggressive attitudes, but there were only one or two in a class. Over the years, however, children have been increasingly affected by the harmful aspects of society at a younger and younger age. Kids of five will tell you now in their first few weeks at school, 'My mum says if I get hit, I hit back; if I get kicked, I kick back.' It's terrible, absolutely terrible.

The old idea of a *tabula rasa* (is that right? I never did Latin) no longer has any validity. Certainly in my experience of infant teaching, kids have grown up with pretty constant television from the beginning. They soak up all sorts of values from it, particularly from the advertisements. The basis of most advertisements, it seems to me, is that if you want things, you have to have them, regardless of how you get them. You find this with the kids in school. They want something and they think they have to have it. It's an instant gratification syndrome, which is very difficult to fight. They soak up these values from advertising and television, so there's certainly not a clean slate, not any more.

35

Exams are Ratraces

Jane Dernley is an uncompromising critic of teachers and the compulsory educational system who has spent many years giving unpaid tuition to its rejects who really want to learn. She has eked out a living by working as a clerk and a telephonist and by doing a few paid evening classes, though in later years she has taken a full-time job in further education. Her attempts to establish close and fruitful relationships with her one-to-one pupils seem to have brought her as much distress as pleasure, but she would not have wanted to live in any other way. She is in her fifties and lives in Wales.

My first job, after I got a degree, was in a grammar school. The school attracted me because it had no uniform so you didn't have to distort your moral senses by convincing unwilling pupils that it was worse to leave their hat off than to tell a lie. I told the head that I didn't intend to attend morning assembly as I didn't believe in it. I was on probation. The inspector who came in to watch me was a nice avuncular figure. I believe he thought I was okay. Whenever the secretary of the education committee – a little, fishy-eyed man – came in, I dried up, I was hopeless. I wasn't happy there, but I couldn't have done too bad a job because later I met by chance one of my ex-pupils, who said that I'd turned her on to poetry, which was a success of a kind.

At the end of the probationary year, however, they told me that I hadn't passed. I protested that I should have been told sooner, because it was up to them to give me advice, so they agreed to inspect me again next term. However, I decided to get away and do another degree. I started applying for scholarships and on the very day when I heard I'd got one, I was told that I'd passed my probation.

After the course, I didn't go back into State schools. I didn't like the tripartite system. I'd always had strong doubts about compulsory education as I believe that people should be able to choose for themselves. You know that Socrates invented unpaid, adult education without entrance qualifications, whereas Plato invented exams. Well, I prefer Socrates. The chances of finding any place where I could feel easy in my conscience from a political viewpoint was also very unlikely. I'm a libertarian anarchist, you see, non-violent.

I'd been a telephonist before and after I got my degree, so I got a switchboard job. I was very involved in the peace movement. There was a young girl in my group who'd been done out of her education. Sally must have been about eighteen at that time. She had gone to a notorious secondary modern school where she'd been told quite openly by the teachers, 'You're factory fodder'. She was going around with Bob, a young science lecturer in the group and, being bright, she realised how she'd missed out on education. So I said, 'I'll teach you'. She was the first of my one-to-one non-paying pupils. Sally was really amazing. It was education she wanted primarily, not certificates. I could teach her a couple of subjects, English language and literature, but she wanted to do other things. Bob was teaching her maths.

Her parents didn't like her going out with Bob. They actually locked her in her room. It was quite extraordinary. So the next thing that happened, she ran away from home and came to live in a spare room in my house, where I was looking after my sick father. Bob used to come and visit her.

Time after time, I've got involved with pupils in most distressing ways, but this one was actually comic. Sally was often worried about her periods. She told me that Bob didn't know anything about contraceptives, so I arranged for him to have a chat with the husband of a friend of mine. But Bob was so damn shy that I had to go out and buy them some contraceptives myself. I'd never bought condoms before as I'd never had occasion. I remember meeting an American friend of mine and asking him, 'Do condoms come in different sizes?'

Then Sally decided that she wanted to do all the books prescribed for English O level. I gave her a reference for a college and they were so impressed with her that they provided her with free tuition, though they couldn't give her a grant. So, without any maintenance money, she went to college by day and at five o'clock went to work in a factory until ten at night. She had no social life, no student life, but she was getting an education. One had to respect her. At that time, I was also teaching night school, but it got too difficult because of my father's health, so I dropped it and continued teaching different people at home without any pay. They were mainly people in the peace movement who needed qualifications to get into college. I suppose I was a one-woman alternative education system, really.

Those secondary moderns were abominable places. Another student of mine, who left a secondary modern without any certificates at all, went on to take a degree eventually. I asked him once, 'How is it Chris, that they managed to put you off education?' and he replied, 'Oh, it was quite simple. They just gave you the impression it was not for the likes of you.' That reminds me of a story I always like to tell against teachers. Chris was always truanting to read books, and one teacher unwittingly did a splendid piece of educational work for him. One day, when Chris was in school for once, a teacher suddenly referred to 'that filthy book, *Ulysses*,' so Chris immediately got hold of a copy.

Teachers are unforgivably awful. They're reactionaries; they're middle class; they will always sell the pass about education. They think their loyalty is to absolutely everything but the bloody thing it should be to. They're not even loyal to their own students. The primary loyalty must be to the truth of their subject. That's the first priority. The truth! The loyalty after that is to the student and after that, quite a long way after that, to the employer, the education authority or whatever. That's never followed, never! Some of their compromises are really rotten. I've always felt guilty about preparing pupils for exams, because exams are ratraces and pupils aren't rats. I do it, because I know too well that exams provide the key to learn more, but I don't feel right about it.

And now the teaching profession has sold the pass about substituting training for education. I wish I was five years older so that I could retire before I see the worst effects. They're going to chuck out everything educational. This childish belief that what pupils learn at school is meant to equip them for a job is rubbish. God help us! It's a con! What the authorities don't want is an educated dole queue.

I've got a lot out of my unpaid teaching, a greater understanding of human beings and how they tick. That really helps me to understand literature better, because that's what literature is all about: human beings and what goes on inside them. I agree mine is a highly individual view, but I have a strong belief that teachers with any sensitivity at all labour under a terrible load of guilt, because they can never do as much as they ought to. Not being paid frees you entirely of that guilt as no one can blame you for not doing enough. It gets you off the hook. It's a way of shedding a little responsibility. It may be self-indulgent, but it also feels good.

No, of course I haven't got private means. I was looking after my parents for years, so I inherited this house, which was what I got in exchange, but it wasn't much. I don't like money. I've always been embarrassed to take it. I really do think it's abominable stuff. I always wished that my one-to-one pupils would bring me flowers occasionally in appreciation, but they never did. When I was teaching Sally, I was very, very poor. I only had a tiny job which made about five quid a week. Sally could run up clothes just like that. I had some nice material for a two-piece, so one day I asked Sally, 'I wonder if some time you could make this up for me.' She never did. I was always a bit sorry, but I didn't do it for a return.

36

Daisies in Our Hair

I'm very much a child of the sixties. Oh, yes! I remember sitting down in Charing Cross station with a group of friends with garlands of daisies in our hair and walking round in the seventies in bare feet and wearing kaftans. I don't feel envious of more conventional people. I don't think they're basically any happier than I am.

After having a son in her early twenties, Philippa Brookwell is just completing her probationary year at the age of thirty-three. She is a tall young woman with short dark hair shaped carefully around her rather pale face, who looked rather tired when she returned from school to her Victorian end-of-terrace house in a trendy area of a city on the south coast. She was dressed in grey harem trousers and had a small blue rucksack on her back. Her casual jacket had two round badges attached to it, one supporting the miners and the other backing the teachers' pay claim for '£1,200 – nothing less'. Her interests range widely beyond maths to include t'ai chi-ch'uan and improvised jazz. Although she likes teaching, she believes that part-time teachers with their deeper participation in life beyond the classroom walls can offer more to the children and feel less threatened by them.

After I left school, I went to university to do a maths degree. I wasn't really forced into maths at school. It was just an assumption that everybody made. My mum was a teacher; my aunt was a teacher; and my dad was an engineer. I could do maths, therefore I must do it, even though I wasn't really very keen on it then. Most of my friends at university were doing English or theatre so I got involved in a lot of other things. After I'd done two-thirds of the course, I failed my exams. I only just failed them, which wasn't bad, as I hadn't done any work at all, so I didn't feel ashamed at the time. I didn't resit the exam as I was going to have a baby. No, I wasn't married. So while I was pregnant, I went to London and worked as a computer operator.

When Stace was born, I went back to the north, because I'd bought a big house there with some money my mum had left me. I just lived there with my baby and various friends. I could share the house with five people at a time. Stace and I weren't getting on too well then, being together just the two of us twenty-four hours at a time. It just drove both of us batty. When he was nearly three, the health visitor got him a nursery place and I got a job in management accountancy. I was earning £15 a week, but it was difficult to make ends meet. It was £5 for the nursery and £5 for the petrol, so we had to live on £5 a week. It was ridiculous really. We were better off with me not working. I did that job for a while. Then I had a succession of jobs, with agencies, as a char in an army barracks. That was good money, better than management accountancy, about £24 a week. By that time I was living with my present husband. In 1977 he came down here to look for work and we came with him.

I got a job in management accountancy again, but gave it up because I didn't like the child-minder. Stace was always grumpy when I picked him up. Then someone mentioned that there was an interesting course at the university, so I just rang up and asked if they had any vacancies. It was a real impulse thing. After I got my degree, I eventually went on a PGCE course which was interesting though I wish I could have seen more teachers at work in the classroom. On my teaching practice, we were doing SMILE, so I was actually working with another teacher; but I still haven't seen a teacher giving a classroom lesson since I was at school myself. Teaching is all very private, almost shameful in some ways, as if no one else ought to see what goes on in your classroom, though I think it would be better if they did. Since I've been on probation, I've had one inspector in, but he was assessing the maths department overall. He pointed out one moment when the class and I came a bit adrift, with which I agreed, but hc didn't really give me any general pointers.

As I'm on probation, I get one afternoon off a week for maths induction. Currently, we're talking about the racist content of maths questions. I can show you an example, if you like. It's a question about Christians and Turks. It's wicked, really wicked. 'Once upon a time, a ship was caught in a storm. In order to save it and its crew, the captain decided that half the passengers would have to be thrown overboard. There were fifteen Christians and fifteen Turks. He announced that he would count the passengers and every ninth one would be thrown overboard. How could the passengers be placed in a circle so that all the Turks would be thrown overboard and all the Christians saved?' That's an American example, but there are others . . . Mathematicians always try to say that their assumptions don't reflect the times in which they live, but they do, they absolutely do. We also discuss how children can be left behind linguistically, because they don't understand the meaning of the words in a maths question. That sort of thing also cropped up on my PGCE course, but it's nice to go back to thinking about those things instead of just having to churn out the next lesson.

When I was on my teaching practice, I probably dressed a bit neater than

I do now, but I'm sure my present head would have said something if she'd found my garb unacceptable. Once I wore a pair of orange dungarees to school, but there were so many remarks from the rest of the staff about mending roads, that I haven't tried it for a while. You get on a lot better with the children if you wear things they can relate to. Well, I find I do, anyway. Like one dress I wore in, and the girls said, 'Ooh, did you make that yourself, miss? Can I have the pattern?' It's particularly important if you're teaching maths which has such a bad odour about it. They can see you as a real person.

I like teaching when it works and when I'm feeling well. I do enjoy it then. But I had flu for two weeks before half term, when we went skiing and I hurt my knee, so for the last month I've been limping which has made me feel a bit burdened. Today, I started feeling that it was quite fun again, that I could be a bit sparky and get something out of it. It's awful when you're feeling flat. The kids just squash you completely.

I back the current industrial action all the way. It's about time we pointed out what a hard job teaching is. I've spent the terms marking till half past one in the morning, not every night, but a lot of the time. Teaching requires an incredible amount of sustained energy if you're not to leave a whole class of moaning kids behind.

When I've finished my probationary year, I'm going to be a supply teacher because my musical career is so important to me. I've already had to turn down a week's tour because I couldn't get leave. Some people say that part-timers aren't committed, but I don't think that's true. While I was waiting to go on my PGCE, I taught numeracy in a college which had a high proportion of part-timers, who were paid at an hourly rate and were on an hour's notice. You've got to be committed to do that sort of job. They stayed there year after year, working part time, because they wanted time to sustain their other interests. You can get a point 5 in schools, but they're still very wary of part-timers because of this commitment thing.

It would really make schools much better places. Full-time teachers just go barmy. They've got so much pressure and don't know of any other life during term time. A real dedicated teacher, that is. If teachers only worked part time, they wouldn't be so desperately eager to ram their opinions down the children's throats. They'd realise there was a bigger world outside. And maybe the children could answer them back without appearing to be so threatening. That's when they undermine you. Your whole world is undermined if you're a full-time teacher.

37

A Practising, Teaching Family

I come from a teaching family, you know, so I turned down going to
university in favour of training as a primary teacher. Both my parents and
my brother had been to teacher training college, so it seemed to make sense
to follow in their footsteps, although my school wasn't too pleased, you
know. They wanted me to go to university.

After a long saga of disillusioning and harrowing experiences with
aggressive pupils and parents and apathetic or trendy teachers, Norman
Beckley has found a safe haven in the traditional environment of an
independent prep school in the north-east. He is a tall, thin man with
fair hair, who sat almost motionless, gripping the side of his armchair
tensely, as he told me his life story, which he seemed to have rehearsed
many times before in his mind. He was wearing casual clothes – an open
neck shirt, a multi-coloured jacket, jeans – which did not seem to
accord with most of his views or attitudes, a paradox which was
explained during the course of the interview.

It was a secondary specialist college, so the academic side was extremely
good; but, as it was an all-male college, the primary department was a bit of a
Cinderella. While I was there, I was pushed quite hard . . . how can I put it?
. . . that somebody with my academic bias would be wasting his talents in a
primary school. That was really what they kept on saying. They tried very
hard to persuade me to do a general degree course, but I wanted to get into
the job, into the teaching practice. That was what I enjoyed most at college.

Having said that, I was agreeably surprised by how much I did enjoy the
purely academic side and my specialist study. I really did enjoy that. My
tutor was excellent. The college was run very much on the lines of a
university department. They prided themselves, you know, that their
students were as good as university students. The standard of lectures was
excellent.

I found the education side less helpful because, coming from a practising,
teaching family, as I've said, I found it awfully difficult to swallow some of
what I would describe as the very airy-fairy ideas of the early sixties. The

other students didn't know much about teaching and swallowed those ideas lock, stock and barrel. Streaming is a good example. I had an awful lot of arguments because I didn't think streaming was all that bad, but I was in a minority of one. Competitive sport was another source of argument because I was quite keen on it. So, all the way through college, I constantly fought these battles with the more progressive people, the trendies and the lefties as I would call them now. One tended to be a little bit of a loner as, against my will, I had been forced to be a day student since my home was near the college.

Probably, I trained for primary because my father was a primary teacher. Nobody in the family had any knowledge of secondary education. I tend to think now that if I had only had more confidence in myself as a person I would have been happier in a secondary school, but I was frightened of the discipline side. At the age of . . . what? . . . eighteen, nineteen, the sixth-formers would have been the same age as I was then. I've always had a fear of a class running riot. Maybe it was something that my father used to be apprehensive of. Certainly, my mother used to worry about losing control. In my parents' day and age, a quiet class signified a good teacher. As soon as the noise level started to get up, I began to think I was losing control.

It would certainly not be true to say that my parents wanted me to be a teacher. They felt that my brother and I had the world at our feet and that we should be encouraged to do something different. What that was I didn't know, as the careers department in my school was pathetic. If you were a success, you went to university; if you weren't, you crept out by the back door.

I have always admired my father. I used to go with him to his football matches on Saturday mornings and the kind of relationship that he developed with the boys there was what I wanted to take into the classroom. As the football master, you were a different person – just a mate, or like dad, or like an older brother. My dad and I had a great dream of both running football teams at our separate schools and meeting up for friendly matches, which did happen before he retired.

When I left college, I wanted to work in the same area as my father, but I didn't think it was a good idea to do that straight away, so I went to a primary school in another part of the country for two years. My first year of teaching wasn't particularly happy. Apart from the head, I was the only man in an all-female staff. The headmaster had built up this empire of ladies, ranging from quite young girls to elderly gentlewomen close to the sixty mark, and he didn't quite know how to handle a somewhat awkward and abrasive chap who had just left college, you know. When he left, I got on much better with the new head. Unfortunately, I had already arranged to go back to the school where I had done my teaching practice. My brother was also working there. I think we set a precedent, made a little bit of history, by having two brothers teaching in the same school, you know. Those were very happy years.

After I had been there for three years, I decided that I really ought to give this secondary business a try. I had become concerned that my specialist knowledge was gradually drifting away and there was also a bit more status attached to being in a secondary school. Furthermore, at that time, the late sixties, people thought you were dragging your feet if you stayed in a school more than two years, you know. So I got a job in the local comprehensive, hoping that they could use someone like me with primary training. My idea was that in addition to teaching my own subject, I could help with the remedial English, or the lower ability children, or eventually, perhaps, become head of lower school. Frankly, the secondary school just didn't want to know. Remedial education? It was a job for a part-timer. It had no status. At that time, if you didn't have a degree, they weren't interested.

It was a huge school with nearly two thousand pupils. I was dumped in a little boxroom in the far corner where I taught a class first thing on Monday morning and didn't see 'em again until first thing the next Monday morning. It was like starting to teach all over again, you know. If it hadn't been for the games . . .

I did two or three afternoons a week on the games pitch, which involved an absolutely horrendous journey on coaches, with people being knifed and all the rest of it. Police cars chasing us. It was unbelievable. You'd usually find that the head of PE and a couple of other senior staff went on the first coach, leaving you, as the youngest member of staff, to cope with a screaming mob of fifth-formers, piled three on a set, with a semi-riot on your hand. The only people who could control them were the coach drivers. As teachers, we couldn't touch the kids; but the drivers were in a different situation. I've known a driver stop in the middle of a town and say, 'Right, you, you and you! Off!'

On one occasion a boy was knifed. Fortunately, it didn't happen on my coach. Missiles, such as tin cans, would be projected from the windows. That was when the police came screeching after us, their blue lights flashing. They had a general shout at everybody, but didn't arrest anyone. Periodically, the coach company would withdraw its services for two or three weeks. The boys thought it was a joke. Probably the majority were upset, but the minority tends to rule.

At that time I met my future wife, who is now my ex-wife, so money and promotion became more important to me than gaining experience, so I elected to go back to a primary school to get a Scale post. It was a very trendy school – open-plan, team teaching, integrated day – in a very tough area. The kids just wouldn't accept a teacher in a suit and tie, so one of the first things I had to do was to go out and buy some different clothes. Yes, I've gone on wearing casual clothes: I just find them very comfortable.

I didn't really fit in there. The head was looking for a whizz-kid to come in and pep the place up, you know, pulling bicycles to pieces all over the place. That really wasn't me. Moreover, I had serious reservations about the teaching methods. With team teaching, which meant four teachers in one area, there was usually one weak teacher – we did have a few around in those days – or a clash of personalities. I didn't like the idea of having no timetable at all. If there was no geography teacher, that subject would be neglected, and it would be all history or science. Topics got repeated every year. Somebody did the Romans in the first year, the second year, the third year and the fourth year.

Then I got a deputy headship in a very big junior school, with well over five hundred pupils, on a very tough estate. It was an absolutely beautiful building on a wonderful site. The kids were tough, but compared to my previous school, they were quite angelic. It was a marvellous job. I was over the moon when I got it. Nobody was more surprised than I was. The first two years, along with the time when I was playing football matches with my dad, were my happiest times in teaching. I clicked an exceptionally good headmaster. He and I ran the school together. He was a very strong disciplinarian and I did the pastoral side. Also I enjoyed going back to a traditional set-up with streamed classes.

The parents were as aggressive as they'd been in my previous school. The door would fly open and they'd storm in. School finished at four o'clock and if it got to a quarter to five without an incident, we all breathed a sigh of relief. The kids would go home and complain that they'd been thumped or that a teacher was picking on them, and their mother would believe them and come storming up the steps. We always said that if the parents didn't hit you in the first thirty seconds, you were safe. My office was right by the front door and I'm sure it had been put there deliberately, you know. The parents went from one extreme to another. They'd come in threatening blue murder, but by the time they had left they were saying that you were a great bloke . . . you could thump their child if you wished . . . they couldn't do anything with him at home either.

When the head left after eighteen months, I was made acting head which I thoroughly enjoyed. The staff was very supportive knowing that I was doing the job only for a few weeks. Finally, a very experienced head, who was about two years away from retirement, was appointed. We didn't hit it off. I don't know why. I don't really think it was my fault, though I'm sure he would think it was. Anyway, he just never consulted me; he shoved me right out. He put me back to teaching a class full time and took the senior mistress, a middle-aged lady, into his confidence. That is why I feel teaching is all a matter of personalities, you know.

Eventually, it got so bad that I decided to apply for a job elsewhere. The stresses of teaching were already beginning to affect my marriage. My wife got more and more fed up because I was rather morose and tired when I came home. I'd sit down in front of the television and fall asleep. Quite often at the beginning of the holidays, the tension would burst and I would have a cold or the flu. Bronchitis would be about the worst. Towards the end of the holiday, she could see the clouds gathering again. Finally I got the headship of a primary school. On paper I had reached the top. I was head of a big school with all those extra allowances; but by this time I had become thoroughly disillusioned with three things: aggressive pupils, aggressive parents, apathetic teachers. And teachers I couldn't identify with – left-wing trendies, if you want to call them that. My new school was in a multi-cultural area and the teachers wouldn't have any reference to God or Jesus in assembly, you know. They were on about their rights all the time. I could see that the job of head was going to be very lonely. Deputy head, you're one of the boys; head, you're not. I wasn't ready to cope with the isolation, particularly as I was increasingly isolated at home. My wife left me for a fortnight, came back, and then, not long afterwards, we separated for good. We were divorced a few months ago. I would have to say, certainly in my wife's eyes, that the stresses of teaching cost us our marriage. I had also been affected by my inability to be a good husband and a good teacher. So I resigned and set about finding a job outside education.

By this time, I'd got a degree part time. I applied for jobs in educational administration, business management, as a toll-booth operator, thirty-five in all, but nobody wanted to know. Finally I started looking at independent schools, which I thought might suit me better because of my style of teaching, the family atmosphere and the absence of discipline problems.

I am very much at home in my present school. Within two days I recognised something that was familiar. It was like going back to my old grammar school, its ethos, its tradition. One of the greatest tragedies in the State sector is the lack of pride in tradition. I wanted to have a celebration in one of my State schools when it had its twenty-fifth anniversary, but the head, who wasn't a young man, didn't want to know anything about the previous heads, or the past, or what the school was like when it opened. We have destroyed an awful lot that was good in our quest to revolutionise education. The curriculum was expanded to such an extent that it was difficult to know what was being taught. Respect is something else that I should like to see returning. I respected many of my own teachers, but I wasn't terrified of them. Instead of being proud of our authority figures, we knock them down.

The boys here are polite but remarkably normal. They can be quite rough, they can hold their own in a fight, but they know when to stop. Lessons are an absolute delight. The largest class is about eighteen and quite often there are as few as ten or eleven. I had a remedial group last year of only six. Where in the State system would they have that sort of attention?

When you get down to it, education boils down to money and little else. We have all this talk about educational philosophy, but I believe that open-plan was only introduced because it was cheaper to build than traditional classrooms. Even the trend towards a core curriculum, which I support, might have come about because the money's dried up. Nevertheless, I'm glad to see some limits set to the ever-expanding horizons. I'd like us to be thought of more as teachers and less as social workers. There was a time when the teacher took on board everything the parents couldn't cope with. I'm a teacher and I'm quite glad to see us returning to that.

38

All Headbangers, Anyway

A somewhat shy man of great sensitivity and intelligence, Frank Shelbrook is a highly dedicated teacher who was forced to retreat into an independent boys' school in Wales after a year's devastating experience of an inner-city comprehensive. His intellectual honesty, however, compelled him to admit that what disturbed him most was not the children, but his own inability to cope. He was conservatively dressed in a dark sports jacket and grey trousers and his fair hair was cut rather short. He spoke quietly with a soft, but pronounced, West Country burr.

After I left university with a degree and a Dip Ed, I got my first job in 1968 at a mixed grammar school on the south coast, which was very pleasant. There used to be about sixty people doing A level English and they got very, very good results. I stayed there for four years and then I moved to another grammar school in the West Country. It wasn't quite as academic, but it was a friendly, easy-going kind of school in a small country town. I felt very much a part of the community. For example, I found, when the milkman came, that I taught his daughter; I went to the doctor, I taught his daughter; I taught the vicar's daughter; and I taught the daughter of my own daughter's teacher. You were on very good terms with all the parents. For instance, after the school play, there was a school tradition that one of the parents would hold a party at his house.

I've always liked the social side of teaching, you know, knocking around the building, knowing the office people, even doing dinner duty. By the time you'd been there two or three years, you knew all the pupils. It was all very friendly, yes, very friendly. Then the school became comprehensive. I taught mixed ability and low ability in the first and second years. At that time, I didn't mind it at all. Everything seemed to be going well; but now, with hindsight, I can see that the whole balance of the school was changing until it reached a point where it keeled right over. I remember one teacher, a very nice man, who had been the backbone of the grammar school. He'd run the debating society, been head of department, and in his fifties, he was finding that he couldn't cope. It was terribly sad. After teaching in grammar schools for thirty years, he found new pupils who had less ability, less interest and less concentration. I don't say that as a criticism of the pupils. It was like an unhappy marriage in a way; they just didn't fit each other. It's very sad, isn't it?

Anyway, I stayed there for three years. I was quite content and then my marriage broke up. I needed to be near my children, so I got a job in an inner-city comprehensive school. I thought to myself, 'I've managed all right so far. It can't be that difficult.'

Until then, I'd been quite content with my teaching; but in this school, I was just terrible. It's a great, great regret, you know, to think how badly I did. I'm quite shy with strangers generally and if you teach in a grammar school, you don't really have to get to grips with a new class until about half-term. You tell them what to do and they do it. But these children were coming at you right from the start. 'What do we have to do now?' 'Where can we put this?' Little things which I'd taken for granted, that people came with pens, just didn't happen. I put a little pot of pens on my desk for them to borrow, but they were always being nicked. I was buying about ten a week. I thought, 'This is ludicrous. It can't be right.'

My style of teaching is more or less as I'm talking to you now, in a quiet, friendly way. The other teachers had an entirely different method. It's hard to describe. I felt as though I was used to teaching in black and white and they were teaching in colour. Words and books weren't enough. There had to be pictures on the wall. There had to be games . . . I mean, for a start, they had about two discos a week, one in the dinner hour and one in the evening. Well, I think I hate discos more than anything else in life.

There were some terrific teachers there, right hard-bitten men who had been in the job for about thirty years, with a kind of built-in megaphone for a voice. By and large the rest of the staff did remarkably well. I don't know if you know this, but in the average grammar school, there'll be about five teachers in a staff of fifty who can't cope. The proportion was much the same there, only, to my regret, I was one of them. In assembly, the kids looked as nice as pie when the deputy head was talking to them. Once, the RE teacher asked the whole assembly, 'How many of you have got a cat at home?' These kids of fourteen or fifteen were putting up their hands and saying, 'I've got one.' I mean, I'd never have thought of asking them that. Why did he ask them? Oh, he was just going to draw some moral from it. That was the level. Other members of staff said it was better to be junior-trained to teach there.

In some ways, the pupils seemed to me very naive and childish in their opinions; but at the same time, they were quite rough and difficult. Try as I would, I couldn't find a good manner of speaking to them or of dealing with them generally. They didn't get out of their seats in class, or attack me, or anything like that; but I felt permanently harassed, not with all the classes, only three of them. The worst thing was this. I felt they knew my teaching was bad. It's very hard to live with the feeling that you're not doing your job well. I used to read books with them like *Shane* or *A Hundred and One Dalmations*, which had always gone down nicely, but after three pages, they just didn't want to know. They were yawning, arguing with each other, asking 'What have we got to do this for?' There were some pupils who would be quiet when you read and others who would be quiet when they wrote, but they weren't necessarily the same.

The main trouble wasn't in class, but on dinner duty, break and outside school. They called out at you and shouted. I remember once chasing a boy who had told me to fuck off for a quarter of a mile through a housing estate. What on earth the people down the street must have thought, I don't know. I heard of one teacher in a nearby school who had a standard form of punishment. He didn't hit them, but he put the kids in a big metal box and hit it with a hammer, three or six times. They were all headbangers, anyway.

I used to visit a teachers' centre occasionally, though not very often, as you couldn't afford to be tired the next day. One night, at about ten o'clock, I was talking to two girls of about twenty-five who taught at a very hard school. You could see they were frightened to go in the next day. They were saying, 'Oh, God, I've got so-and-so tomorrow.' I felt very sorry for them. They looked really anxious, really tense. Some teachers are under a terrific strain, much worse than anything I ever experienced. As I drove home in the evening, I'd always hit a high of happiness about five o'clock. It was fantastic! I used to go in a library and read a book. I felt really happy. And then as the evening went on, I'd kind of tighten up and become more and more nervous. The only thing I can say in my favour is that I never had a single day off. The worst time was Sunday evenings. The anticipation was really dreadful. A lot of teachers suffer in that way. Oh, yes, they feel really bad on Sunday evening.

I only stayed there for a year. Once I had given in my notice, I could have told you at any moment how many days I had left. I'd handed in my notice without having a job. I thought I'd rather go on the dole than stay there. I spent the last half-term holiday looking for a job. There was a job advertised in a betting shop. You know they write the results up on a board. Well, the manager asked me if I thought I could cope and I replied, 'I suppose I can. I'm a teacher.' I didn't take the job as it was clear he only wanted someone as a stop-gap.

Then I got this job in an independent school, which is even easier than the grammar schools I've been in. The boys work a lot harder than they would in a mixed school. They all get loads of O and A levels. The majority are middle class boys who are going to be accountants, dentists, that sort of thing. There's a kind of brightness and intellectual directness in the air, which is quite stimulating, though it's also a bit cheerless and monastic. One of the problems is that as time goes on you start to lose your enthusiasm for literature to a certain extent. It's just the endless repetition. There's an American novel, *To Kill a Mocking-Bird*, which I used to like very much, but

I've taught it, oh, about twelve times and I just can't stand the sight of it any more. It's even worse if a book calls for some kind of emotional reaction like *All Quiet on the Western Front*.

I'm sure that losing enthusiasm is a vocational disease. In English you have to teach an awful lot from your imagination and feelings. Just to give you a little example, I used to do a long project about a deserted planet which had been peopled by different tribes and beings from outer space who had developed their own civilisation there. The children used to have oral lessons and write essays about it. They used to write a fantastic amount, pages and pages. They worked together in little groups and wrote in big scrapbooks. I must have taught that about five times, until I got nauseated and hated the very idea, but the children loved this creative writing. I know there's been a lot of criticism that creative writing leads to sloppy and ungrammatical work, but there's a lot of uninformed criticism about what goes on in schools generally – a fantastic failure in communication. People think that a teacher comes in and puts a record on 'Write, write, write', and says that everything's wonderful. To me creative writing is just writing that involves imaginative and emotional reactions. All writing should be organised and disciplined, so I always made one person in the group responsible for seeing that nothing went into the scrapbook unless it was in decent English. I don't teach analytical grammar. I never have and I refuse to, though I do set factual writing – organising paragraphs, punctuation, all the rest of it – and I do an awful lot of running repairs in the marking.

Marking is the hardest part of my job. Some teachers, you know, won't take books home because they think they contaminate the house. I've got a big cupboard and I put the books in there and never get them out except to mark them. I'd really like to have a separate marking room. If I've got eighty books, I'll only take out ten at a time. It's a very neurotic business, marking. I used to think that no matter what I did, for example, say I'd come home and found this beautiful woman, or say I'd gone out and saved somebody's life, I'd still have to go and mark. Nothing would do away with that. I always have to do it at night so you're still marking at about half past twelve, your eyes are hurting and you're drinking endless cups of coffee. Theoretically, I mark a set of books a night, and if I did that I would never have any late nights. I suppose I mark about a hundred and fifty or two hundred books a week. I think teaching without marking must be brilliant. That would be the perfect job. But these problems are nothing compared with working in a comprehensive: they're not worth mentioning. Compared with State schools, it's like the life of Reilly.

Like a number of other teachers, Frank wrote to me a few weeks later to give me his second thoughts:

In my first letter, I said that teaching was sometimes dreary, repetitive, soul-destroying; sometimes easy, delightful, rewarding. I seem to have had a very happy term. What makes it so?

Most delightful is a feeling of like-mindedness and sympathy with pupils: talking, discussing, reading, maybe a feeling of extending their horizons a little. Introducing an author whom pupils enjoy is very rewarding. We did so recently with Dylan Thomas. It doesn't seem like work at all, just pleasure.

Even marking can be almost enjoyable if done in daylight, when I'm not exhausted, when pupils have written imaginatively and variedly. Sometimes I even reread their homework, which is the highest of all accolades.

Getting to know pupils well is nice, becoming part of the furniture at the school, having pleasant relaxed relationships, e.g. at the end of term, hanging about idly, watching the Christmas decorations go up, chatting to the dinner ladies, all creates camaraderie. Schools can be genuine communities, providing all kinds of satisfaction.

Stephen Leacock said, 'There would be nothing wrong with schools if it could all be like the last day but one', which is true. I always liked the last week of term best, which is almost better than the holidays, though the prospect of three weeks away isn't bad either!

39

Bonfires in the Desks

I started teaching in 1968 straight from university as a biology teacher in what was then one of the county's few purpose-built comprehensives. In those days, I really enjoyed teaching. To see the science department build up from four to sixteen by the time the school amalgamated with its 11–13 feeder was very exciting. As head of science I got a lot of self-confidence and satisfaction out of it.

Thoroughly disillusioned by the conscripted nature of State education, John Thorsen, head of science in a West Country comprehensive has left teaching after seventeen years to open a general store in Wales. Although he expects a significant drop in income initially, the compensation will be greater control over his own destiny. He is married with four children.

Then around 1981 I began to feel dissatisfied, probably because I'd stayed in one school too long. It was also this classic age thing when men of forty or so start to think, 'Am I going to spend the rest of my life doing this?' There was also a change of head and the school became more bureaucratic. The biggest factor, perhaps, was the great increase in unemployment so that a lot more kids became dissatisfied with education because it was no longer a passport to a job.

I thought about packing it in then, but as I'd spent my whole career in one school, I decided that in fairness to the system I ought to try another school first. The idea of getting a deputy headship didn't appeal to me, as I've never been very keen on administration. Eventually, I landed the head of science here in the West Country. I'd hoped that moving from a northern manufacturing city to a country town would make a big difference. There were no bonfires in the desks, which used to happen from time to time in my old school, but the dissatisfaction with the system was just as identifiable. I heard teachers saying just the same sort of things about the kids as my former colleagues had done. I hadn't really expected that.

A lot of it comes down fundamentally to the conscripted nature of education. You get some people saying, 'Bring back National Service', but you don't need to. For many of these kids it's literally here – in the schools.

They are made to come to school by law.

However much you jiggle round with the curriculum, there's an increasing percentage who say, 'I don't want to know'. It didn't happen so much when jobs were plentiful, but it's become far more common now. 'Why should I bother to work?' they ask. 'I'm no good at English, maths, physics or whatever, and my brother's got twenty-three O levels and six A levels and he can't get a job. What's the point in me bothering?' That's very difficult to answer. You fall back on clichés. 'Try to do as well as you can while you're here. You've only got another eighteen months or six months to go.' That's an awful thing to have to say. It's like a sentence. I really believe that even if you ran topless dancing and the local radio at the school, they'd still want to leave and get a job where they'd get a wage and wouldn't have to wear school uniform.

The kids' attitudes have changed a lot in the last ten years. They're treated far more like adults at home with the power to make their own decisions, so when they come to school, where they get much less say, they're reluctant to have any sympathy with anything that might be called authority. I don't mean a respect for authority itself, because that's an old-fashioned concept. Schools have been forced to become more liberal and democratic because it's no longer possible to control them in any other way. They've altered by default, not design. Democracy has followed on from chaos, though perhaps that's a Black Paper view.

Some teachers claim that teaching is a profession, but it isn't really. If you go to a dentist drunk, he'll refuse to see you; if you go to a solicitor and abuse him, he'll tell you to take your problem elsewhere. As a teacher, however, you've got absolutely no control over your conditions of work. If you say in a staff meeting, 'I think there are fifty kids in this school who are beyond the point of control', there's a stultified silence. The administration find it difficult to believe because they don't teach them. I can only say it because I'm a senior teacher with seventeen years' experience. Younger teachers always suspect that it might be their fault.

Kids who don't like school are capable of causing absolute mayhem in the classroom. I've got two or three kids like that in one of my forms. One boy was expelled from a public school for trying to burn it down. Another boy is very disturbed. He has a total inability to sit still or to keep quiet – publicly loud and outrageous behaviour. His home has broken up. His mother went off with the boy-friend of the lad's eldest sister. The educational psychological service is involved, but they say they can do nothing for the lad. 'I'm afraid he's your problem until he leaves.' I've got every sympathy with the boy, but, looking at it coldly, it's not my job to cope with him. I'm not a trained social worker or psychiatrist or child guidance officer. And with social problems as they are, there are an increasing number of children in the same category. It's a sad situation.

Education has been bedevilled by constant change in the last few years.

More and more teachers are taking more and more time developing more and more things that, ultimately, interest fewer and fewer kids. Take this new pupil profile scheme. It's good in some ways, but they're enormous documents. A fifth form teacher was telling me the other day that it took him two hours to interview each child, and he didn't know how he was going to find the time. From the pilot scheme, it seems that most employers aren't very keen on it either. Some kids will soon cotton on the idea that this is just another exercise dreamed up by teachers or the system and that employers don't take it seriously. In fact, they're already doing that in the pilot scheme. Kids are far more cynical, aware and sophisticated now. Take exams. The education system has always served O and A level kids, but whether it's served them as well as it should is another matter. Examinations turn kids into fact gluttons. A lot of O level courses could have up to 40 per cent of their content axed and still not serve them badly. For example, they're expected to know the names and functions of four or five digestive juices. You spend a lot of time getting them to learn about amylase and lipase and this and that, when the whole idea of digestion is just to make food soluble so that it can dissolve in the blood and be carried round the body, because you can't have lumps of bacon floating through narrow blood-vessels. If they got that fundamental idea, it would be quite adequate.

I'd like exams to test people's skills and attitudes to science, rather than rote learning of semi-irrelevant facts which will be forgotten ten days after the exam or which could be easily looked up in a book anyway. It is changing slowly, but it should have changed years ago. One of the optimistic things is that the Association for Science Education and the DES have both been involved in liberalising science teaching. There are lots more integrated courses, incorporating social, political and skill aspects. I hope this new 16+, which we hear so much about, will change it; but CSE was going to do that and ended up as a watered-down O level.

And yet, if you asked somebody what should be the most wonderful thing you could do, it should be encouraging fertile minds to develop, expand, extend. And in primary schools, it's probably still like that. I don't know. But if a teacher with an ordinary personality, who is sympathetic to children, can't see something positive in education, it's very worrying. It shouldn't get to the point where it's only a job for supermen and superwomen – ordinary mortals don't apply. That's the way, perhaps, it's going. I haven't got the stamina I had years ago, and I'd rather get out now and leave on a cloud rather than under one.

X

INDEPENDENT SCHOOLS

40

I'm More Concerned With Character

John Flaxton, who prefers to be known as a schoolmaster, is a tall, thin man of thirty-three, with an aristocratic bearing. He teaches history at a public school in the south. In his first letter he had confessed to being ultra-conservative in his views, having a low opinion of State teachers, and driving around in a vintage Bentley. He also made it clear that he would be happier to be interviewed on his 'home ground', in his London club, where he was waiting for me rather impatiently on the steps. He was impeccably dressed in a well-tailored three-piece suit.

I work very hard, literally from seven in the morning till ten at night, but I don't mind that. The only disadvantage, apart from the effect on one's social life, is that I can become a bit testy at times and somewhat tired. The life is very monastic in a sense. That I do find tiring, especially being with the same age of boys all the time. They're twelve, thirteen, fourteen, coming up to the rebellious age.

I went to a well-known boarding and day-school as a day-boy. My father, who is a company director, didn't want me to be a boarder. I don't know why. I greatly regretted not having been one, as they achieved so much more academically and were more self-confident. Personally, I would have liked to have gone to Eton. I think most people would.

I had the idea that I wanted to teach in my teens. Maybe it was because I liked talking to the masters at school. It was hero-worship perhaps. When I came down from university, however, my mother said that anyone could be a teacher, so my father suggested insurance instead. I went into an office in the City, but I had no real aptitude for financial matters and I didn't really like my colleagues. Too many of them were only interested in going out to play darts at lunchtime. I realised that I might as well do what I wanted, so I went to Oxford to do a post-graduate certificate.

I had a marvellous time there and did no work whatsoever, though I had to go to the lectures which were very tiresome. I didn't write a single essay and spent most of my time entertaining friends or going beagling. Although I liked Oxford very much, too many of the undergraduates seemed to be obsessed by work. There should be a place for those men who may not be very intelligent, but who have money, or whose fathers were up, or who are good rugger players. The most distasteful part of the course was the week I spent on teaching practice in a comprehensive school which was supposed to be one of the best in the county. Admittedly I was taking fourth- and fifth-years of low ability but to have girls and boys of fifteen, only a minority, saying 'Fuck off', throwing things around, walking out, just shocked me. One girl said, 'You want to teach in a posh school, don't you sir?' and I replied, 'Yes, you're quite right, I do.' When I asked what sanctions I had, I was told none. I would have liked to beat the boys severely, as I regard corporal punishment as the punishment of the first resort not the last. It does not leave the sort of resentment that lines, runs, cold showers can do. I find that 80 per cent of boys opt to be slippered if caught doing something wrong, and I am appalled that the government kow-tows to European courts and STOPP.

While I was there, I also formed a low opinion of State teachers. The sort I met were very keen to have left-wing speakers in to talk to the children. I don't like teachers constantly pressurising children to support CND, Arthur Scargill and so on. The boys in my school all know my views, but I would never try to force them on the pupils. In fact, it can be a bit tiresome to hear so many conservative views all the time. It's refreshing to find a boy who's prepared to stand up and voice a different opinion.

I know some comprehensives have marvellous examination results. There's one in London. As far as I'm concerned, however, examinations aren't everything. I'm far more concerned about the boys' characters. The standards which State schools tolerate are disgraceful. We should be pressurising children to conform to high standards, middle class standards and values. Ideally, I'd like to see all schools privatised on a voucher system, so that those who did not care about standards, or were disruptive, could be thrown together in sink schools, where they would not drag others down with them. Egalitarianism is not a Christian concept. We should return to the day when a professional person earned ten times more than a labourer. One of the manifest causes of unemployment is the inability of people to employ domestic servants. Few of my acquaintances can afford to employ full-time staff anymore, so the nearest most of us get to enjoying the standards of personal service we would have had eighty years ago, is when we are at our clubs. The advice I would give to young unemployed people is to petition the government for the abolition of minimum wage restrictions. It must surely be preferable to work for a low wage than to rely upon the State for an income.

Oh, yes, I've had quite a lot of contact with ordinary people. My father was terribly keen that we should learn about money, so he insisted that I took vacation jobs. In one vacation, I worked as a beach cleaner. It was appalling. I had to stick it for seven weeks, but I must say that I did the job better than anyone else. They were all starting late, taking tea-breaks, finishing early. Admittedly, if I had that job permanently, I'd probably take the same attitude. It was difficult to relate to the others at first, but in the end we did have some sort of relationship, even though it was rather formal. I also worked in a mental hospital. We had to clean out the latrines and things like that. There was shit all over the floor. My supervisor was quite annoyed when I was allocated to her, because she thought I wouldn't be able to cope, but within two weeks she was saying I was one of the best workers she'd ever had. I didn't really like the work. It was merely a means of earning some money.

Ideally, I would like to teach on a voluntary basis, part time. I have various friends who don't have to work, so in my spare time I'd simply socialise. When I think about it, I do feel a little anachronistic in a way. Of course I do. I stand out so much. But I don't really care what other people think. It doesn't affect me. I do provide some brightness in people's otherwise drab lives. For instance, when my friends and I drive around in the Bentley, all dressed up in country clothes, that causes a lot of amusement, though it fills some people with envy. At times, I do exaggerate my views, especially for the boys, or if I feel I'm in a hostile crowd. I suppose all people like to seek attention somehow. Not that I am constantly rushing out into the streets to do so, but if I'm at a party and I see people winking at my remarks, I'll play it up. I can't take myself too seriously.

41

More Individual Attention

Before I came here, I was teaching French in a comprehensive. The classes were so big and so many children didn't like the subject, that there were lots of discipline problems. Two or three children would start chatting and you'd get them quiet; then another group in a different corner would start. Children who were going to give up French after the third year were particularly awkward. The worst pupil I have ever had was an overweight third-year boy, who disrupted every lesson and refused to do anything more strenuous than colouring pictures. He went on to become a criminal.

Doris Rookwood was delighted to leave that comprehensive school six years ago to teach in a small independent boarding school for girls near London. The smaller classes provide great benefits for both teachers and pupils.

What surprised me most at my present school was the pleasant atmosphere, the friendly girls and the fact that any work you set them was always done. Quite a few of the girls are foreign. Obviously they all have parents with money, or their fees are being paid by somebody else, a firm. There's very little snobbery among the pupils or the staff. As the girls are aware that a large amount of money is being paid for their education, they are well-motivated on the whole. The head is a pleasant hard-working woman who runs the school fairly efficiently, and my colleagues are congenial.

The main advantages for teachers are the smaller classes, which means that the girls get much more individual attention. Any problems are quickly noticed and usually sorted out. We do quite a lot of teaching of individual girls. Quite a few are not very intelligent, and if they manage to get an O level through their hard work and mine, it's very gratifying. Smaller classes also mean that we have much less marking.

We work longer hours, but we have one or two free periods every day and one free afternoon a week. The main holidays are longer than in State schools: four weeks at Christmas and Easter and eight weeks in the summer. Although we're not underpaid, as we're on Burnham rates, there are very few Scale posts. The highest in the school is Scale 3. When a post falls vacant, it is usually given to someone on the staff rather than an outsider, but there aren't many opportunities for promotion.

Most of the teachers have taught in State schools. On the whole they're very pleased that they've left the State sector, as the conditions here are easier and more pleasant and the work-load is lighter. Obviously, there are times when we rush around like mad, for example, when we're doing exams or reports, which we do three times a year; but the stresses are very few compared with the State system. One rarely gets absolutely exhausted as I did when I was working in a comprehensive.

It obviously isn't fair that parents should be able to buy a better education for their children, but one can't blame them for doing so. I sent both my children to prep school before they went on to a comprehensive. My girl has just left and is about to enter university. My son, on the other hand, has not been stimulated at all by the environment and wants to leave school as soon as possible. I shall be surprised if he gets any O levels. He would have been quite capable of passing Common Entrance and is actually a university-standard child, though obviously he'll never get there. If I'd been able to do so, I would have sent him to an independent school, but I'm a single parent.

42

A Rather Snobbish Reputation

Oh yes, Mr Huggett, I do think it right that parents should be able to pay for education, especially when the State system leaves so much to be desired. If it could be considerably improved, the arguments against parents being able to pay would be stronger; but, you know, those arguments have always savoured of authoritarianism, even tyranny, to me.

During the last thirty years, Albert Radnor has taught in small, relatively inexpensive private schools in Scotland and England and in State grammar and secondary modern schools. As State schools deteriorate, he fears that more parents will send their children to small private schools for snobbish reasons, which may help to depress overall standards even further.

The independent school I teach at in the West Country is quite frankly the kind of school which has got the private sector a bad name. The academic results are pretty disgraceful. I've never made any secret of it. When I had been there just a little while, I told the head that the English results were a disgrace and that I'd be quite prepared to stand down. He said, 'No, no, you're doing all right. You musn't worry. They're no worse than in other subjects.' So I thought to myself, 'Oh, well, if it suits you, I'll just carry on.'

There isn't any pressure from parents to maintain standards. They're quite content that their children aren't going to State schools and so long as nothing happens at the school to upset their children, they're satisfied. To tell you the truth, the school does have a rather snobbish reputation. That's how the head can get away with it. In fact, you may have trouble if you try to put pressure on a child. I remember one girl who was quite bright, cheerful and extroverted; but careless, untidy and lazy. Happy-go-lucky, you know. I kept getting at her, not in an unpleasant way, but firmly, telling her that she could get a good result. Just before she took her O levels, her mother came up to me at open day and said, 'You know, Mr Radnor, you're the only teacher here who has ever criticised Sarah's attitudes.' So I replied, 'Oh, really! Well, other teachers must do as they think best.' It seemed to take the wind out of her sails. I don't know whether she thought I'd apologise.

At one time, I'd have said that private schools like this were only a small minority, but I'm not so sure now. I've read reports about other schools which remind me too forcibly of this one. The first private school I taught in, which was in Scotland, was very different. It was run on a shoestring, but the academic results were very good because it had an excellent head-mistress. She was a Scotswoman who could be quite fiery-tempered and sharp-tongued – Scottish characteristics, you know – but she was a kindly person. She'd had plenty of classroom experience and was a proven successful teacher, two qualifications which other heads I've served under have lacked.

For a short time, I taught in an awful secondary modern school, which was grossly overcrowded and very rough; but the main trouble was that it was badly run. The headmaster, who had spent the rest of his teaching life in a grammar school, had no experience of that type of pupil or parent. He was a ruthlessly self-centred man, who exploited the staff quite disgracefully by setting one member against another with marvellous skill. He could be very charming when he pleased, giving secret favours, particularly to people teaching scarcity subjects. He made sure that they didn't have to teach rough classes, exempted them from covering for absent colleagues, let them slip away from school for a while so long as they came back quietly. Things like that, Mr Huggett. I wouldn't blame people outside teaching for saying that these are just trivialities, but when you're working in that type of school with very difficult conditions, and you find out what is going on, it has a big impact. One of the great needs in teaching is to have a strong team. A teacher spends a great deal of time on his own, away from colleagues, which means that you must have a genuine leader to maintain a corporate spirit.

In Britain, traditionally, the head has enormous power, as they still do today when they complain so much about their power being restricted. It's a job that appeals to power-hungry individuals. The headmasters I've worked for were all crudely autocratic and treated their staff and the pupils outrageously in some ways. On the whole they got away with it. Yet it didn't have to be. I find myself thinking now that they would have tumbled over if you'd blown hard enough on them. They weren't really strong, determined men at all: it was just that no one was willing to stand up to them.

The crying need in education is for a greater orderliness, interpreting that word literally, in everything: curriculum, manners, yes, everything. I've been aware of the deterioration in that respect ever since I started teaching. Education has been mauled horribly by constant changes of direction, experiments in freedom, constant diversification, and interference from outside, particularly by politicians, but not only by them. When well-meaning people commiserate with me on being a teacher, I always say I wonder that the children aren't worse. Yes, it's really a wonder to me, Mr Huggett, it really is.

43

No British Warrior-Queen

Do you want to plug the tape recorder into the mains? . . . Would it be able to hear me if I walked around while I'm warming up?

Shirley Rulton, a highly qualified Oxford graduate in her forties gave up her job as a university lecturer when her child was born and found it difficult to get back into education again. After spending an excruciating year in a comprehensive in the north-west, she got a job in a girls' public school in the Midlands where she feels much more at home. She seemed a little nervous at first, her words running on breathlessly to keep up with her agile mind; but after she had returned from her initial perambulation with two glasses and a well-chilled bottle, she settled down on the carpet and relaxed. She is a tall, slim woman with dark hair.

Teaching is a stressful activity. It would be even if you were teaching the Archangel Gabriel. You are on view all the time and you've got to combine your concern with the children's needs with your concern for your subject. Even now, in a very well-run public school, I occasionally feel absolutely shredded at the end of the day, just keeping my voice pitched to carry over all the interruptions, without sounding too much like a British warrior-queen . . . I didn't know if you were interested in this. You're not a teetotaller, are you?

The classes are twenty or twenty-five, which is big for a public school. That's probably one of the reasons why it's relatively cheap. It's selective, obviously, so the general level is quite good. The academic results vary. This year we had nine Oxbridge places. Most girls go on to some form of higher education.

The staff is rather older than in most State schools. I would think the average age is about forty, though we do have one or two young members of staff. Interestingly enough, nearly everybody, as far as I can judge, has taught in State schools. Where people went to schools themselves, I do not know. I should think it's a fairly equal mix of public school and grammar school. Most of us have honours degrees, though one or two have a B Ed which, I must admit, I still don't entirely regard as a degree. There's a rather hearty, girlish atmosphere in the staffroom – a lot of giggling. Teachers in general, as you must have noticed, tend not to grow up in quite the way other people do. The constant exposure to the very young produces a kind of retardation. I'm afraid, for instance, we tend to giggle at vaguely smutty jokes in the way that schoolgirls do. If we didn't know we were parodying ourselves, it might be serious.

The girls don't have a very exciting life, poor souls. The youngest go to bed at eight and lights out at eight thirty. The older girls go to bed at nine and the sixth form have a certain measure of freedom. They do get out of school, but one of the troubles is that we're in the middle of nowhere with very little public transport. It needs quite a lot of organisation to take them out. Last week, we took a group on a trip, which was supposed to be a joint English and history event, but the arrangements rather broke down in the afternoon, and we ended up by going to a castle with the vague idea of doing a practical history lesson, but the girls just rushed around, shrieking. It was just girlish glee. You couldn't get ratty about it. The fact that they felt the need suggests that they lead a rather sheltered life.

I suspect that there might be a bit of money snobbery among the girls, because a few of the parents are very rich. Most of them aren't, of course. They're doctors, solicitors, even some teachers, who must be scraping the bottom of the barrel to pay the fees. There are a few girls from the Continent whose parents have sent them over just to experience life in an English public school. We don't have many on assisted places, though a lot of public schools use their full allocation. Some of the parents are working overseas. I dare say all public schools keep going to some extent on people who have allowances to pay for their children's education.

The parents can be extremely helpful and co-operative, but there are a few who imagine that just because they're paying fees, you can produce an Einstein out of bank clerk material. One stretches children but doesn't try to push them in any kind of school. And if you get a parent whose only aim is a series of As in O and A levels, you do begin to worry. It's difficult to learn how to handle parents because the very worst will tend to treat you as a sort of paid employee. It's usually the fathers who take that line, though not invariably. Although you're not their subordinate, it's very easy to feel that you are, when you are being addressed in that way. Obviously, you must not be offensive; but sometimes the only effective thing is to adopt that kind of approach yourself. That's something you have to learn. I heard of an old headmistress at another school who once told a parent: 'Ah, well, you just can't make a success out of a sow's ear. If you want your daughter to do that, I suggest a brain transplant.' I don't think any of us could get away with that. Sometimes parents expect you to let them know if their children aren't working, even in the middle of a term. If they thought about it, they'd see that you couldn't possibly establish any kind of trust with the children if you did that. A lot of people in real life as well as schools, if you see the distinction, would like to think that all forms of evil-doing could be controlled without freedom being in any way impaired. It wouldn't work, I suspect. Fortunately, parents like that are a tiny percentage, but just like children who are giving trouble, they tend to stand out, because you worry about them.

Everything here seems terribly easy compared with my previous experience. The girls do understand appeals to reason and to some abstract notions of good behaviour. One tends to get occasional clever-cleverness, but I find myself able to cope with that quite easily. On the whole they don't like wasting time or being unconstructive. It was very different at the comprehensive.

Whenever I see television plays about comprehensive schools, they never reflect the sense I had of something being just barely held in and held down, not only in the particularly unpleasant example I taught in, but even in the other two where I did my teaching practice, which were reasonably successful examples of the genre. There was an incident on television last week when a delinquent boy heaved a carboy of acid over an unpopular teacher. That I could easily imagine happening, though nothing like it did happen in my schools; but the rest of the time the atmosphere seemed curiously tranquil. It's very difficult for anybody who's not been in the situation to imagine the constant tension, the sense of always being watched. This occurs in all teaching to some extent. In bearable quantities, it keeps the adrenalin flowing. In more than bearable quantities, you just get shell-shocked. In fact, that was the metaphor that kept coming back to me in that year. Going out on to the playing fields was exactly like going over the top.

Half of my lessons were with low ability classes, very, very low ability indeed. As you can hear, I haven't got the world's most striking north-western accent, so clearly there was a credibility problem. I probably also appeared very cold and distant, which was probably a result of my being scared and hopping mad at the same time, which two emotions reinforced each other constantly. Also, of course, it was difficult to know what to do with third- and fourth-year classes, where you get the most developed form of adolescent resistance and aggression. I can cope quite well with verbal aggression if I feel I can hit back in kind. The trouble was that I was dealing with people who were less fortunate than myself, so I couldn't really let rip. The other thing was that it wasn't my kind of verbal aggression, largely obscenities and personal remarks of an opprobious nature.

I soon learned that nothing I planned for lessons ever worked. So I tried a lot of self-expression, creative writing. I honestly don't think there is any sharp divide between formal and informal teaching. You slide from one to the other as the thing or the class demands. Some of the children could do good creative writing if they were in the mood. You couldn't go round giving them individual attention because the classroom was so small, you couldn't get past the desks. If you turned your back for a minute, the fruit gums started flying. So the only way to follow up the work was to write comments on it, which is quite inappropriate for that sort of child. They didn't like seeing red ink on what they'd done and they couldn't read what they called joined-up writing. So it was very useless, just a means of keeping them occupied. I must admit that occasionally I fell back on the well-worn elementary school device of writing something on the board and making them copy it. They actually enjoyed that. It gave them the illusion that they were working.

We also did a fair bit of reading aloud. As it was a split site school, you can imagine how convenient it was to carry sixty books across a large playing-field in a north-western gale. I learnt not to wear wrap-over skirts there. The buildings were so designed that the children could watch you from the classrooms struggling across the field. When I was doing end-of-term reports, I used to realise that even in the wildest class there were only six or seven who were really giving me trouble, and the rest were just unwilling accomplices or completely passive. In the two schools where I did my teaching practice, which had a greater sense of staff unity, the Dunkirk spirit prevailed. In this school it was the Belsen spirit: you tried to stay alive and if anybody happened to get killed in the crush, that was tough.

Of course, I'd much rather that people could get a better education without having to pay for it. My education didn't cost anyone, except the ratepayers, a penny. But it can't be obtained now, not dependably. If you happen to live in the catchment area of an excellent comprehensive, it's great. Even then, things can go to the bad very quickly and take much longer to recover, so that a school which was good when your child was eleven may have totally collapsed by the time your child is sixteen. I'd rather that some people should be able to buy a good education than that it should cease to exist altogether, because as long as it exists, it's there as a standard. A few weeks ago, there was a perfectly ordinary Scale 1 post at a former direct-grant grammar school which had gone independent. There were over a thousand applicants. The person who eventually got the job came down from being head of department in a comprehensive school and maybe sent his wife out scrubbing or something to make up the difference.

XI

OUTSIDERS' INSIDE VIEWS

44

Jumping Over the Curriculum

When you talk to Poms, our pay is embarrassingly high. I get about £18,000 a year. I haven't told them at my school, though they were fishing like blazes, because I don't want them to know I get double what a Scale 2 teacher gets over here.

Geoff Miller, an Australian primary teacher in his mid-thirties, is working in a first school in a fairly prosperous area of the West Country. The main differences he has noticed are in pay, curricular directives and work planning.

As Australian teachers get more money, we enjoy, perhaps, a better standing in society. As a group we don't feel markedly inferior to anyone. Some people – doctors, lawyers, dentists, accountants – get a lot more than we do, but teachers come next. After ten years we get three months' leave with pay. I work fewer hours here than in Australia. The school here starts ten minutes later; we have seventy-five minutes for lunch instead of fifty; and ten minutes more for afternoon play, so that's forty-five minutes less contact time a day. In government schools at home, however, there's almost no out-of-school activities unless you're the netball or the football coach.

I have to work harder in Australia to get the same results, however, because there's far more paperwork. In England, teachers do forecasts, which are basically little chats on paper, saying 'I think I'm going to do this, this, this and this', which the head teacher then signs. Back home, the average programme takes me ten hours and I have to do five of them a year. A typical programme on maths or social studies would include objectives, specific things I want the children to do, the types of lessons, the resources I'm going to use, and how I'm going to assess each child's progress. There are ruled-up files to record the children's progress and we've even got a standardised parent-interview record form now.

Education in my state is very much more formalised, though I don't know about the rest of the country. There's an enormous difference in the curriculum. In England, the curriculum documents are very small, only guidelines; at home, they're like phone books. If you stacked the social studies documents for the age range of six to twelve on top of each other, they'd be ten inches high. The music document is two inches high; the maths about three-quarters of an inch. I couldn't step over all my curriculum documents; I'd have to jump. The social studies syllabus, which is produced at enormous expense, is incredible. If you wanted to, you could take your lessons from it page by page. It even gives you the page numbers to look at in the atlas. If you need a syllabus like that, you haven't got any initiative, any ideas. I use it as a springboard, otherwise it can be stultifying. Our system is geared to the worst teacher which is probably a good thing; but they also make you keep records as if you were the worst possible teacher, too.

My English school is a lot more formal. The head always refers to other teachers as Mr or Mrs when they're not there, and he does the same when he's talking about parents or when he introduces me to them. In Australia, if I've got a good relationship with parents, and things are going well with the child, I use first names.

What goes on in the classroom isn't very different really. There are two computers here, but we've only got a 16 mm projector and two overhead projectors at home. England is probably a couple of years ahead in computers. And there's much more paper here in my school. Back home, you have to be very careful with it, but here they use it like it's going out of fashion. Good quality paper, good colours, too.

The size of classes are about the same. I couldn't positively identify a great difference in behaviour between English and Australian children, though the classes I've got here don't say 'Please' or 'Thank you'. I don't like that. I haven't noticed any great difference in teaching methods, either. There's a bit of team teaching here, which I've also been involved in at home. It's especially good here, mainly because we've got a particularly good deputy head. She keeps the school happy. Oh, she's terrific! She does it really well. She keeps the laughter coming and the jokes rolling. In the end, it all boils down to the runs on the board: whether the kids can read. The runs on both boards are the same. The kids in my class here read very well. I was really impressed.

45

Teacher Burn-Out

Dorothy Janeway, who teaches in a Canadian elementary school for children of five to twelve, is working in a middle school in an industrial city in the Midlands. The main differences she has observed are in children's behaviour, parental involvement, resources and curriculum development.

What has surprised me most in my English school? Well, I guess I just couldn't believe there would be the number of interruptions in lessons any day, all day, especially as I'd thought that English children all wore school uniform and had impeccable manners. They just love talking to each other all the time. Although the children are very eager, enthusiastic and wish to please, they all seem deaf when I say 'No talking' and just carry on while my mouth is still hanging open. They are far less apt, however, at expressing themselves in real discussion than they are on paper. They should have far more directed oral work.

There is more shouting and barking at children here, but fewer consequences for bad behaviour. At home, if a parent agrees, a child can receive a one- to five-day suspension. Parents at home are much more concerned with their children's progress, socially, physically and, most important, academically. They have at least two interviews a year and in addition I get constant notes and phone calls. They're far more competitive about their children, while parents here just want their children to like school or to have a nice time. There is far less communication with them about educational matters than about fund-raising. Teachers are constantly collecting money for lunches, crisps, outings, Christmas cards, school diaries, newspapers, whereas money is left to the accountants back home. That was another thing that surprised me here – the amount of time that is spent not only on collecting money but on assemblies, school productions, decorating classrooms, discussions about issues which don't seem to have any solution, and the tooth fairies, or dental people.

We have much better resources in Canada. There is a school library with a full-time librarian; a teachers' library; a printing office; and a resource centre which delivers and collects films, books, videos and so on. On the other hand, we don't have so many museums or such an excellent environmental centre.

The curriculum has become much more structured in Canada in the last few years. In maths, for example, there is a graduated system, definite guidelines and far more prepared texts and worked examples, which is a great time-saver. The children here are required to cover much more in a year, but we stress problem-solving far more at home. In the humanities, however, the curriculum has made teaching less creative. I, for one, feel that imposed topics such as Canadian Government for ten-year-olds is boring and a waste of time. With a more structured system, teachers are not so hassled. Before I go home at night, I have planned the following day's work in my day-book, which means that I arrive at school in a less tense frame of mind. Here, there is often a sudden flurry of activity before the bell, when some teachers decide what they will do. An amalgamation of the two systems would be beneficial, as I do enjoy the freedom to teach in topic.

This is a bad time for teachers in both countries. At home, people with years of experience have lost their jobs as schools have closed, there have been education cuts, no sense of furthering careers. The stress level among teachers is incredibly high, particularly since our first-ever strike last year, which created a rift between parents and teachers, and striking and non-striking teachers. There has been an increase in teacher burn-out, when you reach a point where everything seems old hat, boring, 'ho hum'. I feel burnt out myself every February, but an inspiring course will usually fix it, particularly if I go to the States which runs fantastic courses. I've seen burnt-out teachers here. One at my present school is always tired, sullen, sulky when she arrives; she has a headache or a sore throat; she goes on diets, drags around, can't think of what to do; she is generally negative. Oh, I can't go on!

Teachers over here do not get enough money for the amount of work they are required to do, which leads to a martyred attitude. My salary is $35,000 which is not considered high by professional standards. Although British teachers don't get enough time or resources to teach so many subjects, they keep on saying 'Yes, we'll do it'. In Canada, we're expected to teach too much as well, but we've begun to say, 'If you want to get back to basics, the three Rs, then something has to go.'

46

Too Much Baby Talk

The main differences between my present school and the one back home relate to pride and involvement. That hits pretty heavily, but I have never seen a school so slovenly in its physical plant, and it's not just the one I teach in. The facilities are literally coming to pieces. Now maybe, twenty years ago, the quality of construction was pretty poor, and from what I hear that's true; but I taught in a 125-year-old school in Massachussetts which was in better shape than the one I teach in here. And as for the cleaning, it's a lick and a promise and away you go.

John Edson, who was brought up in the United States and went to university there, has taught in five countries. He now works in a voluntary-aided school in a northern industrial city.

Yet to have a school in a fair-sized city with acres of playing fields, big trees, is beautiful, surprising and very, very pleasant. On arriving here, before the term started, I walked about the campus of two schools, one just up the street which my daughter attends, and the other where I'm working. In each case, the school could have been used as an arboretum, as there were lots of native and quite a few non-native trees: sequoia, Douglas fir and horse-chestnut, which I believe is North American.

Now the involvement, or rather the lack of it! I've yet to be in what I would call a staff meeting here. Information meetings, yes! Very little is decided by the staff or requires a tremendous input from them. I doubt that many North American schools would put up with it. Perhaps that's a measure of a particular situation rather than something general. It probably is, but there's a tendency here in my opinion for the person in charge of a school to become proprietorial. In Canada, there are lots of us who have been school heads and are back in the classroom again. I'm one of them. I've also been head of a department, but I'm not functioning in that role right now, though I probably will again some time in the future. Here, it seems to me, you never go down. That's kind of strange in my opinion.

In Canada, a lot more is expected of the teacher in out-of-classroom activities. If you're told to supervise a school dance, you will be there. The first meeting of the school year back home was called for seven in the morning. More teachers arrive at school before the official opening time and stay longer afterwards. It's not unusual to stay for an hour or even longer working with students and, for that reason, we have a second bus run.

I'd say the relationships with pupils are very similar. Students are not so responsive as they were, so that teachers have to put on some song and dance to keep their attention. Perhaps they take their cue from TV and if they're not being entertained they turn off and turn away. That is not meant to be a criticism of education in any particular country. It seems pretty nearly universal. There are grinds in all countries, people who memorise what they need to memorise and are shooting for the piece of paper. I suspect it is encouraged more here, mainly because of the emphasis on external examinations. I'm fortunate in that the head of the maths department where I'm teaching right now believes our role is to teach people to think. I'm very definitely a believer in that. I try to make people think at all levels, or at least give them the opportunity to do so. Students in both my English and Canadian schools feel free to ask for help most any time. That's actively encouraged and I like it. There is more streaming in my present school than there is back home.

What has displeased me most over here? If I had to lay it on, I'd say that the insistence on retaining the traditional where it's not appropriate is terrible. The teacher who uses the language of the children rather than more technical terms and doesn't teach the necessary vocabulary, isn't delivering. If I never hear the word 'nought' again after I go home, it will be soon enough. And that's not a big thing. To say 'minus' – minus six, minus x – rather than the better descriptions of 'negative' or 'opposite', where they're appropriate, is short-changing the student. We cannot get by with baby talk. That's been my biggest disappointment over here.

47

It Comes Back to Money Every Time

The thing I've noticed most is the lack of funding. I'm rather sad that teachers have to consider money every time they want to make a move for the betterment of the children. At this special school, whenever I take a group of students to the library, we go by bus if the weather's bad. I never think about it. Why should I? But one or two teachers have said, 'Oh, is there enough money in the petty cash for that?' Well, gosh! I'm not knocking the teachers, only the system. It's too bad they have to consider things like that because what does it do for their motivation? Not much!

Laura Bilby, a brisk fifty-year-old, emigrated to Canada with her husband and three children some twenty years ago after working in a grammar school and two secondary moderns – and has never regretted it. She is working for a year in an ESN(S) school for severely retarded children in Wales. At home, she works with mildly retarded children ESN(M) in a special unit in a composite school for infants to thirteen-year-olds. The main differences she has noticed are the lack of funding, organisation and goal-orientation, though she finds British teachers still as nice as she remembered them to be.

In Canada, we're far more safety conscious, so that the buses are built specifically for children in wheelchairs. They have a sort of ramp that lifts the wheelchairs up and once they're in, the top and base are so secure that the wheelchair couldn't move if it tried. I'm not saying that there aren't buses of that kind over here, but I haven't seen them. It's just the same with other forms of communication. My school in Canada, which is six years old, has an intercom, but my British school, which is only four years old, hasn't got one. Films, books, everything to do with A-V are only delivered here once a week, whereas in Canada it's a daily service. Back home, we each have our own mailbox for internal communications and post office mailings, but there are none in my present school. Unfortunately, it comes back to money every time. You do have to question where the incentive is for British teachers. It must rub off on them a bit. And let's face it, if they were given what they were asking for, a reasonable percentage pay rise, surely that would do something for them too, wouldn't it?

I know where I'd prefer to be. There's no hesitation. In Canada. The North Americans are very aggressive, very goal-orientated, which comes from their training. On all the courses I've done over there, the emphasis is on goals and aims, so naturally it's going to become part of their make-up in a work environment. If there's such a thing as better time management, I'll try to find it. I think most North Americans are like that, but I don't see it over here. Teachers here seem to flitter around, doing a triple job, which, if they only thought about it objectively, could be done in one. They go to the supply room, come back to the classroom, and then, oh yes, they have to go back again to get something they need. We use a lot of individual work cards daily, so I've colour-coded them for language, fine motor skills and so on. They'd never done that before. If there's a phone call for a member of staff, someone has to go round looking for him or her. I suggested we could have a board by the phone where the message could be written down. In Canada, I've been at school a few times at twenty past seven, but I've never been the first. We are all in at five past eight. There's only fifteen minutes for morning break and none in the afternoon. We finish at a quarter to four. Back home I go straight to my classroom and stay there. I did that over here, too. One day, soon after I'd arrived, I popped into the staffroom for something about a quarter to nine and everybody was sitting there drinking coffee. I couldn't help it, I wasn't being sarcastic, but I said 'Ooh, is there a staff meeting?'

The heads in Canada are A1. I don't know of any that aren't. They'd criticise themselves before they'd criticise the teachers. The children come first; the teachers second; and they come last. I've even known heads over there come out with a questionnaire, which teachers don't necessarily have to sign, asking if their approach is positive enough and if the staff would like to see any changes. They also place a great emphasis on positive relations with the secretaries and janitors. I think that's very important.

I'm delighted with my head teacher over here. Oh yes, I am. What else do I like? . . . Obviously, nothing comes to mind. That sounds terrible, doesn't it? Isn't that awful? I can't think of anything except that all the other teachers are nice. In my present school, I can't speak of any others, they're always saying, 'Everything okay, laura?' My first morning, I guess within half an hour, I had at least a dozen questions like that. Then the head came in and said, 'Is everything all right, Laura?' and I replied, 'If anybody else asks me that, I'm not sure what I'm going to do.' I was never conscious of being asked questions like that when I worked here years ago, though my main memory of British teachers was that they were very friendly. You wouldn't get that in Canada. Everybody's far too busy doing their own thing, whatever that might be. That's what I've said. They're very goal-orientated. And that's where the aggressiveness comes in.

48

No Class Snobbery, Not Any More

Françoise Pride, who was born in France some thirty years ago, is married to an English businessman and lives in a neat, middle class estate in a county north of London, from where her husband commutes to work. An Amnesty International poster was prominently displayed in one of the windows of her freshly-painted, detached house. She is a striking woman with a statuesque figure who was dressed in blue bib-and-brace overalls. She took a B Ed in this country, teaches in a preparatory school and is an active member of the PTA at her boy's infant school. She speaks virtually perfect English, with a very slight French accent.

Everyone's so very conscious of class in England. You don't mix with people who have the wrong accent, though a foreign accent can be okay. some people socialise with me just because I'm French. I don't like that, because where does that leave *me*? Class division isn't just a question of money. It's very subtle, so subtle sometimes that you can't put your finger on it, though you're always conscious of its being there. English people will do anything to climb another rung of the social ladder, so that, even within the State sector, it's very important which school you send your child to. Mothers think that if they take their car every morning and drive far, they are doing good for their children, but often they are just trying to maintain the social structure. Most mothers round here drive their children to a traditional primary school in a very middle-class village because they say it has a better class of mother. I've had that said to me.

I send my son to the nearest infant school, just around the corner near an estate of lower-priced houses, because I think it's a far better school educationally. The classes are much smaller for one thing, and the headmaster doesn't put pressure on the children or the staff. For him, each child is just as important as another. He doesn't want to show the school off to parents, but does things in a quiet way. More and more teachers, nurses and people in the paramedical professions are sending their children there, so some of the other mothers are beginning to wonder now if they've made the right choice. Before that, I used to drive my son to a play group, because there wasn't one in walking distance. Once I gave a friend of mine a lift and when she saw the play group, she was really shocked and asked, 'How can you possibly send him there? It's right beside a huge council estate.'

School uniforms are another way of trying to uphold social distinctions. In France, some girls at selective secondary schools used to wear white aprons, but that doesn't happen any more. When I was at school, the select – not selective – private schools had a uniform, but they don't now. They were religious schools and the girls wore navy blue, because it's the colour of the Virgin Mary, I suppose. On practical grounds, a school uniform may be an advantage, as every morning my son knows what he's got to wear, and we might have a row otherwise. That's the only advantage. It doesn't blur social distinctions even within the same school. Some of the children will have a really big hole in their sleeve or their uniform will be filthy, so if they're sitting next to a child with a clean, smart uniform, you can see the difference anyway.

Parents shouldn't have too much say in education. I really hear so much rubbish from them. They're always saying that what they did at school was right, but when you look at them and hear them speak, you ask yourself, 'Was that really the right thing?' Education isn't an easy subject. You have to study it very carefully and you need a lot of experience, which I feel I haven't yet got. Parents should decide the aims of the school, but how they are to be achieved should be left to the educators, the professionals. This idea of a parents' take-over is wrong. The parents who think they know best are often the ones who know least.

Parents will do all sorts of things for their own children that they wouldn't do for their neighbour's child. They don't seem to realise that by helping other children, they would be helping their own children in the long run as well, because it's all one community. We regard professional and office people very highly, but the manual people are always underrated. The purpose of education should be for children to fulfil themselves and to produce a better society, but we're not achieving that because we have such a competitive system. The whole mentality has to change. The 1968 revolution changed a lot of things in France, including people's mentality, not everyone's, but people of my age. We've got other forms of snobbery in France – fashion, expensive holidays – but not class snobbery, not any more.

49

Life Can Be Lonely

We have much more docile and apathetic children here. They've no great desire to gain qualifications or to go on to further education. There is a very large tail of less able children and many social problems as the divorce rate is very high and there is also a high proportion of alcoholism. Unemployment has doubled in the last three years, but it's not really a problem because, once the tourist season starts, there are plenty of jobs. There is no unemployment benefit. Each parish has its own money and the unemployed must report usually on Monday to be given relief in cash.

Mark Pinchard has been teaching in Jersey for a number of years after spending fifteen years in half-a-dozen secondary schools in England. Education on the self-governing island is financed by the States of Jersey and is completely independent of the DES. In addition to the States schools, there are a number of private schools, all grant-aided. The children of tax exiles are usually educated privately on the mainland, though a few go to States or private schools on the island.

The comprehensive schools offer O levels, CSE and link courses, with a 14+ transfer to the high school for about twenty-five per cent of the children. This is based mainly on continuous assessment profiles by teachers, though parents can elect to transfer their children against recommendation and a foundation course is now available for those unable to meet academic standards. The FE college offers a full range of courses from A level to RSA, B Tec, TVEI and CPVE. Parents have to pay fees of £2,500 to £3,000 a year and there is an equivalent subsidy by the States. All students get a basic grant of of £100 a year and a bigger grant if the parents' income is below a certain level, but it's nothing like the grants on the mainland. Jersey students from middle class homes are therefore very much the poorer.

The cost of living is very high. Our mortgage is almost £1,000 a month. Goods are zero-rated for VAT, but retailers slap on transport costs. All fuels cost as much as fifty per cent more than in UK, except for petrol which is currently £1.33 a gallon. Perfumes, cosmetics, wines, spirits, some foods are cheaper than in UK. The low rates of tax are very pleasant and as we pay them retrospectively, we have the advantage of the money being in a deposit account accruing interest. Conversely we do not have the same allowances as UK, so we reckon to be, overall, little better off.

Until 1984 our salaries were on the Burnham rates, but in January all the Jersey teachers, union and non-union, said they would withdraw goodwill if their demand for an immediate £1,500 increase was not met. The Education Committee offered £501 immediately, with the proviso that in June, 1984, we would receive the same percentage increase as local civil servants and manual workers, which proved to be six per cent. Teachers do enjoy a slightly higher status in the eyes of the public here, but they are definitely looked down on by other professional groups. Attitudes tend to be twenty to thirty years behind those of UK.

Our educational situation here is very privileged, particularly from the point of view of resources. In our school, money is literally no object. There is, however, a noticeable dissatisfaction with the lack of promotion pro- spects. One particular stress is the difficulty of getting off the island. It costs a minimum of £200 for a family of two adults and two children to reach the mainland by sea or air. We do feel very cut off from UK, especially when bad weather means that we are cut off literally. I would recommend teachers to work here only because the teaching conditions and resources in UK are so much poorer than they used to be. For young people, life here can be very exciting. It can also be very costly and very lonely.

Glossary

Advisory teacher A teacher who is seconded to the authority's inspectorate to advise practising and probationary teachers on ways of teaching a subject or an age range of children.

A-V Audio-visual aids, such as films, video recordings.

B Ed Bachelor of Education. A first degree, which incorporates a teaching qualification. It has replaced the three-year Certificate of Education qualification, which was phased out from 1979–80.

Behavioural objective The observable and verifiable changes which a pupil is expected to exhibit after instruction.

Black Paper A collection of articles by educationists and politicians which was critical of modern methods and called for better academic standards. The first was published in 1969.

Bridging The possibility of moving from one level or one course to another which is built into some training courses.

B Tec (General Award in Business Studies). It was introduced in 1984 to provide a general education for the 16+ group who were interested in a clerical or sales career.

Burnham A committee, composed of representatives of the secretary of State, local education authorities and teachers, which decides teachers' pay.

Catchment area The area from which a school recruits its pupils.

CEE The Certificate of Extended Education, designed for CSE pupils who want to stay on for another year. It included a number of subjects related to the world of work and was due to end in 1985.

Chalk and talk An authoritarian style of teaching involving a liberal use of the blackboard, lecturing and even the dictation of notes.

Child-centred A method of education which focuses on the whole child rather than subjects.

City and Guilds (of London Institute) An examining body set up in 1878 to provide and assess schemes for technical and commercial education.

Common Entrance An examination taken at thirteen for entry to public schools. It is produced collectively but marked by the individual schools.

Community schools Those which keep open beyond normal school hours and encourage the rest of the community to use their facilities. They were recommended by the Plowden Report of 1967.

Contact time The time actually spent with pupils in the classroom.

Contract of employment At present much of the teachers' work is voluntary. It is proposed to draw up a new fixed contract in return for which teachers would get a new professional-grade pay scale. Their contract would include covering for absent colleagues, doing some lunchtime supervision, and having their work assessed by the head every year.

Core studies Life skills, such as communications and numeracy, which students following one of the new vocationally-orientated courses are expected to develop.

Cover Taking a class for an absent colleague.

CPVE The Certificate of Pre-Vocational Education, a one-year, full-time course which aims to prepare the 16+ group for adult life, including work, by means of vocational and additional studies, and work experience. It also includes integrated core studies covering ten areas.

Creative writing Assignments which allow children to express their thoughts and feelings in an imaginative way.

CSE Certificate of Secondary Education, which was started in 1965 for less academic pupils. It is being incorporated in the new GCSE.

Curriculum development The designing of a new course of study and a structured set of learning experiences to achieve identified aims and objectives.

DES The Department of Education and Science, which replaced the Ministry of Education in 1964, is responsible for English State schools, while primary and secondary schools in Wales and Scotland come under the respective secretaries of State. It controls finance and can make legally-binding regulations. Under Sir Keith Joseph it has assumed much greater powers in the actual content of education, the development of courses, teachers' conditions of service etc.

Dip Ed Diploma of Education, a teaching qualification for graduates which was replaced by the PGCE.

Education Act, 1944 It consolidated the tripartite system of grammar, secondary modern and technical schools; raised the school-leaving age from fourteen to fifteen; and abolished fees in all maintained secondary schools.

English from 5 to 16 An HMI report, published in 1984, which recommended what children should know at certain ages. It also proposed that they should receive more instruction in the rudiments of grammar, spelling and punctuation; how to speak and express themselves properly; and how to write formal and informal letters.

EPA Educational priority areas, with a large proportion of deprived children, which were given extra resources and a special allowance for teachers following the Plowden Report of 1967.

ESN Educationally subnormal children who are educationally retarded for various reasons. Some are mildly handicapped, ESN(M), and others severely handicapped, ESN(S). Because of their pejorative connotations, these terms are going out of fashion.

FE Further education, a loose term which usually means all post-secondary education provided in colleges, but not universities.

First school A school for children from five to nine, followed by attendance at a middle school.

Foundation year A course designed to give students the foundations of knowledge to progress to another course.

GCSE The General Certificate of Secondary Education, due to start in 1988, which will replace O levels and CSE. There will be seven pass grades from A to G, but it is planned to set different questions for different ability groups.

Hargreaves A report published by the Inner London Education Authority in 1984, which proposed greater parental and pupil involvement and the formation of staff development committees to raise the level of achievement by working class children, girls and ethnic minorities in the authority's secondary schools.

Hidden curriculum The implicit ways in which a school imposes values and attitudes on its pupils, e.g. respect for hard work and authority.

HMIs Her Majesty's Inspectors, responsible to the secretary of State, who inspect schools, advise teachers and run in-service courses. Under Sir Keith Joseph, their reports on individual schools have been published, and their advice has become much more frequent and wide-ranging.

Houghton A committee under the chairmanship of Lord Houghton, whose report, published in 1974, recommended big pay increases for teachers. Their average pay rose by 25 per cent.

Illich, Ivan Born in 1926 in Austria, he originated the de-schooling movement, which believes that schools should be replaced by community learning using libraries and networks of tutors.

Induction courses Training courses for new teachers. The James Report of 1972 recommended that one-fifth of a probationer's first year should be spent in further training.

In loco parentis Latin for 'in place of the parents'. A vague legal phrase governing the teacher's responsibility to pupils.

In-service courses Training of teachers on short courses after school hours or at weekends, or on longer courses for which leave of absence is granted. (Now called 'in-service training of teachers'.)

Integrated day A method of teaching in which children follow their own interests either individually or in groups for most of the day, though there is also work on the basic skills of numeracy and literacy.

JMI Junior mixed and infant school in primary education.

Laboratory technician An assistant, not a trained teacher, who assists science teachers.

LEA Local education authority responsible for providing education in its area.

Link course Courses for secondary and special school pupils using the facilities of a further education establishment.

Middle school A school for children from nine to thirteen, eight to twelve or ten to fourteen, who have previously attended first school.

Mixed ability Children with a range of general abilities who, in theory, are taught together in a class, but in practice often have to be taught individually or in small groups.

Modes Methods of conducting secondary examinations. In Mode 1, the paper is set and marked by the examination board; Mode 2 allows teachers to set part of the paper; Mode 3 allows teachers to set and mark examination papers, which are then moderated by the board.

Modules Self-contained training programmes in new courses designed to lead as a series to a certain level of attainment.

MSC Manpower Services Commission, set up in 1973 to co-ordinate vocational training and employment.

NAS The National Association of Schoolmasters, founded in 1919, which merged with the Union of Women Teachers in 1976, to form the NAS-UWT.

Neill, A. S. A Scottish educationist (1884–1973) who pioneered progressive methods of education at Summerhill, his school in Suffolk.

NFER National Foundation for Educational Research, funded by the government and local education authorities, which carries out a wide range of research.

NUT The National Union of Teachers, founded in 1870.

Open-plan Schools, mainly primary, built without enclosed classrooms but with large open areas in which more than one class can work.

Pastoral Care for the personal and social welfare of pupils, provided in secondary schools usually by heads of year or house masters or mistresses.

PGCE Post Graduate Certificate of Education, a one-year teacher training course for graduates.

Piaget, Jean A Swiss psychologist (1896–1980), whose theory that children go through four successive stages of intellectual development between birth and adolescence has had a seminal effect on primary education.

Pre-vocational courses New courses, such as CPVE, designed to prepare pupils mainly for the world of work.

Probationary year The first year of teaching during which the newly qualified teacher has to show his or her competence. There are plans to increase it to three years.

Profile A method of evaluating a pupil's separate attainments and characteristics, instead of giving an overall assessment of some of their skills in an examination.

Project A report or piece of work done as a result of studying a topic from various angles.

PTA Parent/Teacher Association. A voluntary body which raises money, holds social functions and discusses the running of the school.

Reception class A class for children who are attending infant school for the first time.

Remedial class A smaller class providing more individual attention for slow learners.

RSA Royal Society of Arts, founded in 1754, to encourage art, manufacturing industry and commerce. It started examinations in the middle of the nineteenth century. Its commercial examinations are still widely taken.

Scale posts Incremental pay scales. Teachers are promoted from the basic Scale 1 to higher Scales (up to Scale 4) for taking on extra responsibilities.

Secondary modern schools Non-selective secondary schools for children who did not enter grammar or technical schools. Most have been transformed into comprehensive schools.

Selective system Deciding what form of secondary education a child shall have by means of an examination such as the 11+ or teachers' assessments and reports.

Self-assessment A method which allows pupils to test their own performance and diagnose areas for improvement as in some profile systems.

Setting Putting children with similar levels of ability in a specific subject in a group, or set, for instruction in that subject.

Sixteen plus examination *See* **GCSE**

Sixth-form colleges These started in the 1960s to provide 16+ education for pupils from a group of smaller comprehensives which had no sixth form of their own. They are usually open access.

Skill An organised and co-ordinated pattern of physical, mental or social activity.

Skinner, B. F. An American psychologist, born 1904, who pioneered work on the conditioning of animals and developed programmed instruction.

SMILE Secondary Maths Individualised Learning in which children progress at their own speed by using work cards and other individual items.

Split sites Two or more separate sites, usually some distance apart, which continue to be used after the schools have merged.

STOPP The Society of Teachers Opposed to Physical Punishment. As a result of the Society's pressure, and judgments in the European Court of Human Rights, the government plans to bring in a Bill to allow parents to veto corporal punishment for their children in schools.

Streaming Grouping children in classes according to their general ability.

Subject-based Teaching which is centred on a subject rather than the needs of the child.

Super-teacher A scheme to pay outstanding teachers merit money. The idea was abandoned in 1984 in favour of a plan for teacher fellowships which would give some teachers an extra £1,000 a year for three years and a one-term sabbatical.

Supply teacher A teacher who is employed temporarily in place of an absent teacher or one who has not yet been appointed. He or she may be employed on a daily or a permanent basis.

Swann Report A 1985 report which found that West Indian children do less well in schools because of racial prejudice in society and recommended that there should be more multi-cultural curricula, a non-denominational approach to religious education, and more recruitment of ethnic minority teachers.

Teacher assessment A plan under which the head would appraise a teacher's performance each year and be able to refuse promotion to the next increment if his or her work was unsatisfactory. There would also be a triennial review by a senior colleague and an outside inspector or adviser.

Team teaching Teaching by a group of teachers instead of one to a class, in which each can use his particular interests and skills for the benefit of several classes.

Three-six-five (365) The City and Guilds vocational preparation course, introduced as a pilot scheme in 1981–2. The course allows pupils from the age of fourteen to sample a wide range of vocational activities and to develop personal, social and other skills.

TP Teaching practice undertaken by students under supervision of their tutor.

Tripartite system The system, consolidated after the Second World War, in which secondary education was divided into grammar, modern and technical.

TVEI The Technical and Vocational Education Initiative, launched in 1982, for pupils of fourteen to eighteen of a wide range of abilities, to prepare them for the world of work. It is financed by the MSC.

Voluntary-aided A school, usually run by the Church of England or the Catholic Church, which receives a government grant for the building and repair of the school, usually 85 per cent, and controls its own religious instruction and appointment of teachers.

Voucher system A proposal to issue all parents with vouchers which they could then 'spend' on State or private education.

Warnock Report A 1978 report which recommended that special education for handicapped children should start as early as possible and that the children should be integrated into ordinary schools as much as possible.

Wendy house A model house or room large enough for children to play house in.

YTS The Youth Training Scheme, started in 1983, to provide a year's occupation-based training and off-the-job education for school leavers. It is proposed to increase the period to two years.

Index